MW00991579

Defending Heaven

出师夫捷身先死，长使英雄泪满襟

杜甫

The general dies before the battle is won,
His breastplate covered with a hero's tears.

(Du Fu, Poet of the Tang Dynasty)

正气歌

天地有正气　杂然赋流形
下则为河岳　上则为日星
于人曰浩然　沛然塞苍冥
…
时究节乃见　一一垂丹青

文天祥

Zheng Qi Ge [Ode to Virtue's Force]

A force of nature permeates Heaven and Earth.
It is embodied in all physical forms
The rivers and mountains on earth.
The sun and stars in heaven
In man, it manifests itself as a boundless spirit
So vast it fills the universe . . .
The strength of character is revealed
Only in times of crisis and peril
They are remembered by history.

Wen Tianxiang, Song loyalist before his execution by the Mongols

Defending Heaven

China's Mongol Wars 1209–1370

James Waterson

Foreword by John Man

Frontline Books, London

Frontline Books, London

Defending Heaven: China's Mongol Wars, 1209–1370

This edition published in 2013 by Frontline Books, an imprint of
Pen & Sword Books Limited, 47 Church Street, Barnsley, S. Yorkshire, S70 2AS
www.frontline-books.com

ISBN: 978-1-84832-660-6

CIP data records for this title are available from the British Library and the Library of Congress

For more information on our books, please visit
www.frontline-books.com,
email info@frontline-books.com
or write to us at the above address.

Typeset in 11.5/13.8 point Plantin MT by JCS Publishing Services Ltd,
www.jcs-publishing.co.uk
Printed and bound by CPI Group (UK), Croydon, CR0 4YY

For E, H, K, D and 37

Contents

Maps and Illustrations

MAPS

ILLUSTRATIONS

Timeline

880s	Tang Dynasty controls China in name only after revolts and a collapse in central authority.
890s	Tang emperor a puppet of northern Chinese warlords.
930–47	The Kitan, a Turkish confederation, emerge as an important force in the political chaos of northern China. They briefly invade northern China and finally occupy the 'sixteen prefectures', a strip of territory on the northern edge of Chinese lands. They form a state, taking the Chinese dynastic name of Liao.
954	Kitan and Northern Han invade Shanxi. They are defeated at the Battle of Gaoping. The Tang General Zhao Guangyin is rewarded for his part in the battle by promotion to grand commander of the chief of the palace troops. He begins to form the nucleus of the military clique that will bring him to power from the leaders of the palace guard.
960–74	Zhao Guangyin establishes Song Dynasty during the chaos of the Five Dynasties and Ten Kingdoms period. The Song capital is established at Kaifeng.
974	Song reduces the last of the Five Dynasties and Ten Kingdoms.
979	Song goes to war with Liao over the 'lost sixteen prefectures' of the Tang state but fails to regain them.
1004–19	Repeated wars between Song and the Tangut tribal confederation in the northwest of China.
1038	The Tangut form the Xi Xia state in northwest China.

1044 Gunpowder first noted, in a Song military manual.
1068–86 Attempts at reform of Song government by minister Wang Anshi.
1115–17 The Jurchen, a Manchurian tribal confederation, rebels against its Liao overlords, defeats the Liao army, and creates the Jin Dynasty in northern China.
1118 Song army struggles in a losing war of attrition against the Xi Xia on the northwestern border.
1122 Pact on the Sea formed between Jin and Song against the Liao Dynasty.
1123 Jin armies take Beijing from the Liao.
1125 Liao Dynasty overthrown by Jin.
1125 Jin assault on Song territory.
1126 Kaifeng lost to Jin.
1132 New Song capitals south of the Yangzi River, northern China lost to the Jin Dynasty.
1130 Naval arms race between Song and Jin as the Yangzi and Huai rivers become the new front lines of the conflict between the two dynasties.
1134–5 The Song General Yue Fei retakes much of the territory lost to the Jin.
1142 The Shaoxing Peace between Song and Jin. Yue Fei is betrayed and poisoned by the Song court to appease Jin.
1161 A massive Jin attack is repelled on the Huai River defence line by a powerful Song fleet.
1167 Probable date of Chinggis Khan's birth.
1169–70 Emperor Xiaozong of the Song expands his navy and brings his army to parity with the Jin. He creates the Sealed Treasury for war expenditure.
1189 Emperor Xiaozong abdicates.
1206 Chinggis Khan proclaimed universal khan of the Mongolian plateau tribes.
1209 Mongol campaign against Xi Xia.
1211 Invasion of Jin empire by Mongols.
1212 Mongol siege of Jin city of Datong.
1215 Chinggis Khan's Mongols slaughter tens of thousands of people as they take Beijing.

1218 Fall of Kashgar, Kara-Kitai defeated by Mongols.
1220–3 Mongols at war in Persia and Russia.
1220 Song forms an alliance with Xi Xia against the Jin as the Mongols continue to press the Jin Dynasty.
1221 Final Jin offensive against Song.
1223–5 Xi Xia enters into 'fraternal relationship' with Jin as 'younger brother'.
1224 Jin makes peace with Song in a desperate bid to gather all their forces to fend off the Mongols.
1226 Mongols obliterate the army of Xi Xia.
1227 Xi Xia destroyed by Mongols. Death of Chinggis Khan.
1227 Li Quan, the bandit ruler of Shandong, goes to war against Song, and allies with the Mongols.
1231 Song army kills Li Quan in battle. His son, Li Tan, is recognised by Mongols as ruler of Shandong.
1231 Mongol siege of the Jin cities of Hezhong and Kuju.
1232 Mongol siege of Jin capital of Kaifeng.
1233 Song retakes lands from the Jin lost in 1125.
1234 Mongols storm last Jin stronghold of Caizhou and kill last Jin emperor. The Song general, Meng Gong, seizes the Jin imperial seals.
1234 Song launches the 'Luoyang expedition' against Mongols occupying Jin lands, and suffers heavy defeats.
1234 Song economic crisis begins.
1235 Mongols form the *heijun* or Black Army of Han Chinese troops to fight with them against Song.
1236 Mongols begin an invasion of Song on three fronts. Song resists in both Sichuan and on the Huai front, and the Mongols withdraw.
1237–43 Mongol campaigns in Russia and Europe.
1237 Further Mongol invasions of Song repelled by General Meng Gong. General Lu Wende and his family become famous for their battles with the Mongols.
1239 Review of the Song navy shows glaring deficiencies, reforms begun.
1239–64 A series of floods, droughts, locust swarms and earthquakes strike China.

1241 Death of Ogedei Khan.
1242 Song defences strengthened under the guidance of General Meng Gong.
1246 Death of General Meng Gong.
1248 Death of Guyuk Khan.
1251 The Toluid branch of the Mongol royal family becomes dominant in Mongol politics and brings Mongke to the throne.
1251–9 Mongke Khan launches attacks on the Middle East and Korea.
1256 Wen Tianxiang graduates from the Song imperial university.
1258 Mongol offensives begin in Yunnan, Sichuan and across the Yangzi.
1259 Death of Mongke Khan during campaign in Sichuan. Minister Jia Sidao takes control of the Song government. General Lu Wende enhances the reputation of his family during the war by his leadership.
1259–60 Qubilai's Mongol army held by Song on Yangzi River front.
1260 Qubilai and Ariq Boke engaged in conflict over Mongol throne.
1260–3 Mongol civil war. Mongols defeated in Syria by Mamluks.
1262 Shandong unsuccessfully rebels against the Mongols.
1262 Li Tan killed by Mongols, Shandong comes under full Mongol control.
1265 First defeat of the Song fleet at the Battle of Diaoyu. Mongol fleet-building gathers pace.
1267 Mongols begin siege of the Song twin cities of Xiangyang and Fancheng.
1270 The Song general, Lu Wende, dies while defending Xiangyang.
1271 The Mongols take a dynastic name, the 'Great Yuan'.
1272 Persian engineers employed by the Mongols bring counterweight trebuchets to the siege of Xiangyang.

1273 Xiangyang and Fancheng surrender to the Mongols. Massacre of entire population of Fancheng by Mongols. Lu Wende's brother, Lu Wenhuan, defects to the Mongols.

1273 Peace between Mongols and Korea.

1274 Mongols' first attempt on Japan fails.

1274 Mongol campaign along Han and Yangzi river valleys.

1274 Jia Sidao leads a disastrous campaign against the Mongols and falls from power.

1275 Mongols cross the Yangzi.

1275 Mongol armies reach the Yellow Sea to the east of Song lands.

1276 Wen Tianxiang made general commander of the Song armies.

1276 Fall of Hangzhou. Song emperor captured by Mongols and abdicates. Mandate of Heaven passes to the Yuan but two other Song princes escape and a new Song court is set up in Fuzhou.

1277 Fuzhou falls. New Song court relocates eight times in one year.

1277 Revolts against Mongol rule all over former Song lands.

1277-8 Mongol campaigns in Guangxi, Yunnan and on east coast squeeze Song from all sides.

1278 New Song emperor dies. Six-year-old child placed on throne.

1278 Song resistance centres on Guangzhou.

1279 Wen Tianxiang captured while fighting in southern Jiangxi. Naval battle at Yashan Island. Song navy destroyed, last Song emperor drowned. Fall of Song Dynasty.

1279 Former Song cities in Sichuan continue to resist Mongols until famine forces their surrender.

1279–83 Wen Tianxiang imprisoned in Beijing. He refuses all Mongol offers of high government position. He is finally executed by Qubilai. He becomes an icon for anti-Mongol sentiment.

1281 Mongol fleets fail against Japan.

1280–90 Continual revolts against the Mongols in southern China.

1290–1315 Mongol laws mandate harsher punishments for Han Chinese than for foreigners, make Mongolian the national language and ensure government exams are made easier for non-Chinese.

1315–30 Mongol attempts at tax censuses cause further large-scale revolts across southern China. Piracy is rampant on the Yangzi River.

1323 Mongol rule in China begins to break down, with assassinations, factional struggle and civil war. Five emperors are enthroned in ten years. Plague spreads over China.

1333 Child of thirteen placed on Yuan throne as Emperor Toghan Temur.

1340 All central control over Yuan China lost. Many rebellions called in the name of the Song Dynasty.

1344 Yellow River floods cause massive displacement of people, Yuan attempts to 'straighten' the river require the conscription of vast numbers of corvée labourers. Among this large concentration of Han Chinese workers there is a further resurgence in secret societies and cults.

1350 Major outbreak of plague in China.

1356 Millenarian 'Red Turban' revolution takes Nanjing from the Mongols.

1363 The Red Turban 'northern insurgency' against the Mongols halted after twelve years of war.

1361–7 Three warlords, Zhu Yuanzhang, Chen Youliang and Zhang Shicheng fight for control of southern China. Zhu Yuanzhang is finally victorious.

1368–70 Zhu Yuanzhang topples the fading Yuan Dynasty. China returns to native rule as Zhu Yuanzhang forms the Ming Dynasty.

Dynasties

Chronological List of Chinese Dynasties and Emperors

Northern Song Dynasty Emperors: 960–1126

Taizu	960–75
Taizong	976–97
Zhenzong	998–1022
Renzong	1023–63
Yingzong	1064–7
Shenzong	1068–85
Zhezong	1086–1100
Huizong	1100–1125
Qinzong	1126

Southern Song Dynasty Emperors: 1127–1279

Gaozong	1127–62
Xiaozong	1163–89
Guangzong	1190–4
Ningzong	1195–1224
Lizong	1225–64
Duzong	1265–74
Gongzong	1275
Duanzong	1276–8
Dibing	1278–9

Xi Xia Dynasty Emperors: 1032–1227

Jingzong	1032–48
Yizong	1048–67
Huizong	1067–86
Chongzong	1086–1139
Renzong	1139–93
Huanzong	1193–1206
Xiangzong	1206–11
Shenzong	1211–23
Xianzong	1223–6
Mo Zhu	1226–7

Jin Dynasty Emperors: 1115–1234

Taizu	1115–23
Taizong	1123–34
Xizong	1135–49
Hailing Wang	1149–61
Shizong	1161–89
Zhangzong	1190–1208
Weishao Wang	1209–13
Xuanzong	1213–23
Aizong	1224–34
Mo Di	1234

Chinggisid Family Tree and Yuan Dynasty Emperors 1227–1370

I. Chinggis Khan d.1227

- Jochi d.1227
  - Batu
    - Khans of the Golden Horde (Southern Russia)
- Chagatai d.1242
  - Chagatai Khans
- **II. Ogedei r.1229–41**
  - Qashin
    - Qaidu
  - **III. Guyuk r.1246–8**
- Tolui d.1233
  - **IV. Mongke r.1251–9**
  - **V. Qubilai r.1260–94**
    - Yuan Emperors
  - Hulegu
    - Persian Ilkhans
  - Ariq Boke

Yuan Emperors: 1294–1370

Temur Oljeytu Khan	1294–1307
Qayshan Guluk	1308–11
Ayurparibhadra	1311–20
Suddhipala Gegen	1321–3
Yesun Temur	1323–8
Arigaba	1328
Jijaghatu Toq-Temur	1328–9 and 1329–32
Qoshila Qutuqtu	1329
Irinchibal	1332
Toghan Temur	1333–70

A Note on Transliteration

In my first history involving the Mongols I named the greatest of the khans as 'Genghis', but after being severely admonished by a leading Mongolist I have ever since called him Chinggis. The reason for my original sin is easy to discover, however: it is that most of us grew up, so to speak, with Genghis. Furthermore, I do not know of too many non-Italians who delight in the work of Raffaello Sanzio da Urbino but I know plenty of Italians whose blood boils when the name Raphael is substituted for it, and not too many people in China would know who Confucius was but they can tell you quite a lot about Kongzi, as this is how the famous sage is most commonly referred to in the Middle Kingdom.

This leads us to a real dilemma when we write about China. I am a disciple of the modern Pinyin system of transliteration, but most readers will be used to at least some of the names of places and individuals being in the nineteenth-century Wade-Giles system, and this system is still being used even in some very recent academic books. I hope this situation will change but that seems about as likely as Italians not continuing to call Beijing 'Pechino'.

I am prepared to go halfway on this matter, so readers will find the Yangzi flowing through these pages rather than the Changjiang River, along with the more common Western names of sages and poets. For the names I have rendered in Pinyin, tone marks have been omitted, for the sake of simplicity.

Foreword

This book is about one of the most significant events of the last millennium, yet it is – to westerners – one of the least known. It is also extremely surprising. That the Mongols, a mere million 'barbarian' nomads, as the Chinese regarded them, a people with just one small town, should take on and actually conquer the world's grandest, most ancient empire, with perhaps a hundred million inhabitants and hundreds of cities – why, the very idea would have been ridiculous to any intelligent Mongol or Chinese child in, say, 1210. Yet within the life-span of many children alive then, it happened. All China, and much more besides, became part of the greatest land empire in human history.

The significance of the conquest is hard to overestimate. It was not simply that under the legendary Kublai [Qubilai] Khan China joined a family estate that reached from the Pacific to the Black Sea, for that empire broke apart soon after Kublai's death. No: the true significance of Kublai's conquest lay, and still lies, in its consequences. For Kublai's China is today's China, with the exclusion of one notable area, Kublai's original homeland, Mongolia itself. Why is Yunnan part of China? Why Tibet? Why the western regions of Xinjiang, with its restless population of Muslim Uighurs? And why, come to that, does China not include Japan, Vietnam, Java and Burma? In each case the answer is: Kublai Khan, his ambitions, his conquests, his failures.

You may ask: what on earth drove Kublai to undertake a venture seemingly so far beyond the capacity of the Mongols?

The answer is two-fold.

Firstly, he was inspired by an astonishing vision of world rule, a vision he inherited from his grandfather, Genghis [Chinggis] Khan. Genghis has a reputation as a mass-murderer, which he was. But he was no more simply a murderer than Napoleon was simply a corporal or Hitler simply a private. He started as a nobody, the son of a murdered clan leader and an outcast mother. Despite this unpromising start, or perhaps because of it, he dreamed of empire. A leader of genius, he turned dream into reality with a big idea – that heaven itself had given the world to the Mongols, and that it was his task, and the task of his heirs, to make the world accept this astonishing fact. To us, now, the idea is quite daft, but we must remember that no one, let alone a small-time clan leader in the back of beyond, had any idea of the size of the world.

By the time his grandson, Kublai, rose to power, Genghis's empire was already much larger than Rome's and Alexander's combined. He died when on the verge of invading north China, a realm named Jin, separate from south China (Song). Kublai's inheritance lay in Jin. His elder brother, Mongke, became the emperor in 1251, and gave Kublai the task of starting the conquest of south China by seizing the then-independent state of Yunnan. So the second part of the answer to the question – what drove Kublai to invade the south? – is that when he himself became emperor in 1260, he was well on his way, inspired not only by his grandfather's vision of divinely ordained world rule but also backed by an empire that could draw on the resources of both north China and the Muslim world.

It took twenty years, until 1279. That is the major part of the story told by James Waterson. It takes in what I believe to be one of the greatest of sieges, an epic which, if it could be written, would be an Asian equivalent of the siege of Troy. It centres on the city of Xiangyang (now absorbed into today's Xiangfan). Xiangyang was the key-stone to the old south: it guarded the river Han, which runs into the great Yangzi, which is the river highway to the old Song capital of Hangzhou. Xiangyang, with its three miles of stone walls, its broad moat and its river frontage, had to be taken before the invaders could take Song, had to be held if the beseiged were to save Song. The siege lasted five years (1267–73). Thousands of little ships from both sides ferried troops to attack, defend, reinforce and relieve. Blockades were mounted and destroyed, all without conclusion, until the Mongols brought to bear overwhelming force in the form of heavy artillery – a giant catapult, a counterweight trebuchet such as those that Muslims had used to batter down the walls of Crusader castles. Kublai knew this, because his nephew Abaqa was ruling Persia. Off went a message by pony express. Back came two Muslim engineers. Nothing could have shown better the advantages of empire, the importance of a free flow of information between west and east. Their product was the mightiest catapult ever seen in China: a 40-tonne monster that would toss a 100-kilogram stone 200 metres. Perhaps there was one of these giant machines, perhaps several. It – or they – did the job. Xiangyang surrendered, the door to Song opened, Kublai's immense force moved on to the Yangzi, to the capital Hangzhou, and to victory.

It was not easy. Song had been in existence for three hundred years, and this was a catastrophe so intense that hundreds of its top people committed suicide rather than kowtow to a foreign conqueror. The Song court fled Hangzhou and ended up on an island off the south coast. It only finally expired in a great naval battle, during which the most senior Song official took the five-year-old emperor in his arms and jumped into the sea with him.

So it was that in 1279 Kublai's China assumed its current borders, though these at the time included Mongolia. It is one of history's great ironies that China's sense of itself derives from the vision of a down-and-out Mongolian who decided that heaven had ordained that Mongolians should rule the world.

Mongolia is no longer part of the great Han family. It slipped away almost a century ago, when China was weak and the new Soviet Union a force to be reckoned with. Though traditionally part of China, Mongolians were not happy under Chinese rule, and broke away to fall into the Soviet sphere. But because Kublai established a Chinese dynasty, the Yuan, and because he backdated its foundation to his grandfather Genghis, he allowed the Chinese to believe that Genghis and his people were, and are, Chinese. As one of my guides once said to me, 'We are proud of Genghis Khan because he was the only Chinese leader to have conquered Europeans.' She was referring to the Mongol conquest of Hungary in 1241, fourteen years after Genghis's death, but I let it pass. The point is that in their heart of hearts, Chinese people know that if one day Mongolia returns to the bosom of the Han family, well, things will again be as they should be.

So you can see why the events related in this book are significant: they are key not only to an understanding of the past but to the future as well.

John Man, 2013

Introduction and Acknowledgements

> Victory is not glorious, those for whom it is glorious delight in killing human beings.
> Those who delight in killing human beings will never control the realm.
> When there are mounds of dead one should weep with sorrow.
> When one is victorious, observe the mourning rites.
>
> *Laozi, Dao De Jing*

As an undergraduate I was warned by several tutors that it was well-nigh impossible for anybody wishing to complete a history degree at the School of Oriental and African Studies to escape the Mongols. They were right and I now find myself composing a fourth book in which they are the *sine qua non*. However, I also once again find myself writing more genially of their enemy than of the khans. It has been a consistent theme in my work that the Mongols were, as the authors of *1066 and All That* would have had it, 'not a good thing'. I recorded their absolute devastation of Persia and Iraq in the pages of *The Ismaili Assassins* and the blessed fact that they were stopped from reaching the Mediterranean by the Mamluk dynasty was a central theme of *The Knights of Islam*. They appeared once more as a bête noire in *Sacred Swords* as they choked the Tigris with bodies before moving on to massacres in Syria in an attempt to extinguish Islamic civilisation.

Mongolists would argue, I hope passionately – or perhaps dispassionately, as most of the major arguments for the Mongols being a constructive element of world history rely on a detached appraisal made through the long lens of history – against my opinion, but the rehabilitation, through books and film, of Chinggis Khan that is currently taking place would seem to suggest that my viewing him and his offspring as one of the worst man-made catastrophes ever to strike Eurasia will not harm the khans' image too much.

The above very probably seems somewhat out of character for any writer of history or professional historian. It is integral to our line of work that we commonly recount the deaths and miseries of thousands in simple telegraphic detail before moving on to a more detailed dissection of the consequences of victories in the field or of a resulting *Pax*, whether that be of a *Romana*, *Mongolica*, *Britannica* or *Americana* variety. Engels was not too far from the truth when he wrote, 'history is about the most cruel of goddesses, and she leads her triumphant car over heaps of corpses,'[1] I, however, feel that undertaking a too detached approach to history leads us into a moral void. I take Wellington's observation that 'next to a battle lost, the saddest thing is a battle won' very seriously indeed.

Then there is the question of historical relativism. Following Benedetto Croce's dictum that the historian's task is one of 'criticism, criticism and then criticism' is vital for our craft if history is truly to offer modern man anything at all in the way of guidance. Accepting that any atrocity or even misguided governance can be framed as being tolerable by the standards of its time just will not do, for as Croce also said, 'every historical judgement gives to all history the character of contemporary history, because however remote in time events thus recounted may seem to be, history in reality refers to present needs and present situations wherein those events vibrate.'[2] If we condone the sins of the fathers we run the risk of excusing them in ourselves, particularly if they might obtain what we consider to be desirable ends. Furthermore, it is dismissive of the humans of the past to suggest that we are any more civilised or less capable of accepting barbarism now than our forefathers were. Liu Ji, a Yuan Dynasty writer wrote that:

> Weapons are instruments of ill omen, war is immoral.
>
> Really they are only to be resorted to when there is no other choice. It is not right to pursue aggressive warfare because one's country is large and prosperous, for this ultimately ends in defeat and destruction. Then it is

> too late to have regrets. Military action is like a fire – if not stopped it will burn itself out. Military expansion and adventurism soon lead to disaster.
>
> The rule is 'even if a country is large, if it is militaristic it will soon perish'.[3]

Then there is the question of how it was to live through profoundly destructive times. Discounting or not acknowledging the immediate effects on a society, and on men's thinking, of brutality, indifference to suffering, incompetent or absent governance and inhumanity will not get us any closer to achieving the goal of every historian as dictated by Ranke: '*wie es eigentlich gewesen*'– show simply how it really *was*, and not how it looked later.

Even given the above, there still are undoubtedly dangers in a partisan approach to history but my 'purely academic' argument for its partial application in this work is that there is currently available no single-volume history of the Mongol invasions as seen from the standpoint of the Chinese dynasties they were unleashed upon. There are several studies of the Mongols' military achievements and government, and if I had taken up a strictly neutral point of view in my recounting of the defence of China I would have risked merely creating a pale imitation of such superb books as Timothy May's *The Mongol Conquest in World History*, David Morgan's *The Mongols* and Morris Rossabi's *Khubilai Khan: His Life and Times*. The virtue of creating a work that generally reflects the action from one point of view is that it allows for an understanding of perceptions. The perceptions of both the governing and of the governed, however erroneous they may have been and as difficult as they may be to reconstruct, are vitally important when we want to understand why some dynasties or governments last and others do not, and why some wars are lost that should have been won. Not to accept that any Chinese citizen or official would have attempted to make sense of the Mongol invasions and subsequent Yuan government through an application of Confucian morals and philosophy is frankly disingenuous, and the same must be said of every other culture that ever had contact with the Mongols. The fact that our primary sources are coloured by the often-unconscious influence of their authors' milieux should not surprise us, and whilst we must seek truth from the facts presented to us by contemporaries of the events of the past we cannot escape the very basic idea that facts presented themselves to contemporaries as a series of impressions; this is how every human experiences their world and, more importantly for the historian, how they respond to it. It may be trite to comment that only hindsight is perfect but it is an important point for any historian interested in relating 'how it really was'.

Much 'quantifying' of the Mongol invasions of both China and of the Middle East has been undertaken by historians, usually with the intent of rationalising the figures given by medieval historians. Generally speaking, the trend has been towards making far more conservatively sized mounds of dead than the original sources had portrayed. In some respects this is commendable. Historians have a duty to create hypotheses about the past: it is, after all, a social science that we are engaged in, and the question of magnitude is always a question we are likely to ask and be asked. But, even if we can 'prove' such suppositions as 'each household should be multiplied by five to calculate the population affected' or that 'the square hectarage of the remains of a city could not possibly have supported as many people as the contemporary historians claimed were slaughtered there', I would suggest that this is still not as useful, historically, as gauging the psychological impact of having nearly all your neighbours killed and next year's crops destroyed. Whether the number killed was seventy thousand or seven thousand does not in fact matter; the question of magnitude of terror depends, in fact, on the numbers left alive, and the sources make it very clear that this number was a fraction of those who died.

Further to this, contemporaries of the Black Death, the single greatest killer ever to be visited upon mankind, commonly wrote not just of the volume of death they surveyed but of the fact that society's mores had been degraded, and even hypothesised as to whether the breath, pus, sweat and stench of the ill had corrupted the souls and conscience of the healthy. Boccaccio's *Decameron* was very clear on what damage mass death could inflict on those who survived:

> E in tanta afflizione e miseria della nostra città era la reverenda auttorità delle leggi, cosí divine come umane, quasi caduta e dissoluta tutta per li ministri e essecutori di quelle, li quali, sí come gli altri uomini, erano tutti o morti o infermi o sí di famiglie rimasi stremi, che uficio alcuno non potean fare; per la qualcosa era a ciascun licito quanto a grado gli era d'adoperare.[4]

It is notable that the right degree of *simpatico* for Boccaccio's words can only really be found in the 1620 English translation commonly accredited to John Florio, who entered into the task in a time not unused to sudden death and contagion. Perhaps we who write of the Mongols in comfort and security might take note of a how a man living in rather different times brings to us an account of what terror, whether biological or man-made, could do to pre-modern societies:

> In misery and affliction of our City, the venerable authority of the Lawes, as well divine as humane, was even destroyed, as it were, through want of the lawfull Ministers of them. For they being all dead, or lying sicke with the rest, or else lived so solitary, in such great necessity of servants and attendants, as they could not execute any office, whereby it was lawfull for every one to do as he listed.[5]

We will return to this subject at the conclusion of the tale of the Yuan and how the collapse of their dynasty was recorded by Boccaccio's peers in China.

Most Mongol historians certainly accept that terror was an acceptable practice in war for the khans (just as it is in the modern world, though now in our post-Douhet age it is delivered from the air rather than from the saddle), and if we set out to cause terror by killing enough of the populace to cow the remainder, then the question of whether the populace we slaughter is seven thousand or seventy thousand does not really matter. The end is terror, the means are proportionate to that and equally so is the fear, discord and loathing that terror is likely to arouse in populaces subjected to it.

I hope I have not – and many times my draft work was rescued from it by peer reviewers – fallen into a trap that far greater historians than I have been lured into. Even J. Saunders claimed that the Mongols suffered from 'blind unreasoning fear and hatred of urban civilisation'.[6] I thank Dr David Morgan for drawing to my attention to this back in 2007 and to the work of Professor Joseph Fletcher, who noted that a major cause for the huge destruction that the Mongols wrought was that they came, 'too fast'. Fletcher was in fact discussing the damage done by the Mongols to Persia when he wrote that they had no time to acculturate themselves to the desert habitat and continued with 'attitudes nurtured in the East Asian steppe: disdain for peasants, who like the animals that the Mongols herded, lived directly off what grew from the soil . . . With the steppe extortion pattern in mind, the Mongols did violence and used terror, reinforced by their ideology of universal dominion, to induce their victims to surrender peaceably.' Fletcher argued that the Mongols, 'came to understand settled society . . . quickly', but, 'by that time the Mongolian juggernaut had done its dreadful work'.[7] My argument is that something very similar happened in China. I do not argue that the Mongols were inherently savage – or no more so than any other peoples ancient or modern who had been instructed that they might please their generals not with prisoners but with killing and burning – but rather that the means they were forced to apply to the conquest of China, as they were pushed so hard by the Song, were terrible and then untameable in the post-conquest period, and though they may even have wished to govern in the 'style' of a Chinese dynasty, the vested interests within their state – the very interests that had brought them to power – were by this point ungovernable. They had opened a Pandora's box by taking on China, and the infrastructure of government that they brought with them into the Middle Kingdom was not up to the task of governing what they had won. Song's long resistance revealed the fault lines in Mongol government, and the Yuan Dynasty was in trouble so early on after finally defeating the Song that its leaders never had time to adapt or to tame the forces that would soon enough begin to tear it apart. With this in mind, it is notable that the Ming Dynasty, albeit brought to power by force of arms and through an internecine civil war, grew up within the existing cast of Song government and lasted nearly three centuries.

In my recording of China's confrontation with the Mongols I have recorded the Song Dynasty's long war against the khans in more detail than that of the Jin and Xi Xia. I chose to do this because the history of Chinese civilisation is more extensive and complex than that of any single Western nation, and the profusion of names and the sheer 'density' of Chinese civilisation and society risks producing a book that is both vast and indigestible for Western readers. Furthermore, Song *was* China. It is no accident of editorial judgement that Jin and Xi Xia, are placed along with the Mongol Yuan Dynasty in Volume 6 of the magisterial *Cambridge History of China*: *Alien Regimes and*

Border States. All these dynasties took on 'Chinese characteristics' but all three were transmitters of this tradition whilst Song was both a vessel of the past achievements of China and a continuing locus of production for the vital elements of Chinese civilisation. Certainly the Song viewed all these aliens in the same light; the Jurchen of the Jin and the Tangut of Xi Xia were no better than the Mongols of the Yuan in their eyes, and that essentially xenophobic perception of its enemies was certainly part of Song's undoing.

It is also no accident of history that the rebellions which finally toppled the Mongols in China started in what had been Song lands and not in the former lands of the Jin. Song China's long resistance to the Mongols, and the memory and myth of it, was fundamental to the Mongols' eventual fall from power in China and to the birth of the Ming Dynasty.

Acknowledging mentors and friends is always the most pleasant part of writing any book and my thanks go out once more to Dr David Morgan, who first introduced me to the Mongols 'at the safe distance of eight hundred years', and to Dr Brian Williams, who is, I am sure, right now somewhere in Central Asia discovering the history of tomorrow. Their ongoing kindnesses and words of wisdom and encouragement are beyond value. I would like to thank Professor Morris Rossabi for replying to an unsolicited and decidedly cheeky email that I sent him from the depths of depair whilst trying to structure this book. The fact that the good professor responded with a full, thoughtful and insightful message whilst travelling hotfoot beween Ulan Bator and Tokyo speaks volumes both for his goodness and for his encyclopedic knowledge of the subject.

The generosity of John Man appears to be as limitless as the oceanic Mongolian grasslands of which he has written so eloquently in his marvellous renditions of the lives of Chinggis and of Qubilai Khan. The Foreword he has gifted for this book is every bit as insightful and vibrant as the piece he fashioned for my first book. Betsy Kohut of the Smithsonian Institute's Freer and Sackler Galleries has also been unstinting in her kindnesses and invariable in her expertise in the provision of images for both this book and for my previous Middle East 'trilogy'.

For keeping me on the straight and narrow I would like to thank my editor Kate Baker and my anonymous peer reviewers who steered me back again and again from a course of ruin and who can bear no responsibility for any of the errors that may remain. For continual kindnesses I would like to thank Jane, Liz, Wayne, the two Marks, Minna, Wael, Boris, Svetlana, Di, Melinda, Mandie, Chris, Jan Marie and Brent.

Simply priceless is the love, understanding and intellect of my dear wife Michele, she is also *sine qua non.*

~ 1 ~

Heaven Inverted

China on the Eve of the Mongol Invasions

See the Southern Gate of Heaven, Deep Green, Crystalline, Shimmering Bright, Studded with Jewels.
On Either Side Stood Scores of Heavenly Marshals, Tall as the Roof Beams, Next to the Pillars,
Holding Metal-tipped Bows and Banners. All Around Stood Gods in Golden Armour . . .

Wu Chengen, the Monkey King's first view of Heaven, The Journey to the West, c.1580

China's 'Mongol problem' was not unique to the thirteenth century. Many a Chinese dynasty had expended much revenue and blood countermanding the threat of Turco-Mongolic tribes from the north. Indeed, this dated from far back into the second century BC with the invasions of Han Dynasty lands by the Xiongnu, who may or may not have been the same individuals who were known in Europe as the Huns and who would one day be led by Attila to the gates of Rome.

Chinese policy, in brief, was constructed to a degree of appeasement called *heqin* or 'harmonious kinship', which entailed payments to the barbarian,[1] trading with him through frontier markets, and making the outlaw into an in-law through the giving of imperial brides. Along with this conciliation of the barbarian went construction of defensive lines, and agitation and intrigue among the northern tribes to foment wars among them and thereby to divide potential confederations. There was also recruitment of Central Asian cavalry to serve in Chinese armies and the application of military science in the form of early warning stations and systems for mobilising impressively large forces for the defence of the state and for punitive expeditions. The application of this policy over the period of more than a millennium was, give or take a few glitches, generally a successful one, but in the Tang Dynasty it began to crumble.

Arguably the Kitan, a Turkish confederation lying to the northeast of the Tang state, began their movement into Chinese territory as a direct and slightly panicked response to the chaos that the Tang state had collapsed into by the 870s. The Kitan were forced to undertake an occupation of Chinese territory as the Tang court had become a powerless vessel among a raft of more than fifty Chinese warlord states and was incapable of raising tribute in the form of bolts of silk and silver to pay off the Kitan and of ensuring its safe transport to the Kitan court.

The Kitan occupation was unusual, as Turco-Mongolian confederations aimed, generally speaking, to exploit China through the seeking of tribute, often disguised as 'gifts' by the imperial courts, through plundering Chinese wealth and through carrying off manufactured articles that could then be sold on through the Central Asian trade system. Indeed, before the establishment of their 'state', it was common for the Kitan to build 'Chinese' cities in their own lands as centres of production and commerce. Captured and refugee Chinese artisans were commonly relocated to these centres.[2]

Occupying Chinese territory and becoming one of the settled, as opposed to one of those who fed off the settled, was always likely to be a dangerous policy for any steppe tribe, as it would strain its political system. The organisation of these steppe tribal confederations was based on a very simple principle of exploitation of a cowed state and not on conquest of that state per se, and certainly not on the careful management, administration and husbandry of a settled state. For a tribal confederation leader to demand that his followers give up the saddle and bow and take up the administrator's chair, as we will see, was always likely to cause dissent among his own people. Furthermore, a steppe tribe, being made up of nomadic cavalry capable of striking randomly and quickly and at multiple locations, was not suited to controlling a region, and if it did take on garrisoning and consolidation as military tasks it sacrificed its very essence. Indeed, great steppe politician though he was, Chinggis Khan's invasion of China was arguably one of history's greatest political blunders.[3] Any chance of longevity for the khan's steppe empire was essentially destroyed when he embroiled his nascent state in the conquest of China.

By the 890s, the Tang emperor had become a puppet of northern warlords who had formerly served as his generals. As China disintegrated, the Kitan moved into Chinese territory, and by 947 they had settled and formed their state in modern-day Inner Mongolia and taken the Chinese dynastic name of Liao. The beginning of the end of the chaos that had gripped China for most of the tenth century occurred a few years after the formation of the Liao state. China's slow march back from anarchy began at the Battle of Gaoping in 954, which halted the Kitan and Northen Han's invasion of Shanxi. This battle was part of a campaign that brought together a small group of commanders who would form the nucleus of the nascent Song Dynasty. The man who became the first Song emperor was General Zhao Guangyin, who after the battle was promoted to grand commander of the chief of the palace troops. It was in the palace guard that he formed the military clique that would bring him to power.

In February 960 the new Song Dynasty, having unified much of China, established its capital at Dongjing, modern Kaifeng. The verdict of one historian, that 'Chinese Empires were built slowly at immense cost in blood, and a lot of its history is not dynastic at all but the chaos in between'[4] seems justified if we review the bloody and destructive wars that the Song waged to put the former Tang lands under Song control and to solidify the border with the Liao.

That the Song army was a capable force at this juncture was shown in December 964, when two columns of thirty thousand men marched into Sichuan province over high mountains in the dead of winter. Meanwhile a further column to their east forced the Yangzi River defence line via pontoon bridges with a mass infantry attack under General Pan Ai, possibly the first time this had been done by any army on such a vast scale, to force the capitulation of the Shu kingdom. In 970 the army also showed itself capable of operating with the close support of a riverine navy when the Southern Han kingdom was defeated.

A peace accord with the Liao that was struck in 974 allowed Zhao Guangyin, who had taken the throne name Taizu, to reduce the remaining small kingdoms that the Tang empire had shattered into. The Southern Tang and Northern Han were conquered, and in 979 the Song turned their attentions to the 'lost' sixteen prefectures, which had been part of the Tang Dynasty's lands before being lost to the new Liao state. Unfortunately, despite the army sent to undertake this task being led by General Yang Ya 'the invincible', it was badly mauled at the Battle of the Gaoling River, just west of modern Beijing, with the Song Emperor Taizong fleeing the battlefield, severely wounded, in a donkey cart. This unlucky ruler then faced a rebellion in his capital and he was forced to exterminate much of the royal family in order to bring it to an end.

The consequences of the year 979 on the Song Dynasty were to be immense. The crushing defeat of Gaoling and the Song's failure to annexe the sixteen prefectures became a festering wound that blinded the Song court to its own interests in almost every subsequent strategic decision it made about the northern border. That the sixteen prefectures were Song lands and the Liao were illegitimate monarchs over them became a virtual doctrine of the Song court. This obsession with the 'lost' prefectures grievously misguided the Song emperors and their counsellors at key junctures during the later contests with the Jin Dynasty and then with the Mongols. Furthermore, the near annihilation of the imperial family by Taizong also required the emperor to create an extensive bureaucracy to assist him in ruling. The Chinese government exam system predated the Song, but Taizong and his descendants formalised it as the only route into government and professionalised the roles of bureaucrats. While there were undoubted benefits to this system of government, a major drawback, as we shall see, was that the Song court often acted like a veritable ivory tower: narrow in its vision and often almost deliberately cut off from the realities and dangers that the state faced.

In the novel *Der Glasperlenspeil* Hermann Hesse created a fictional city named Castalia, where scholars played the glass bead game, an abstract game of pure intellect. Similarly, the intelligentsia of the later Song court did historians a great service to posterity in that they anthologised and thereby saved for us much of China's military history prior to their dynasty and maintained censuses of a standard that would challenge many modern states to replicate. Indeed, Sima Guang's monumental 'Comprehensive Mirror for Aid in Governments' (*zishi tongjian*) was produced within the court's cloistered walls in the late eleventh century. But this vast body of work – the censuses aside – is equally a great potential trap for the historian. There was no Caesar, Guderian or Musashi to recount the achievements and failures of the Chinese military in the field, and the civilian officials assigned to the History Office (*shi guan*) rewrote, condensed and altered records to suit the court's world view and to make recorded events fit the accepted configuration of dynastic Chinese history and follow the rules of writing historiography as laid down during the Han Dynasty by the great Sima Qian. Their creations were, then, in many ways far removed from the reality on the ground.

There was certainly plenty of material for these Song historians to draw on. China was a paper-rich society, and records of eyewitness accounts, proclamations and appointments and rewards abounded. Unfortunately, once the court historians had steamrollered much of the reality out of them to create a record in harmony with the court's view, even documents such as the *lubu* or announcement of victory and *xingzhuang* or government accounts of conduct, akin to being mentioned in dispatches, lose much of their primary source credibility. The *lubu* give us quite exact dates and locations, but often grossly overestimate the numbers of the enemy. They also record the number of enemy killed without recording Song losses.

In simple terms, the *shidafu* – the scholar-officials who recorded Song's martial history – give us very little military detail because they were not military men. Troy had Homer, Antioch had the anonymous soldier-author of the *Gesta Francorum*, but the Mongol siege of Xiangyang, despite lasting some five years, had no directly involved author to record the Song's defence of the city. The lack of military authors is not surprising, given the divorce between the

Song's general staff and the world of the bureaucrats of the court. A Song general could not aspire to be of the literati who governed and recorded the actions of the state as the Roman Ammianus Marcellinus had done. That we have virtually nothing recorded on battle, tactics or details of combat is a result of the fact that those who led in the field did not write.

The men of the pen also set a genre through their hegemony over the culture of the Song state, and their writings are loaded with conventional literary expressions rather than fact. Even Song poetry avoids any narrative about the battle and the clash of arms, whilst in the texts generals are often found quoting from Sunzi, Confucius and Mencius. Such polished reciting of classics is unlikely, given that Song generals were usually part of dynastic clans of soldiers from the lower nobility. Indeed, it is entirely possible that military men had no contact whatsoever with *The Art of War* and that its frequent quotation in Song records was in fact a mechanism used by civilian authors, designed both to put military men in their place and to intimate a knowledge of martial affairs.[5] Our other source, individual posthumous *xingzhuang*, are also unreliable. The Chinese practice of ancestor worship ensured that relatives or clients of deceased generals eulogised them in these accounts with little regard for fact. The court's detachment from the realities of war also meant that any general reporting success was likely to receive lavish rewards, whilst those who spoke truth to power and admitted reverses were likely to suffer death.

During its early years of existence the new dynasty set itself two tasks that would both define the state and cause it enormous problems in later years. One has already been described above as an unhealthy obsession, and the Song Dynasty spent the first forty-five years of its life attempting to reconquer the sixteen lost prefectures. In this endeavour it was entirely unsuccessful, and from 999 the dynasty moved to a passive defence of the northern border with a series of canals, paddy fields and dykes running east to west across Hebei. This wall of water severely impeded Liao cavalry manoeuvres and, whilst the Liao commonly continued to defeat Song field armies, their incursions were limited and they always withdrew from Song territory after failing against the Song's second line of defence, their fortified cities. The lost provinces, however, remained a deep psychological scar that was only deepened by the Liao's frequent hostility.

The second task that the Song emperors and their ministers set themselves was to depoliticise the army and bring it from under the control of regional military commanders and more fully under the newly strengthened civilian central court's control. In the modern world this would be recognised as a standard approach to the question of command and control in successful states, and in fact the first Song emperor, Taizu, had begun this policy in a highly effective and civilised manner. It is recorded that military leaders were relieved of their command 'over a cup of wine' with the emperor. That Taizu and his descendants should follow this policy is not surprising. Taizu himself had risen to power from being just a popular palace guard who organised a particularly effective palace coup, but what was even more important than this was the fact that a military coup had been the key event that had started the collapse of the Tang empire. The rebellion of the overly powerful military commissioner of the northeast, An Lushan, lasted from 755 to 763 and was the catalyst for other previously loyal generals to break away from imperial control and seek independence as warlords. The over-reliance of the Tang on An Lushan and their imprudent showering of honours and military power on him was a lesson from history that the early Song emperors were willing to listen to. In fact, there were other examples of military coups entirely similar to An Lushan's revolt dotted throughout China's history prior to the Song Dynasty. A close reading of the dynastic texts would have indicated to the Song government that the army had consistently been an inherently unstable and unknown quantity in all of the country's various states and dynasties down to their own. The early Song emperors and their ministers therefore decided that the army had to be kept out of politics in order to ensure the survival of the state.[6]

There were clashes between Song and the Liao until 1005, when the Liao invaded and tried to take Chanyuan. Their general, Xiao Talin, was killed by a Song archer acting as a sniper with a long-range bow, and this one arrow caused the Liao advance to stumble. A peace pact, the Treaty of Chanyuan (modern Chanzhou), was subsequently signed and gave birth to one hundred and twenty years of peace.

During this time Song culture flourished, but many influential voices at court viewed the Chanyuan covenant with distaste, even at the distance of over a century, and the unhealthy obsession with the recovery of all the old Tang lands continued to exert its malign influence. Continued payments of tribute in the form of two hundred thousand bolts of silk and one hundred thousand ingots of silver every year to the Liao doubtless added to the revulsion of Song ministers for the accord.

The peace also added power to the process of defanging the military. Peace with the Liao ended the requirement for large-scale mobilisations, it accelerated the demise of the military men's influence at court and hastened the renascence of the ever-present concept in Chinese intellectual life that *wen*, high culture, was superior to *wu*, the martial art.[7] In this respect, therefore, the Song civilian officials were just an extreme example of how men of the pen, throughout Chinese history, had commonly prided themselves on actually avoiding any involvement with military office.

Peace also directly damaged the body of the army itself. The contemporary writer Ouyang Xiu wrote, 'for thirty three years there has been peace. All the soldiers who have had any experience of war are either dead or decrepit. Those who have been recruited later know nothing of actual war.'[8] Some reforms were, however, undertaken by the minister Wang Anshi before his fall from office in 1085. In Wang Anshi's copying of the Tang *fubing* system, every household with two or more adult males contributed one man as a reserve archer who would train regularly in peacetime and be called up in time of war. This 'people's army' was only a short-lived phenomenon, as were Wang Anshi's other reforms that granted finance to farmers between harvests, created waterworks to encourage productivity, prohibited feudal service and moved land-holding tax burdens to landowners and away from peasants.

Wang Anshi's reforms indicate that at least some at the Song court understood that one advantage the Chinese state had over the northern invaders was the strength of its economic base. In Wang Anshi's view, sustaining the military was only possible through careful husbandry of the land and looking to the rights of *lao bai xing*, 'old one hundred names', the ordinary peasants who both supported the state through their agrarian labour and who could be called upon to defend it. Wang Anshi's fall from power was, however, indicative of a contrary trend within Song government that favoured exploitation of the populace, accumulation of economic power in the hands of only a few and reliance on a 'mercenary' army that lay outside the people. The changes he made – particularly the forging of a relationship between the ordinary populace and the state, and the ordinary Song citizen's identification with the dynasty – were, though, to have profound effects at the demise of the Song Dynasty and during the collapse of the Mongol Yuan state.

By 1038, many battalions were at only one-third strength and few men could even pull the heaviest crossbows. The frailty of the *yangping* army recruitment system that had been introduced in the 960s to supply employment as soldiers for unemployed city folk was in danger of total breakdown, with new recruits only receiving a tenth of their stipend in the 1040s. Defections of entire units to form bandit companies had been common right from the outset of the early wars against the Liao, and in 1043 an entire army that went on to name itself the 'Winged Tigers' defected to the rebels they were supposed to be suppressing in Shandong province.

A war of some seven years that started in 1038 against the Tangut, a Turco-Mongolic tribal confederation on the northwest border of China, and the Song army's poor performance in this conflict, did force some changes on the court. The *jiang*, a distinct legion of between two thousand five hundred and four thousand men became the standard unit. Previously fighting units had been made up as amalgams of smaller groupings, with all the attendant problems of communication and *esprit de corps* that this involved. Later campaigns against the Tangut were, however, also unsuccessful despite the reformed Song army performing well, chiefly because the lack of range of largely infantry-based forces denied the Song generals a knockout blow. The nature of their enemy, made up as it was chiefly of swift-moving horse archers and a mobile court also gave little hope of a distinct objective for the Song campaigns or opportunity to seize the initiative. The Song would face the same problem later when tackling the Mongols.

Better weaponry also came along during the reforms of Wang Anshi and the reign of Shenzong. There was an increase in the number and quality of crossbows, including the extremely powerful 'divine arm bow'. Heavier bladed shields were also produced and simple spears were replaced with heavy axes and long swords.

There was also a large increase in the volume of gunpowder-enhanced arrows, in the catapults used for city defences and large-scale production of other pyrotechnic weapons such as flamethrowers, mines and explosive bombs hurled by trebuchets. The Song had been the first dynasty to deploy gunpowder weapons in large numbers, but their enemies soon copied any innovations. Secrecy therefore often surrounded the development and deployment of any new arms and the infantry weapon known as the 'fire-lance' was not recorded in any Song military manuals until the late twelfth century, despite appearing on banners from the tenth century and having various fanciful names applied to it over time, including 'the pear flower spear' and 'the enemy-exterminating yin-yang shovel'. The basic design of this weapon seems to have been that of a spear shaft, combined with a pyrotechnic which shot out flames, smoke and sometimes small projectiles. The psychological impact on steppe warriors and their mounts of such weapons must have been significant.

Wang Anshi also created the *baojia* system that organised townships and even the smallest villages into defence units based around the service of ten families undertaking watch and guard duties. The system did nothing for the imperial army per se, but it did militarise the lower society and encouraged villagers to identify themselves with the defence of the dynasty. Both these effects would, when combined with the loyalty tie described above, have tremendous significance at the end of the Song Dynasty and for the Mongol Yuan.

As discussed above, the reforms of Wang Anshi were never fully implemented across the army or across the state, and by the early 1100s the Song army did in fact begin to look more and more like a mercenary army without any real connection to the society it was paid to protect, and its ranks were commonly filled with criminals and vagabonds. In fact, from Tang times the main source of recruits to the army had been the landless, desperate and destitute, but in the early eleventh century the Song also took to branding their soldiers' faces to prevent them from deserting, although in the case of convicts who were recruited this would have been somewhat redundant as they were already branded. This branding worked to deepen further the divide between military men and men of the court. Gifted commanders such as Di Qing, who had risen from the ranks to become military affairs commissioner for the dynasty retained, very literally, a mark of low birth.

This weakness would soon be shown when the Song court decided that the time was ripe for revenge upon the Liao for the humiliations of the past. The Liao had in fact been no real threat from the 1060s onwards, but Song tribute payments had continued to be demanded and the Song saw their chance for retribution and to free themselves from the Liao yoke with the rise of the Jurchen, a tribal confederation hailing from Manchuria. The Jurchen leader, Aguda, rebelled against his Liao overlords and comprehensively defeated the Liao army. Aguda would go on to create the Jin Dynasty in northern China, and he took the imperial name of Taizu in 1115.

Emperor Huizong of Song moved quickly to ally with the Jin against the Liao. This may have been a reaction to the Song's failure to complete the destruction of the Tangut and their newly formed state of Xi Xia, as the Tangut were now allying with the Liao against the Jurchen, but it is more likely to have been simple opportunism and related entirely to a hope of recapturing the sixteen prefectures. The two emperors met aboard a ship and formed the so-called Pact on the Sea against the Liao – the state that Song still considered to be its greatest enemy. Taizu was wary of the Song and could not believe that they wanted to go to war over just the sixteen provinces. He may have feared that the Song intended to move a powerful force into the region to try to dominate the lands beyond their current borders once the Liao were destroyed by the Jin. Despite these misgivings he agreed to a pact and joint attack upon Liao in 1122. He need not have been concerned over the Song army's capability to project its power into the northern plains of China. Its heavy defeat at the hands of the Xi Xia in 1118 on Song's northwestern border would have fully reassured him about the Song military's frailties when fighting in the open country of the north.

Under the terms of the pact the Song were to reclaim their lost provinces in the north and pay the tribute they normally ceded to the Liao to the Jin. The weaknesses of the Song army soon became apparent during the joint campaign. The Jin quickly captured the western and central Liao capitals but the Song failed to take Beijing. The eunuch Tong Guan had been charged with the task but his army was utterly defeated and the panicking emperor ordered a retreat. In November another attempt was made on the city by a large force and the advance guard took its outer walls but was then beaten back by citadel guards. Then a Liao relief army arrived and ended all hope of success. An untidy retreat followed that included an ambush of part of the Song army and the panicked flight of the remainder of the troops.

Taizu took Beijing for the Song in January 1123. The Jin burned and looted and carried off numerous inhabitants before handing over the city. Taizu demanded one million strings of copper coin for this service, and when the Song demanded the return of the sixteen prefectures to them the payment expected by the Jin was increased to six hundred thousand units of silver. The remnants of the Liao Dynasty went on to form the Western Liao of Kara Kitai in what is today Kazahkstan and Kyrgyzstan.

The wreckage that the Jin made of the once flourishing city of Beijing was seen by the Song as a sign of Taizu's duplicity, whilst the failures of the Song military had made Taizu realise that the Song army was a paper tiger and that all their possessions in northern China might easily fall to him.

The almost inevitable Jin attack on Song was made in 1125 on the pretext that the Song court was harbouring an unsubmitted Liao general. They made a two-pronged attack on Beijing and Kaifeng. Much of the Song army that faced the Jin had not made effective war for over forty years and many of its commanders were collecting pay for troops that simply did not exist. Indeed, it was perhaps an 'open secret that generals over-reported the number of their soldiers, and exaggerated their military achievements'.[9] Beijing fell, but the fireships that the Jin sent against the water gates of Kaifeng were pinned in place by grappling hooks handled by specialist Song troops and then sunk by a barrage of rocks from the city walls. Other Song 'shock troops' took to ascending and descending on ropes to destroy Jin siege ladders and to cause chaos among the Jin troops trying to scale Kaifeng's walls. At the siege of Taiyuan, despite severe famine,

Song troops fought house to house against superior Jin forces, and their commander, Wang Bing, refused to submit and eventually killed himself in the Fenshui River, after 270 days of siege.

The Song court was caught entirely by surprise by the Jin assault and by January 1126 all of the recently regained sixteen provinces were lost. By the end of the year the Jin army was approaching the walls of Kaifeng and Emperor Huizong abdicated in favour of his son and fled south. The new emperor, Qinzong, immediately treated with the Jin, ceding territory and vast amounts of gold, silk, camels and horses after witnessing the defeat of a Song army close to his capital.

Qinzong then made a series of strange and contradictory decisions. He sent ninety thousand men into Hebei and sixty thousand men to relieve Taiyuan. Both armies were crushed, but he continued to disperse his forces to territories that were already beyond saving. He still reportedly retained about one hundred thousand men at Kaifeng, a force that should have been capable of fending off the Jin offensive if the other Song forces available had been used effectively. The eventual fall of Kaifeng was then not directly related to the number of men in the field but to a series of appalling strategic decisions made within the walls of the Song court. This was the same egregious process that the Song leadership would repeat over and over in their wars against the Jin and the Mongols.

On 9 January, during a heavy snowfall, the Jin brought siege engines to Kaifeng's walls. They lost about three thousand men in the ensuing battle, but it was a characteristic of the Jin and of the Mongols that their leaders found heavy losses of their own troops perfectly acceptable as long as objectives were attained, and by secreting away the bodies of the dead the Jin generals were able to maintain morale. Only three hundred of the Song garrison were killed during the assault but the Song commanders failed to undertake the same subterfuge as the Jin and bodies were left lying among increasingly demoralised troops.

The siege of Kaifeng only lasted thirty-three days and ended on 5 March 1126, when the Jin's second assault smashed all Song resistance. Emperor Qinzong gave them free entrance to the city and ensured that they were provided with loot, horses and young women. Many palace women drowned themselves to avoid their fate.

Both of the Song emperors – the 'retired' Huizong and Qinzong – had now been captured by the Jin, and a Jin puppet regime named Chu with Huizong and Qinzong as its nominal heads was formed in the old Song lands of north China.

Right from its inception Chu was a troublesome state for the Jin. Their brutality caused local rebellions, and they had also failed to 'decapitate' Song effectively, despite their capture of Huizong and Qinzong. Another prince of the Song line, Zhao Gou, was safe in Nanjing and his elevation to the Song throne as a new emperor gave a focus for general anti-Jin feeling right across China. It is also of course possible that the Jurchen had never been intent during their attacks on Song on undertaking an extensive conquest or state building per se but rather on large-scale raiding and the simple extortion of tribute from Song. Song's spectacular military collapse may have taken the Jurchen by surprise, and the rapid cobbling together of the state of Chu was then forced upon them by events. Either way, it soon became obvious that the state of Chu was not fit for purpose.

Zhao Gou came to the throne very unprepared and with greatness thrust upon him. He was installed as Emperor Gaozong in the new Song capital of Nanjing in 1127. He seems to have considered seeking a comprehensive peace with Jin in order to secure his regime but to have realised that such an undertaking would have undermined his legitimacy. Of course he also had the uncomfortable fact that two other 'legitimate' emperors were in the hands of the Jin weighing on him. For simple good form's sake he had to give the impression of trying to retrieve them from their captors through negotiation, whilst fully recognising that an alternate reign to his own, with tacit Jin backing, might spring from either Qinzong or Huizong and challenge him for his Nanjing throne.[10]

Gaozong ceded every city north of the Huai River to the Jin, along with a tribute of ten million gold ingots, twenty million silver ingots and ten million bolts of silk, but also brought a minister, Li Gang, known for his hostility to the Jin, into his government and undertook some impressive sabre rattling. Li Gang was then quickly removed from power, but the belligerent mandarin was always kept at court, as if to back up Gaozong's posturing and claims that he would invade the north. The Jin's continued problems in Chu, and the fact that their troops were losing their effectiveness as steppe warriors among the rivers and canals of the new front line, assisted Gaozong in his policy as the Jin court's appetite for the war also waned.

Furthermore, competent military leadership was now finally emerging among the Song, and the examples of resistance at Taiyuan and Kaifeng described above show that there did already exist both sophistication and courage in the Song military. Working against any renaissance of the Song military's fortunes, however, was the superiority of the Jin in terms of cavalry and the suitability of lands north of the Yellow River for mounted archery. The Song army was strongly infantry based, and the effects of the long peace that the Song army had 'endured' had still not quite been washed away.

In the next period of conflict between the Jin and the Song, we see three trends emerge that would remain constant throughout the rest of the history of Song's resistance to both the Jin and to the Mongols. Two of these are interrelated: the increasing importance to the dynasty's survival of the Song's navy, and Song's harnessing – albeit sometimes not totally successfully – of southern China's powerful economy to fund long wars. This was something that the alien dynasties never really seemed to be able to achieve, as they tended to exploit rather than nourish the economy. Indeed, it has even been hypothesised that, had Kaifeng remained under Song control, it could have been the hub of an industrial revolution in China some seven hundred years or so before Europe's. Jin occupation destroyed all that the Song had achieved there, which included by 1021 the presence of five hundred thousand official residents, and an impressive transport and manufacturing industry.[11]

The last of the three trends that grew throughout the long wars with Jin was the development of a lore of great heroes of resistance, whose mortal deeds, while impressive, were in fact less important than what later generations made of them. The first of these new heroes was General Yue Fei, a man of humble northern Chinese origins:

> who repelled the enemy assaults in 1133 and 1134, until in 1135 the now confident Song army was in a position to recover all of north China from the Jin Dynasty . . . [In 1140] Yue Fei initiated a general counterattack against the Jin armies, defeating one enemy after another until he bivouacked within range of the Northern Song Dynasty's old capital city, Kaifeng,

> in preparation for the final assault against the enemy. Yet in the same year Qin [Hui] ordered Yue Fei to abandon his campaign, and in 1141 Yue Fei was summoned back to the Southern Song capital. It is believed that the emperor then ordered Yue Fei to be hanged.[12]

Yue Fei's successes against the Jin and against bandits in his own lands were partly because of his innate talents but also the result of the court's sense of shock over the loss of northern China and a subsequent campaign to rebuild the army as an effective fighting force. The Jin assaults had spurred local government in the northern region into action far ahead of any response from the court at Nanjing, and after 1127 local Song military forces were the largest of any time in Song history. The population of Song at this time was about one hundred and forty million, or twice that of the Tang, and the army had grown along with the population and pro rata had outstripped it. It reportedly numbered 378,000 men in 960, 900,000 men in 1000 and 1,259,000 men in 1041. In this year it also effectively required some 80 per cent of the state's revenue simply to maintain it.

These local initiatives were undoubtedly a reaction to the tardiness of central government in responding to the crisis, but when the court did finally react these units were rapidly amalgamated into the Song army. Carrying out this unification was enormously expensive, but it effectively repaired the damage done to the army in the 1125–7 campaigns and reduced the risk of local defections.

This increase in manpower, married to the emergence of a crop of good generals such as Yue Fei, who were tutored by war and not by the peace of forty years, and the Song's ability to use the Huai River as a defence line and transport medium brought hard-won successes. The year 1130 saw the Song army and navy operating in harmony under General Han Shizong in a battle on the Huai River near Zhenjiang. The general, tradition tells us, led a cavalry charge against the enemy, whilst his wife beat drums aboard her war-junk to encourage the sailors. Han Shizong surrounded and cut off the Jin army for forty-eight days, and when they tried to re-cross the river to escape their small boats were turned over by chains and grappling irons thrown from Song ships.

Between 1134 and 1135, Yue Fei retook much of the territory lost in the 1120s, and that this was a campaign of grim attrition is demonstrated by the general's deployment of men with axes to hack at the horses' legs of the Jin *guai zima*, a very heavy cavalry unit comprising mailed troopers linked together by chains. The traditional steppe warrior Jin system of rapid cavalry charges by mounted archers had evidently failed among the waterways of eastern China and by 1141 a parity between the two opponents was evident as Song loyalist forces began to emerge and coordinate in Jin lands, and the state of Chu disintegrated in 1137. The Jin resorted to direct control of Chu; the garrisoning that this required further depleted the front-line forces available to them. The undertaking of the management of a settled state also practically forced the Jin Dynasty to become Sinicised, and the change in role this thrust upon the Jin dynasty's ruling elite tore at the fabric of the Jurchen tribal base of the state. The Jin army comprised a variety of ethnicities and, whilst Han Chinese were by this stage the bulk of the army, the Jurchen were the cavalry elite. That so many of these tribesmen deserted the Jin state and joined Chinggis Khan's army when the Mongols began their incursions in the thirteenth century is almost entirely explainable by the loss of connection between them and the centre of the Jin government. This dangerous tension between the steppe warriors that could rapidly bring a Turko-Mongolic dynasty to power and the transformation of such a confederation to a state by its leaders has been a constant of Eurasian history. The desertion of the Ottoman Sultan Bayezid's troops to Timur Leng at Ankara in 1402 and the ongoing antipathy between the Mongol Chagataid *horde* and the Mongol *state* of Persia are just two examples of a quandary that was only ever successfully resolved by the genius of the Ottoman Sultan Mehemmed the Conqueror. The Jin evidently never fixed on a solution.[13]

The Song court therefore chose this moment of perceived weakness in their enemy to negotiate with the Jin. However, the Jin's acceptance of peace overtures hinged on the sacrifice of Yue Fei, since he was now the sole belligerent voice at court and continued to advocate an invasion of Jin lands. The Song Emperor Gaozong wrote personally to Yue Fei to thank him for his efforts and then had him poisoned. In fact, the assassination of this political general fitted as much with the Song court's aspiration of controlling the military as with the need for peace with the Jin. General Yue Fei became a figure of veneration and his patriotic cry of '*huan wo he shan*' (literally 'return my rivers and mountains' but usually rendered as 'give me back my country') would be remembered much later by Song loyalists during their resistance to the Mongols. The murder of Yue Fei was the direct result of the fact that the Song court was caught in a dilemma, as it had become both suspicious of but also highly dependent on the military from 1127 as armies were shifted to the northern border. Civilian officials had taken over the bureau of military affairs in the eleventh century, but the legitimacy of Gaozong's rule, as we have seen, depended on a pretence of retaking the north from the Jin. The difficulty with this stratagem was that successful generals such as Yue Fei found influence through victory in the field and not through honours and privileges bestowed by the court. There was a potential threat of the military becoming a dangerously independent body within the state. The fall of Yue Fei was just one example of the court's attempts to curtail the influence of military men in political circles. In fact, the loyalty of the military caste to the Song court up until the final defection of the Lu family in 1273, which signalled the beginning of the end of the dynasty, is quite astounding given the often appalling response to their fealty and courage by the Song court.

The Shaoxing Peace accord of 1142 placed the Song in a ritually inferior position to the Jin and was entirely unsatisfactory to both sides, but the war had reached a stalemate and would not be reignited until Hailing Wang, Prince Hailing, of the Jin began planning a massive assault on the Song in 1159. His mobilisation, although on a vast scale, was ignored by the Song court until Emperor Gaozong began a belated and hasty defensive preparation in April 1161 after receiving an insulting embassy from the Jin demanding lands beyond the Huai and Han, two rivers which were by now effectively Song's defence line.

The attack came on 25 September in a four-pronged assault across the Huai River, with Jin forces reportedly totalling about six hundred thousand men. The Jin forced the river with a pontoon bridge, but once across it they made little headway, and whilst many border cities changed hands repeatedly in the ensuing months, the action on the river and off the coast of Shandong was decidedly more important. The Jin navy was totally outclassed by that of the Song in every encounter, and the Jin General Wu Zhu neatly summed up the strengths and weaknesses of both sides when he said, 'the Song are as good with their boats as we are with horses.'

Prince Hailing was assassinated by his own generals, who then entered into negotiations with the Song on 15 December 1161, whilst simultaneously attempting to put down a rebellion among Chinese peasants called in the name of the Song in their lands to the north. The Jin managed a fighting retreat that also tried to cause enough damage to Song lands to encourage Gaozong to hurry along an offer of peace.

The following year, 1162, saw the Song court in a state of inertia about how to deal with the Jin. Its courtiers were divided into factions following various personalities; this tendency for the court to pursue partisan politics rather than a cooperative approach to governance was another feature of the government bureau exams system that would severely hamper the court's response during the later Mongol war. Acrimony was common between established courtiers and 'new men' entering the court, and the potential for factions to form was always present.

Eventually, one faction led by the minister Zhang Jun won the new Emperor Xiaozong's favour, and an assault on the Jin was made across the Huai River on 18 June 1163. There is little doubt that the Jin were massing for a further assault and that Zhang Jun's pre-emptive strike was both timely and well delivered, but as the expeditionary army fought its way further and further north from the river, both the loss of naval advantage and the Song's weakness in cavalry became more and more significant. The Song histories tell us that the expedition failed because of a dispute between General Li Xianzhong and one of his subordinates, who enticed many of the army's senior officers into deserting just as Li Xianzhong was poised to crush the Jin. This may be true, but the 'rout of the Fuli expedition' and Li Xianzhong's subsequent costly retreat was in fact as much related to the Song court's overestimation of its army's ability to operate beyond the Huai River line and to political and strategic overreaching as it was to one man's treachery.

However, the Jin were also exhausted by the contest, and their request for peace probably saved both Zhang Jun from disgrace and the Song's illusory claim on the sixteen prefectures from extinction. Negotiations between the two sides finished in January 1165 with a reduction in the payments made to the Jin and less humiliating terms in the peace treaty, as the payments were not listed as 'tribute'. The fact remains, though, that much blood had been shed by the Song army and none of the territory lost in the treaty of 1141 had been regained. Like the sixteen prefectures, this loss of lands would rankle with the Song court and cause further blunders of strategy in the future.

Four decades of military stalemate followed and, to some degree, the question of being a hawk or dove as regards the Jin took second place at the Song court, behind reform of both domestic and military affairs. Perhaps the work of strengthening central and local military administration and improving economic resources was aimed at an eventual recapture of the provinces lost to the Jin, but if this was the case then the emperor was a very patient man and it is just as likely that much of the changes undertaken by Emperor Xiaozong were in fact aimed at gathering more power and control over policy into his own hands and away from those of his ministers. His reign was certainly the most independent of any of the later Song emperors. Limiting his ministers' tenure of office and interfering in all aspects of authority wielded by their respective offices effectively freed him of the risk that any minister would become overly powerful. However, he did sow the seeds of later problems when he gave the chief counsellors of state, the so-called counsellors of the right and left,[14] the concurrent positions of commissioners of military affairs. Further power was given to these men and their assistants when the bureau of national finance was also taken into their charge. Xiaozong's habit of bypassing his counsellors of the right and left with direct orders to the lower ministries largely negated the immediate effect of these changes, but later, weaker, emperors did not have the strength of personality to overrule their senior counsellors and the Song state would suffer from his negligent act of placing these all-important levers of state in only two pairs of hands. By the end of the dynasty it was possible for a skilled politician such as Jia Sidao to encapsulate all the power of the emperor and the court and to implement a personal autocracy.

In order to counteract the power of his official or outer court, Xiaozong also nurtured the development of an informal 'inner court' of confidants made up chiefly of palace attendants who were given low-ranking ceremonial positions which nonetheless gave them virtually unlimited access to the emperor. On one occasion when the outer court challenged the emperor over his favouring of the inner court with a demand that he transmit all imperial orders through the established bureaucratic channels, Xiaozong responded that doing so 'would mean that even when the palace wishes to get a drink or some food, it would have to obtain court verification. Now, would that not be over-restraining?' The imperial recorder, Hong Mai, also recorded the fact that Xiaozong commonly issued orders directly to the bureau of military affairs, completely bypassing his chief counsellors and their entire secretariat.[15]

Xiaozong worked hard to secure a fuller central control over agriculture and the state's financial system. He evidently understood very clearly that these were the chief strengths of the Song state during both peace and war. Irrigation schemes were encouraged to increase agrarian productivity along the Yangzi, and a secondary effect of this was to produce large tracts of ploughed land along the border with Jin that could severely hinder the progress of any northern invaders' cavalry. Willow trees were also planted along the border as they too disrupted cavalry trains and any hope of a war of rapid movement.

Statements of official spending were demanded from every bureau and from all prefectures on a monthly basis by the emperor, as Xiaozong attempted to force prudence upon all parts of the government and to reduce fraud from within the system. Even religious ceremonies became victims of Xiaozong's austerity drive but, despite initial attempts to do so, the military budget was not to be cut. Initially this seems surprising as the state was at peace, but 80 per cent of the state's funds were still being consumed by the army and the army had actually grown to four hundred thousand men since 1165.[16] Perhaps one particular analect of Confucius – 'if pacific negotiations are in progress, warlike preparations should have been made beforehand' – had caught the emperor's eye, or perhaps he just felt that given the uneasy peace between his state and that of the Jin a further confrontation was inevitable.

Officer recruitment became a major preoccupation for the government after an imperial recorder brought to the emperor's attention the fact that many descendants of military officials were failing to maintain their families' traditions of service in the army out of a sense of shame, now that the position of 'soldier' had slid so far down the social scale. Xiaozong tackled this unfortunate development by the giving of special honours to suitable men from the families of former generals and by allowing his military commissioners to recruit new generals personally.

Much of the government's spending on fortification went to the area north of the Yangzi and Huai regions and also on wall repairs to the great fortress of Xiangyang. A new priority was also given to the northwestern frontier, particularly in Sichuan province, where a refinement of Wang Anshi's *baojia* system was made through the reform of the local militia. These peasant-militiamen were trained during the winter months when they were not occupied with tending their fields and could form, by the end of the reforms, a force of some twenty-four thousand men who effectively made no salary demands on the imperial treasury. The same process was repeated in the Huai and Yangzi regions and in Hubei and Henan, and special rewards were given to any exceptional citizen-soldiers.

A step beyond this was the creation of military farms or colonies, populated by soldiers on the borders of the state, where rather more time was devoted to the military than would be expected of ordinary peasants. However, this scheme faltered early on and, whilst some colonies were successful, many were abandoned as financial and agrarian failures.

By 1169 Xiaozong's policy towards the Jin had turned a corner and was, if not expansionist, at least provocative. His renovation of the fortifications of Yangzhou, a city across the Yangzi, and his dispatch of some twenty thousand troops to complete the project indicates that he was, at least to some degree, in harmony with his minister Yu Yunwen, who proposed sending envoys to the Jin, requesting the return of territories containing Song imperial tombs. The request was refused by the Jin court, and to increase the diplomatic pressure on them the hawkish Yu Yunwen was then dispatched as military commissioner to Sichuan. The emperor and his former minister then argued over Yu Yunwen's perceived reluctance to push on with reconquest plans, but upon minster Yu Yunwen's death Xiaozong lauded his memory with honours and was delighted when he discovered how far the minister had improved the Sichuan army in terms of the quality of its troops and the increase in the number of its cavalry.

Xiaozong's pleasure at the re-strengthened army of Sichuan is evidence of his desire to see his state outstrip Jin militarily, as is his statement of 1176, when he lamented that whilst his dynasty was domestically far superior to that of the Han and Tang, it had not matched their military achievements. His military posturing against the old enemy continued with large-scale military exercises being undertaken in 1177 and 1185, in which the emperor played an active part. Archery training was also a common sight in and around the imperial palace. The emperor involved himself in this training and in horsemanship. The learning and honing of archery skills was also required of imperial university students before they could graduate. As scholars began to learn more of the military arts, government offices began to welcome just a few soldiers. Prefectural offices, formerly the preserve of men of the pen, were given to men of the sword, provided that they were capable, and the emperor appointed generals himself rather than giving this power to the civilian officers of his outer court.

The emperor's confidence in his state's ability to defend itself encouraged him to test the limits of his relationship with the Jin. Under the agreement of 1165 the Song emperor was required to leave his throne to receive any messenger from the Jin court. In 1182, the traditional New Year's greeting from the Jin emperor was received by a comfortably seated Xiaozong. The affront was obvious; the 'younger son' or junior emperor Xiaozong was clearly stating that he was now the equal of the Jin emperor and no longer needed to stand as a sign of respect for his 'father'. There was diplomatic expression of anger from the Jin but no immediate military response. Xiaozong must have felt at this point that he had reached at least parity with the Jin's military forces.

Xiaozong also effectively created a war chest on a huge scale when he created the Sealed Treasury in 1170. Both the palace and the state had independent treasuries, and Xiaozong created this third treasury to allow for direct expenditure on the military, which was administered by the outer court but maintained by the palace treasury officers. In this way, Xiaozong could continue to pump funds into the military without waiting for cycles of taxation to cover expenses.

By the time of his abdication in 1189, Xiaozong had gone a long way to rehabilitating the Song state from its decrepitude of the first half of the twelfth century. Its status militarily versus the Jin had improved, in terms of the domestic economy it outclassed that state easily, and the treasuries, including the war chest, were full. The emperor's power was also almost unbridled and he took direct control of much of the state's business, including the military. Such direction was an asset to the state as long as the emperor was as charismatic, focused and committed as Xiaozong; it was a liability if any lesser man should ascend the throne.

Xiaozong abdicated following the death of his adoptive father, the 'retired' Emperor Gaozong, in 1187, but did not officially withdraw from the mandate for another two years while he attempted to mentor his son, Guangzong, in the duties of the emperor. Xiaozong therefore observed two years of the three required years of mourning rites for his father whilst still guiding his heir. The effect on Xiaozong of the death of his adopted father was evidently profound. Normal court life was suspended for more than a month, and when Xiaozong did eventually return to public life he reportedly appeared frail both physically and psychologically.[17] Perhaps, in his heart, he also knew that, despite his attempts to leave Guangzong with a body of good counsellors, a well-functioning state and his own significant investment of fatherly advice, his son would ultimately fail in the role of emperor. Indeed, at the outset of this mentoring arrangement, with his father working 'behind a curtain', Guangzong panicked and refused to take on the burden of the empire, although he did eventually return to the office of co-emperor under his father's more direct stewardship.

Immediately following Xiaozong's death, Guangzong withdrew completely from political life and Song China went from autocracy to effective anarchy before the inner and outer courts combined – despite their own mutual antipathy – to force abdication on the emperor in 1194. The creators of the *Songshi*, the official history of the Song Dynasty, point the finger at Guangzong's wife, the Lady Li, for driving the emperor to insanity through her selfish indulgence, arrogance and jealousy, and there may be some truth in this. Certainly finding the severed hands of a court lady whose beauty Guangzong had praised the day before, in a jar of food he was about to help himself to at lunch, was not what the doctor would order for a man with a documented heart condition.

A son of Guangzong, Ningzong, was chosen for the throne in 1195, but he came to the mandate with no governmental experience and having had a lifetime closeted within palaces. His highly dysfunctional family life and the docile and subservient nature this had in imbued in Ningzong ensured that the court and the women of the imperial family had placed a mere cipher at the head of the Song state. It is recorded that the dowager empress did not inform the new emperor of his impending accession, that his coronation robes were ordered without his knowledge and that when Ningzong refused the honour, standing before the coffin of his grandfather, the imperial robe was thrust upon his shoulders and officials appeared out of nowhere to kowtow before their new emperor.[18] Ningzong's emotional frailty and apparently trusting nature naturally led him to value the closer relationships to be found in the inner court over the more austere and officious outer court, and he rapidly sacrificed many of these men – men of great experience going back to the days of Xiaozong – in order to protect one favourite, Han Tuozhou. This courtier steadily accrued offices and titles, including that of prince, and by the 1200s effectively ran the state. Part of the problem was that many men of the outer court favoured a form of neo-Confucianism called *daoxue* or 'study of the way' which stressed propriety, respect for ancient rites and correct manners and a frugal lifestyle. Against this stoic rigor, perhaps rather easier to admire than to imitate, Han Tuozhou was a boon companion of the emperor, who was now frequently to be found with female entertainers. When Han Tuozhou began a campaign of persecution against the neo-Confucianists in the late 1190s and used it as a vehicle through which effectively to purge the outer court, he enjoyed the emperor's full backing.

Many of these purged and disgraced officials were later officially rehabilitated when Ningzong felt the need of their advice as his regime, under Han Tuozhou's stewardship, mired itself in the early 1200s, but virtually all refused to serve again. The naivety of the foreign policy decisions made in the early thirteenth century by Ningzong and minister Han Tuozhou are partly explained by this intellectual decapitation of the Song government.

Ningzong signalled his intent to challenge the Jin emperor in 1201, when rumours were allowed to travel abroad that he intended to appoint Han Tuozhou to the post of manager of national security, a position that only existed in times of war that would have essentially made Han Tuozhou a generalissimo with power over the entirety of the military apparatus of the Song state, as well as unbridled sway over civilian and financial affairs. There was also a Song military build-up in Sichuan in 1202, as the court began to respond to intelligence filtering out of the Jin state.

From 1200, Jin had begun to move much of its military from its southern border to the north, as the pressure on its lands from steppe tribes had been increasing year on year. This new requirement for military preparedness had also severely strained the Jin state following a series of disastrous floods in the Yellow River valley. Of course the Jin had never been as careful in their husbandry of the state as the Song emperors had been, particularly Xiaozong. They had never built up a state grain reserve and they now found themselves facing banditry on a vast scale as the state tipped towards an anarchy born of desperation, while foodstuffs disappeared from markets and farmers abandoned ruined lands. In 1203 a Song ambassador passed through Jin lands and reported to Ningzong's court that the Jin rule was run ragged throughout the lands; further confirmation was given in 1205 by another senior government envoy to the Jin court who reported a similar scene.

However, in 1203 the Jin began to swing some forces back to their southern border and, whilst this movement was probably primarily directed at putting down banditry and preventing the flight of Han Chinese peasants into Song lands, the Song court could not discount the fact that the Jin were reinforcing the area north of the Huai River, possibly as a preliminary to an invasion of the south. Large-scale raids or even an attempt to occupy the Huai valley born of desperation at the conditions in the north were not beyond imagination.

The belligerent stance of the Song court led it to commit to a further bolstering of military strength along their side of the Huai but there was no immediate response to this from the Jin, bar further reinforcement of the border and a flurry of conciliatory diplomatic initiatives. At first glance this is surprising, given that every previous encounter between the sides had been initiated by the Jin; this time things were different. The entirety of Shandong province had required famine relief efforts from the Jin government for the last decade, and the Jin emperor could be sure that any war with Song would stir up the dissatisfaction of his Han citizens to new heights and was likely to cause mass defections of Han Chinese to his opponents at all levels of the state. The succinct and pithy statement of the Shandong bandit Li Quan sums up nicely the Han Chinese population's attitude to their foreign overlords: 'I would rather be a southern Chinese ghost than serve as a Jin official.'[19]

Song reorganised its command structures for the war it was now planning to initiate. Court officials took up new commands in the Huai central, western and eastern regions. By moving civilians into these posts, Han Tuozhou and the inner court hoped to neutralise the effects of Xiaozong's restoration of military command over the armies, but they also sowed the seeds of disaster by removing experienced generals from the field of grand strategy and by restricting them to the care of the battlefields alone. The mistakes began with mobilisation and with the readying of the army for the campaign. The Song border defences along the Huai were not ready to withstand any Jin counterattack that might be launched, logistical support for mobilised troops was haphazardly available at frontier stations and the army had barely exercised since the death of Xiaozong.

Han Tuozhou ran an effective propaganda campaign for the coming war of aggression, with the posthumous rehabilitation of Yue Fei and the denigration of his opponent of the time, minister Qin Hui. Yue Fei's body was disinterred and reburied at a temple near the famous West Lake of Hangzhou. Nearby to the temple a small statue of Qin Hui and his 'equally treacherous' wife was also later erected. These days it is difficult to make out the features of the disgraced minister and his spouse as they kneel in humble apology to Yue Fei. They customarily wear a thick mask of dried spittle, courtesy of the numerous Chinese tourists visiting the temple on a daily basis. Han Tuozhou also sponsored the creation of new histories of the Song Dynasty that strongly emphasised a glorious time when all of China was held under the sway of the Song emperor. He failed, however, to act with any decisiveness at the outset of the war, and depended on sponsored bandit raids along the border and on inciting rebellion deeper within the Jin lands, primarily in Shandong, rather than relying on the Song army. Even when these proxy bandit wars brought a fairly ineffectual response from the Jin, Han Tuozhou failed to act and to take the initiative.

The Song army was finally deployed in May 1206 and even then we cannot be certain whether the offensive unleashed by the commanders stationed on the central Huai front had official sanction from the court or not. Be that as it may, the war went well for Song on this front, with the rapid capture of Jin territory in Anhui and east Henan provinces, but further west, offensives in both west Henan and Sichuan ended in total defeat for Song. If the Song strategy for the war was dependent on the simultaneous success of both the eastern and western operations, as seems likely, then the campaign was doomed from this point. The Song were, in fact, weak in troop numbers in the east, and the thinking seems to have been that success in the west would draw Jin troops to that region to defend their flank, and that this would equalise the numbers of troops facing each other across the central and eastern Huai. This did not occur, despite the large numerical advantage the Song held in the west. The armies of the central and eastern Huai front therefore fought an offensive and later defensive war against numbers that they could not hope to overcome. Given this, their initial successes are quite surprising and of course proved to be unsustainable.

That there was such an imbalance between the forces in the west and the east can only be explained through the unusual relationship the Song court had with the province of Sichuan and its military. In truth, given the slow speed and fragility of medieval communication, even in an advanced state such as Song China, Sichuan was geographically far beyond the direct control of the court and a degree of freedom from central control had always existed in the province. The court tried to control this dangerous independent-mindedness by a regular rotation of civilian and military commissioners, but there was still the problem of military dynasties and of noble families accruing the loyalties of the army to themselves rather than the troops maintaining a direct adherence to the state. The Wu family was such a military clan, and Wu Xi was the general charged by the Song court with bringing success in the war of 1206.

Strong personal links between General Wu Xi and his army of some sixty thousand men meant that transferring these men from his charge to the commanders of the Huai front was impossible and that replacing Wu if he showed either insubordination or ineptitude was likely to cause a mutiny on the Sichuan front. Despite his considerable forces Wu Xi obtained no victories in the west, and his failure to overcome numerically inferior Jin forces at two strategic points about 200 kilometres west of the ancient city of Xian led to the total unravelling of the Song war plan. The offensive consequently ground to a halt, but Han Tuozhou still pushed ahead with a full declaration of war on the Jin; or rather, he tried to declare war but in a strange form of passive resistance to the war the bureaucrats given the task of drafting the declaration refused the undertaking.

By this point, the conventions of war and peace were largely academic as the Song failed to make any further headway over the next three months and were then pushed into retreat by a masterly Jin counterattack. Seventy thousand Jin troops pushed back through Anhui and towards the Huai and they were only held there by the presence of a courageous Song prefect, Bi Caiyu, who, though outnumbered ten to one, managed both quickly to bring forward fresh troops to plug the gaps that were appearing all across the narrow front and to burn the Jin's provisions in a commando attack. After three months the Jin retreated, but this was only one of nine Jin columns that pierced the 1,200-kilometre Song front in both the east and the west. Of Song's major defence points, only Xiangyang withstood the Jin. They retreated from the fortress city after three months, but everywhere else the Song army was pushed back.

During this assault the Jin pushed the majority of their one hundred and forty-five thousand men to the east to smash through the thinly defended Huai frontier, but in Sichuan only a fraction of the Jin army counterattacked against Wu Xi's army of ninety thousand men and the twenty-four thousand men of the Sichuan militia. The Jin, despite their limited forces, met with many easy successes in the west. Given Sichuan's mountains and valleys, which favour the defender, and the province's later stubborn defence against the invading Mongols, this success is only explicable by the personal actions of Wu Xi.

The general was directed by the court to respond to the Jin thrusts into the region around his headquarters of Xingzhou in the summer of 1206 but, even as the Jin approached to within 30 kilometres of the city, Wu Xi failed to respond. Wu Xi has not been treated kindly by history for his actions that summer or subsequently, but his case is in many ways indicative of the problems that existed between the Song court, directing war policy and attempting to interfere in the strategies that would bring about the policy, and the Song generals, resentful of interference and, often as not, more bound to a region than to the state per se. This was the complete reverse of the Mongol state, arguably the most successful medieval military entity. Mongol strategy at 'khan level' was broadly set and freedom was given to the generals in the field to meet objectives. Mongol higher command was more interested in timetabling events than in micromanaging them. Qubilai Khan is traditionally credited with having said, 'that a general during the campaign need not follow court orders is sound military law.' This made for a more adaptable response to the enemy's riposte and other difficulties, and one of the greatest strengths of the Mongol military was its ability to concentrate forces that had been separated for logistical reasons right up until the point that their unification was required. In short, the Song approach to war was simply too rigid, as the Song military theorist He Yanxi identified in his commentary on Sunzi (*c.*1000):

> Now in war there may be one hundred changes in each step. When one sees he can, he advances; when he sees that things are difficult, he retires. To say that a general must await commands of the sovereign in such circumstances is like informing a superior that you wish to put out a fire. Before the order to do so arrives the ashes are cold. And it is said one must consult the army supervisor in these matters! This is as if in building a house beside the road one took advice from those who pass by. Of course the work could never be completed!
>
> To put a rein on an able general while at the same time asking him to suppress a cunning enemy is like tying up the Black Hound of Han and then ordering him to catch elusive hares. What is the difference?[20]

During the autumn of 1206, Wu Xi studiously avoided deploying his forces in any place where they might engage with the enemy and he effectively halted the entire western Song army from any action. It seems most likely that he was assessing his options between Song and Jin and who would prevail in Sichuan. He was certainly acting antithetically to Sunzi's ideal general, 'the jewel of the kingdom', who 'advances without coveting fame and retreats without fearing disgrace, whose only thought is to protect his country and do good service for his sovereign'. Wu Xi eventually defected during the Spring Festival of 1207. Jin records indicate simple financial bribery, but the title of prince of Shu that the Jin gave him and the possibility of avoiding the destruction of an occupying Jin army in his lands probably helped with negotiations too.

By his defection Wu Xi had inordinately weakened Song in the war but he had also opened up a Pandora's box of deceit that soon enough caused the Jin so many problems in Sichuan that their success in the west swiftly collapsed amid assassinations and double-dealing. Wu Xi attempted to woo other military commanders in Sichuan to his banner and to bring them into an independent government rather than have them either remain loyal to Song or defect to Jin outright. Two men, An Ping a former city commander, and Cheng Song, Wu Xi's superior in the province prior to the debacle of 1206, both accepted the new Jin prince's offer of posts.

The arrangements did not endure. Wu Xi had Cheng Song assassinated soon after, and this led quickly to a grand conspiracy against Wu Xi, led by An Ping. Seventy assassins infiltrated the prince's residence, despite a guard of one thousand men, and Wu Xi was seized and hacked to pieces. His head was placed in the marketplace, the people apparently rejoiced and his entire extended family was murdered. The princedom of Shu ended after only forty-one days and the Song court was not only uninvolved in its fall but during its demise was even trying to tempt Wu Xi back to loyalty by outbidding Jin.

Han Tuozhou then finally seems to have acknowledged the reality of the situation in Sichuan, and he plumped for placing a few men of known loyalty in official positions in the province. He was forced to replace the now deceased Wu Xi as assistant pacification commissioner of Sichuan with An Ping because, given the way one thousand guards had neglected their duty on the night of Wu Xi's fall, he evidently had the army in his pocket. The semi-independent lords of Sichuan then quickly retook all of the Jin's gains in the province and everything looked set for a return to nominal Song rule in the region. However, these quick victories against the Jin fostered rivalries and a round of poisonings, assassinations and banishments occurred, mostly under An Ping's guiding hand, before all his rivals were eliminated and An Ping was promoted to grand military commissioner in chief by Han Tuozhou. The infighting, in some ways, aided the Song court in that an effective military dictatorship now took hold in Sichuan and imposed stability, but the judicial murders of popular and valorous generals such as Yang Juyuan and Li Haoyi reportedly brought the common soldiery to tears. The army's morale was dangerously corroded by the acts of its leaders.

The war went into stalemate. The Song armies of Bi Caiyu and Zhao Fang steadfastly defended the central border regions, and with the Jin having overcommitted to this front and to unproductive sieges of Xiangyang and other fortresses there was little hope for them of a second breakthrough in the west. Clashes between the two sides became less frequent, though at Xiangyang two Song generals had led a spectacular special forces raid on the Jin camp, and by the end of 1207 negotiations that had actually begun back in 1206 at the behest of the Song court were pursued once more.

Initial Jin demands were, however, too harsh for the Song to accept and included territory, an increase in tribute and the surrender of the instigator of the war, Han Tuozhou. The Song's chief negotiator kept this last demand from the Song court when he returned in September 1207. Han Tuozhou dismissed the envoys from their position, but by doing so he may have sealed his fate, as the Jin demand for the minister's head as one part of the price for peace became the common currency of conversations between the unhappy ex-envoys and other dissatisfied men at court. Han Tuozhou had also been losing influence at court since 1206, as he had been summarily dismissing military leaders who failed to achieve immediate victories. His appointees had done no better and in some cases worse than the men they replaced, and both the inner and outer court began to distance themselves from a minister whose policies seemed to be leading to military humiliation at the very least, and total disaster at worst. Han Tuozhou also made the mistake of sacrificing the few loyal followers he had in an attempt to shift the blame for the war from himself. With a string of banishments placed upon previously loyal men he effectively stripped himself of his last supports and seemed to be relying entirely on escalating the war both as an exit strategy and to resecure his grip on power.

The almost inevitable coup came at the end of 1207, when the hungover minister was stopped on his way to his morning audience with the emperor by the palace guard, who then dragged him outside the walls and murdered him. That a minister should be beaten to death was shocking by Song standards of behaviour towards scholar-officials, but what was more surprising was that the most likely instigator of Han Tuozhou's fall was the empress.

Empress Yang was Emperor Ningzong's second imperial bride; he had married her in 1200 after the death of his first wife, Empress Han, who was also Han Tuozhou's niece. Empress Yang owed nothing to Han Tuozhou and the minister undoubtedly feared her. He was right to do so, for the empress was exceptionally politically astute and went so far in her plotting as to exclude even the emperor from the conspiracy until the minister was in the custody of the guards. She had also criticised both the handling of the war and Han Tuozhou himself in the summer of 1207. Her absolute scorn for Han Tuozhou is reflected in the fact that she also ordered the public flogging of one of Han's widows. The empress was more merciful with most of Han Tuozhou's former associates, but one of his notable ex-ministers and favourites was specifically recalled from his banishment in Guangzhou to be summarily executed.

Men untainted by association with Han Tuozhou were promoted to be counsellors of the left and right, and the peace talks with Jin were restored. The Jin dropped their demands for territory and a downgrading of the Song emperor in his relationship to the Jin emperor, but the annual 'gift' to the Jin court was increased from two hundred and fifty thousand to three hundred thousand units of account, to be made up in silver and bolts of silk. The head of Han Tuozhou was also demanded and given. The Song managed to reduce the shame of having the corpse of their former high minister being publicly defiled by their enemy by having Han Tuozhou's head placed on public display in Hangzhou, as would be done with other executed criminals, before it was dispatched north.

The minister Lou Yue neatly summed up Song's need for a conclusion to the war, saying, 'The peace negotiations represent an important matter which awaits only this to be resolved. Why should the already putrefied heads of treacherous traitors merit our concern?'[21] Song needed peace very badly. The military, financial and political reforms and energy of Xiaozong had succeeded in producing a state that was able to survive an incredibly ill-thought out and badly run war and the many failures of the two emperors who followed him. However, new trials still awaited the dynasty and the people of China in the form of the Mongols, who were just beginning their incursions into the Middle Kingdom.

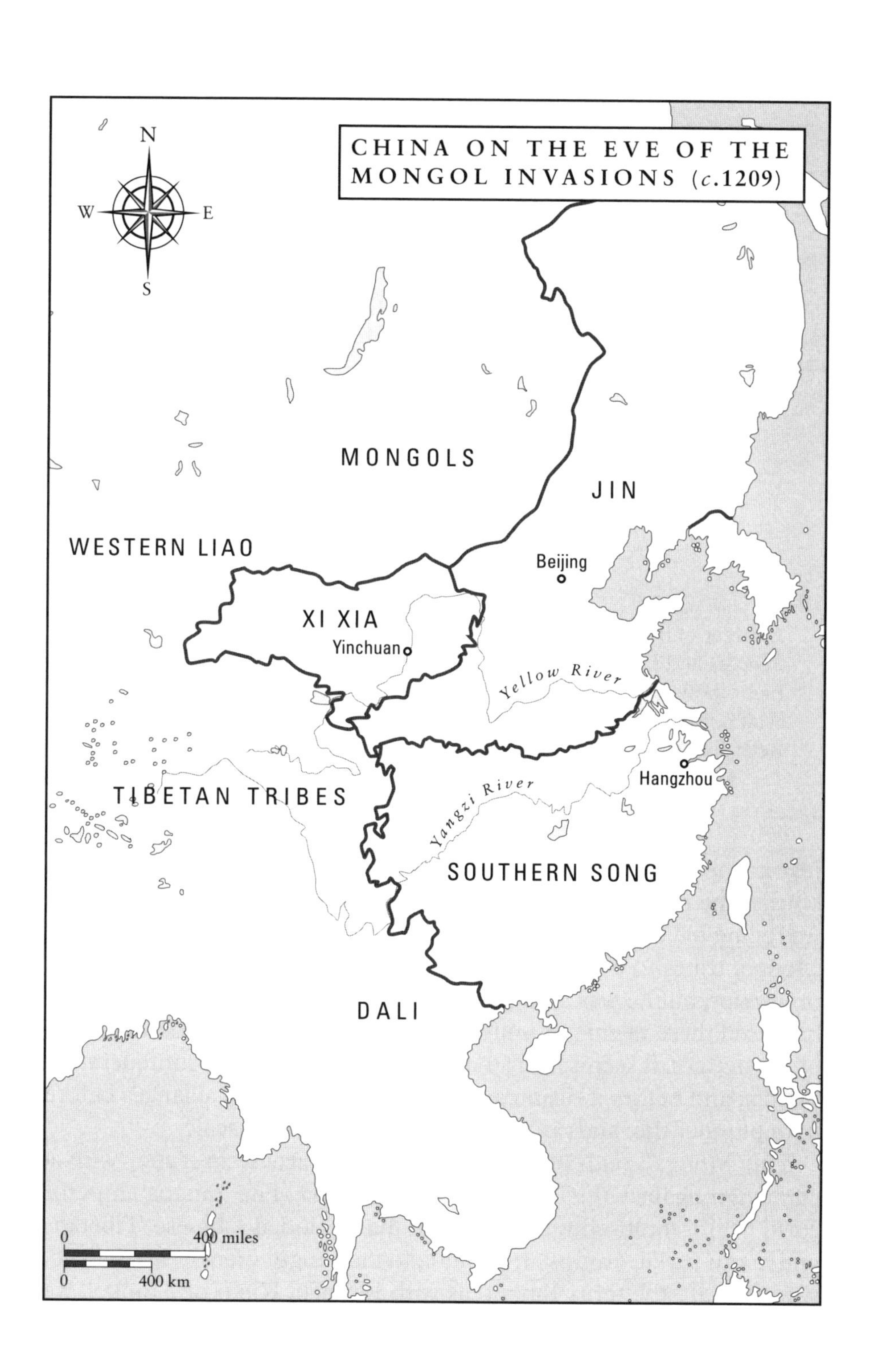
CHINA ON THE EVE OF THE MONGOL INVASIONS (c.1209)
N
S
W
E
MONGOLS
JIN
WESTERN LIAO
Beijing
XI XIA
Yinchuan
Yellow River
Hangzhou
Yangzi River
TIBETAN TRIBES
SOUTHERN SONG
DALI
0
400 miles
0
400 km

~ 2 ~

Bystanders to Destruction
The Mongol Reduction of Northern China

> A career of thirty years,
> Success and fame now turned to dust,
> Eight thousand li on the road gone with the wind,
> Wait not until your young head turns white,
> Revealing a lifetime of useless regret.[1]
>
> *Yue Fei, Song general and Chinese folk hero*

Just as the Jin were being challenged by the Song on their southern border, the man whose ambition would bring about their destruction was being hailed as universal ruler or great khan by a confederation of Mongol tribes to their north. Chinggis Khan was not a great general or warrior, but he was a skilled and compelling political strategist who had used these talents to unite the disparate and often-warring tribes of the steppes. It seems likely that his plan was to use this confederation rapidly, and before it disintegrated like so many tribal alliances before it, to plunder the lands of northern China on a vast scale.

The Mongol raids on China began in earnest in 1209, with a campaign against the Tangut state of Xi Xia. The Tangut emperor ruled over a multi-ethnic population that included Chinese, Tibetans and many Turkic groups, in addition to the Tangut themselves. Indeed, when we use the term Tangut, as with Jurchen, Kitan or Mongol, we should remember that we are really only naming the leadership of these states or confederations. In reality, each of these entities were multi-ethnic and, particularly in the case of the Mongols as their empire grew, the leading group was very much a minority.

The Tangut emperor's state also bordered the Jin state along the northwestern reaches of the Yellow River and extended into the Gobi desert and modern Ningxia. In the past the Tangut had lived a nomadic existence, with their only ties to the settled state being their trade in horses with the Song and their raiding of Song merchant columns. The nomadic past of the Xi Xia state, its largely Turkish population and its extension into the steppe made it a natural first target of the nascent Mongol confederation of Chinggis Khan. Its subjugation would give the Mongols access to the northwestern flank of the Jin state, from which they could raid the Yellow River plains, and if the Xi Xia state could be brought to full submission the Mongols would also gain access to its army of horse archers. Added to this was the fact that the Xi Xia state had never fully escaped the orbit of steppe politics, and the Mongol conquest of the state was also part of a 'tidying up' of loose ends, as all the Turco-Mongolic peoples on China's perimeter were absorbed either voluntarily or otherwise into the Mongol *ordus* or horde. That Xi Xia could never escape its own steppe history is obvious from the fact that many Turkish princes seeking refuge from Chinggis Khan's father found dubious refuge at the Xi Xia court and that royal daughters of the Xi Xia state were not uncommonly married to members of Chinggis's own family. To add to this confused mesh of amiability and animosity, one Kereyid prince sought refuge from Mongol vengeance with the Tangut, but then gave a daughter in marriage to Chinggis's son, Tolui, and she bore the great khans Mongke and Qubilai and the Persian Ilkhan Hulegu. Another of the dissident prince's daughters married into the Tangut royal family and an unlikely romantic tale has her beauty being the catalyst for Chinggis Khan's final annihilation of the Xi Xia state. Be that as it may, the Mongols certainly used the harbouring of Kereyid royal fugitives by the Xi Xia court as a pretext for their first extensive incursions into Xi Xia territory. Mongol raids across the Xi Xia state began in 1205 and the presence of their troops in an area bordering Jin also drew the Onggid tribes, a grouping of previously loyal barbarians whom the Jin had relied on to stabilise their northwest frontier, to join Chinggis's horde.

The Mongols stayed in Xi Xia territory for the next two years and the Xi Xia sent a series of embassies to the Jin emperor, calling for alliance against the Mongols. These appeals were rebuffed by the Jin emperor with the curt comment, 'it is to our advantage when our enemies attack one another. Wherein lies the danger to us?'[2]

The autumn of 1209 saw Chinggis launching a major invasion of Xi Xia and defeating three Tangut armies before investing the capital Chong Xingfu. The Mongols then attempted to divert the waters of the Yellow River's irrigation canals to flood the city, but succeeded only in deluging their own camp, which effectively broke the siege. However, they had done enough damage to the Xi Xia state to ensure its capitulation, and in 1210 the Tangut emperor, Xianzong, became a vassal to the Khan.

That Chinggis was only interested in Xi Xia's submission as a prelude to the greater havoc he wished to wreak upon the Jin is evidenced by his almost immediate employment of Tangut horsemen in raids upon Jin borderlands. By 1214 Xi Xia troops, under Mongol direction, were extensively raiding Jin's southwest provinces. By this point the Jin were becoming more and more dependent on this region for finances and for horses, as the Song had ceased the payment of the tribute that they had agreed to in 1207 and the Mongols were pressing hard from the north and gobbling up Jin pastureland. The city of Lanzhou slipped from effective Jin control in 1214, as the Xi Xia sponsored a rebellion there against them, and then the Xi Xia sent proposals to Song for a joint action against Jin in the west. At this juncture the Song sat on their hands and did not, in fact, act against Jin in alliance with the Xi Xia until 1220, and even then only in a half-hearted fashion. Perhaps it seemed more logical to the Song to let the Mongols destroy the 'auld enemy' for them than to engage the Jin directly themselves or even ally with them against the new foe. The lessons of the past and the debacle that had followed Jin's conquest of Liao with Song complicity had evidently either not yet been learned or simply forgotten.

The encroachment by the peoples of the northern steppe on Jin lands had begun almost at the beginning of the Jin dynasty. In some ways, the Jurchen's descent into 'China proper' in the first quarter of the twelfth century had created a power vacuum in the northern lands beyond the Middle Kingdom's borders, and this had been rapidly filled by new confederations. As early as the 1130s, the Jin had been compelled to send punitive expeditions into the hinterlands at the edge of the Gobi. They suffered many reverses on these expeditions, but through them they also managed to retard any progress towards unification by the tribes as they exterminated much of the leadership in the steppe. Possibly as a result of this policy, the words 'a Jin Emperor killed one of my forefathers. Let me have my revenge!' have been put into the mouth of Chinggis in traditional Chinese histories to explain the Khan's invasion of Jin. We can be certain that no such justification was in fact required for the ensuing carnage meted out to Jin by Chinggis Khan and his descendants; invoking the will of Tenggeri the Sky Father or Eternal Heaven would have been sufficient. But there is tenuous evidence to support the fact that Chinggis could have been intent on revenging the death of Ambaghai Khan, whom the Tatar tribe had handed over to their Jin overlords for execution after they captured him. Chinggis Khan considered himself a legitimate successor of Ambaghai as leader of the Mongols. In 1194 Jin had also made a temporary alliance with the man who became Chinggis Khan. This had helped to stabilise the border but had also unfortunately increased the Mongols' power, as it aided their elimination of tribal rivals. Chinggis Khan's unification of the tribes was, then, in many ways, begun by the Jin's actions in the steppes, and it was at the head of a vast confederation army of Mongols, Kitan and Tangut[3] that Chinggis set out in March 1211 to launch what was in effect a vast raid or *chevachee* across the Jin state.

The word *chevachee* is the most apt way of describing the Mongol raiding tactics in 1211, for it is an act of plundering on a relentless and extensive scale, in order to make control and rule over a region untenable for the enemy. It also deprives the enemy of legitimacy if they cannot effectively respond to the terror inflicted upon their citizens. The taking of territory would have rendered Chinggis's forces open to a Jin riposte, so the tactic of 'burn and move on' also served Chinggis well at this juncture. It is arguable that it failed the Mongols later, when they moved on to attempt to conquer Song, through

Sichuan, a region that would not support the rapid movement of cavalry, and they then became bogged down in the garrisoning of territory and a long war of attrition. Later the genius of Qubilai Khan and his commanders was shown in their co-opting of Chinese infantry and engineers to operate where cavalry could not, thereby freeing up the horsemen to go where they could be most effective and to stretch the Song's defences by lightning strikes. On a more philosophical plane Mongol warfare is a perfect paradigm of Clausewitz's theory of 'total war', in which the ends of war are consumed by the means taken to achieve them. The brief lives of both the Yuan Dynasty and the Mongol Ilkhanate of Persia are both, perhaps, partly explainable by the 'total war' origins of both states, and we will look a little later in more depth at how an inability to muzzle the dogs of war once they had been allowed to slip the leash completely contributed to the Yuan's rapid demise. That such all-enveloping concepts of warfare were alien to China before the Mongols' rise seems evident, given Sunzi's five governing factors, the first of which is the Moral Law, which requires accord between the ruled and the ruler, and the fact that the Confucian definition of war was that it was a punishment for both the defeated and the victor.

In the spring of 1211 two Mongol armies totalling about one hundred thousand warriors entered China from the northwest, through lands formerly 'guarded' for the Jin by the Onggids, and from the northeast, through mountain passes near modern Beijing. They devastated great portions of the northern provinces and the northwestern army essentially split the Jin army of Shensi from the rest of the Jin forces in the east. This northwestern army, however, failed to take the key border fortresses as the Jin forces in the region outnumbered them by about four to one and the Jin garrison infantry were well equipped with cavalry pikes and crossbows. Initial defeats in the open field and a devastating famine across the entire state seem to have decided the Jin on a defensive strategy by which they hoped either to bring about the break-up of the Mongol army or to bring Chinggis to a negotiation where a modus vivendi similar to that enacted between the Mongols and Xi Xia could be formed. Given that Mongol warriors were unpaid and that therefore commanders were entirely reliant on booty for paying them, the Jin might have been hoping that Chinggis's horde would disintegrate for lack of plunder. Certainly this was the norm for such barbarian confederations, but unfortunately the tribal army that had invaded China this time was perhaps exceptional in that it was composed of men who were 'more obedient to their masters than any other men in the world, be they religious or secular'.[4]

The strategy therefore failed. The Jin could keep the Mongols from taking their fortified cities through the technological advantages they held over them, the chief of these being gunpowder and trebuchet-fired 'thunder crash' bombs – some of which were moulded from wax to burn slowly, whilst others were hollow ceramic creations holding molten metal or barbs that would stick in wooden shields and make them impossible to carry. Naptha or 'Greek fire' was thrown in pots at the enemy and fire-arrows could also break up Mongol attacks, but the Jin could not match the Mongols in the field; the Jin had long ago abandoned the 'battue' or nomadic hunt and their stature as mounted archers had gone into decline.[5] The slow-moving, often largely infantry-based field armies the Jin deployed against the Mongols, perhaps a product of the long, static, cold–hot war the Jin had fought against the Song, were easily defeated by the Mongols, and those Jurchen among the Jin armies who did retain the warrior skills of the steppes soon enough joined the Mongols. The cavalry that the Jin did retain was also denied pasture by the Mongols' continual traversing of the northern plains. Each Mongol trooper had about six horses, and one 'tumen' of ten thousand troopers also meant the presence of forty thousand 'civilians' and six hundred thousand sheep or goats. Additionally, Bactrian camels and giant carts pulled by as many as twenty oxen were part of the Mongol army's train. This vast caravan had been known to travel up to six hundred miles in nine days and its capacity for consuming pasture would have been almost locust-like. To worsen matters, the Jurchen homeland of Manchuria, from which they drew horses, cattle and Jurchen warriors, then slipped from the Jin's grasp as leftovers of the old Liao Dynasty took the opportunity of Jin's misfortune to desert their cause. Virtually all the Liao–Kitan cavalry and soldiers that had formerly fought with the Jin army swore their allegiance to Chinggis Khan in 1212. A Jin punitive expedition failed to regain Manchuria from the rebels in 1214 and, to make matters worse, its commander then went on to set up his own independent state in northeast China.

The Mongols withdrew for the winter, which gave the Jin forces some respite, but soon enough the Mongols were back again, and over the course of the next two years they also began to enrol Han Chinese deserters into their army. The engineers among these men would make a very valuable contribution to the later Mongol campaigns.

The poor showing of the Jin in this early contest lured the Mongols further into China than they may have planned to go. Certainly, by the time they had taken the Juyong pass and the environs of Beijing, they had in fact overreached themselves. They were unprepared for the siege of such a large city, and what was almost certainly meant as a simple large-scale raid had now got them wrapped up in a territorial war in China. The equipment of the Mongol troopers of this period makes it clear that there was no developed weapons industry available to the army that could produce siege weapons capable of tackling the walls of Beijing; in fact, even with the later acquisition of Chinese centres of industry, many Mongol troopers still lacked crafted metal weapons. The average Mongol soldier wore a simple heavy coat with a belt sword, dagger and axe, and carried dried meat and curds for rations,[6] along with a stone sharpener. The heavy cavalry had lamellar armour, presumably purchased or looted from Chinese manufacturing centres, and every trooper carried a composite bow of yak horn, sinew and bamboo. Other weapons – round wooden shields and lassoes – were decidedly crude compared to the crafted and cherished Mongol bow.[7] The myth that Mongol silk undershirts 'wrapped' arrowheads and prevented injury to the wearer has long ago been exploded, but the lamellar armour that the Mongols favoured was certainly more effective than mail against arrows,[8] and this may have been particularly significant given the Jin and Song reliance on archers and crossbowmen.

By 1213, with Beijing resisting them even though it was effectively cut off, the Mongols were simply roaming the central plains of northern China and had lost the initiative. They were therefore fortunate that the Jin court was in the act of imploding at this juncture. The Emperor Weishao Wang had been assassinated in 1213 by Hu Shahu, a general who had lost the western Jin capital of Datong to the Mongols. Hu Shahu may have decided to strike first, as the punishment for such failure was bound to be harsh. A new emperor, Xuanzong, was installed, but the Jin state was unravelling fast and, in an attempt to replace the high-ranking Jurchen who were deserting the dynasty for service with the Mongols, the normally xenophobic court[9] opened military and civilian posts to all races within the state. A further symptom of the collapse of Jin confidence was seen in the spring of 1214 when the Jin sent peace envoys to Chinggis, and offered a daughter of the late emperor for the khan's marriage bed. The breathing space this gained them was used by the court to abandon Beijing and desert the troops left there. The court fled to the southern capital of Kaifeng which, it was hoped, was beyond the reach of both the Mongols and of the drought and famine that had struck the north and had once again crippled the logistics of the Jin army.

The Mongols marched on Beijing but could do little except sit beneath its walls and terrorise the surrounding environs. The city was encircled and defended by four fortified villages with four thousand Jin troops in each. Each village also had its own granary and arsenal and was linked by tunnels to Beijing. The city was also protected by three moats fed from Kunming Lake and a 15-kilometre rectangle of rammed earth walls that were 15 metres thick at their base and 12 metres high. Each of its thirteen gates and nine hundred guard towers was protected by double and triple crossbows, capable of hurling 3-metre quarrels over a kilometre, and traction trebuchets with a range of some 300 metres for 25-kilogram projectiles. The Mongols had units in their army trained to use both siege crossbows and trebuchets, the so-called *nujun* and *baojun*, but the technology they used was, at this juncture, almost certainly not a match for that of their opponents.[10]

The Mongols suffered enormous losses through pestilence during the siege, which lasted a year, but then the city suddenly surrendered in May 1215, as it was evident that no relief force was coming from Kaifeng. The capitulation, it seems, did not temper the Mongols' rage at the city's long defiance, and even in 1216 a visiting envoy could still attest the fact that the bones of the slaughtered formed mountains and the soil was greasy with human fat. Sixty thousand maidens had thrown themselves from the walls rather than fall into Mongol hands and only masons, carpenters and – oddly enough – actors were immune from the risk of summary executions.

By now the Jin were ready to accept having the khan as their overlord, but Chinggis seems to have interpreted the dynasty's move to Kaifeng as a dangerous act of separatism and he responded with further devastations of the Jin's Chinese provinces. Elsewhere, control was slipping away from the Jin too. The grain supplies of northern Hubei were gone and the refusal of Song to pay its yearly tribute had reduced the Jin to near penury. The collapse of local government that this and the Mongols' rapine had precipitated reduced whole provinces to chaos and in Shandong it made bandits the only form of authority. Many of these groups sought Song support and proclaimed loyalty to the dynasty in exchange for secret supplies of food and money. The Song particularly favoured a large confederation of outlaws called the Red Coats, possibly because red was the traditional 'fire' colour of the Song court. If this was so, then the Song were sorely misled, as the Red Coats, in fact, showed no particular loyalty to anyone but themselves. However, they resisted all Jin efforts to bring Shandong back under control, and this was probably reason enough for the Song court to support them. In 1218, with the Yellow River flooding and Shandong effectively beyond Jin control, the Song went further and recognised the ruthless Red Coat commander Li Quan as their 'prefect' of Shandong.

Song's sponsoring of bandits such as Li Quan was a direct response to Jin assaults on Song in 1217 as the Jin went to war to try to extract payments from the Song government. Making the Jin fight a proxy war in their own lands would certainly distract them from assaults on Song lands. However, the policy also had a secondary aim: by maintaining a viable state in Shandong the Song may have hoped to prevent a mass movement of Jin's Han citizens to the south, which would have effectively swamped Song with refugees or even with a mass movement of Jurchen households. It is impossible to make a judgement on the great unanswered question about this period of Jin history: where did all the people go? The drop in population was immense and there was, no doubt, massive emigration from north to south and also death through disease and famine. How many were simply slaughtered by the Mongols and how many died as a result of the invaders' damage to agricultural infrastructure and destruction of cities is impossible to decide. Certainly nowhere was safe; cities were refuges of a sort, but were also the key strategic goals of the Mongols and were wealthy enough to attract them for plunder alone. The number of refugees fleeing to Song must have been immense; if any member of the 'local elite' fled there would also be a movement of his kinsmen, retainers and tenants as an organised community of several hundred households.[11] Certainly there are other occurrences of this phenomenon of a 'tsunami' of people in Asian history, and there was never a pleasant outcome for either the displaced or the settled peoples involved. For example, the Jurchen destruction of the Liao's Kitan state in 1125 had pushed immense numbers of Turkish tribesmen into settled Islamic lands and had within only two decades sounded the death knell of the great Saljuq sultanate of Iran.[12]

The Jin assaults on Song served them badly; they offered peace for tribute, but made little progress in their war and in 1218 the Song were so confident of their ability to resist that they did not even allow the Jin envoys to enter their territory. A third and final Jin offensive was launched in the central border region in the spring of 1221. Initially, the Jin met with success and penetrated over 200 kilometres into Song territory, but the Song, in partnership with Li Quan, then counterattacked and pushed the Jin out.

Jin morale was eroded by their defeat in this campaign and was damaged further by news from other fronts. Despite the Mongols being distracted by their need to complete outstanding 'steppe business' with war against, and assimilation of, the Naiman and Merkit peoples of Mongolia, Chinggis's lieutenant, Mukhali, had used the opportunity of Jin's war on Song to take the cities of Taiyuan and Daming in 1218 and 1220 and to enter Shandong in 1220. The army that Jin had mustered to eradicate Li Quan was then destroyed by Mukhali. Western Shandong effectively fell to the Mongols and a three-sided war, fought through proxies recruited among bandit clans, ensued between the Mongols, Jin and Song in eastern Shandong. Li Quan attempted to exploit the war for personal gain and, in this increasingly dirty little war, the Song accepted his false proclamations of loyalty to their camp whilst attempting to break up his army by extending generous offers to his subordinates. Song chicanery of this ilk came to Li Quan's ears whilst bandits in the Mongols' employ were besieging him at Qingzhou in 1226. He therefore turned to the Jin for support in 1227, but when it became obvious that they were a failing star he opted for the Mongols.

Meanwhile, in the west in 1218 the Tangut of Xi Xia, after attacking the western borders of Jin but failing to make any headway, had then refused to honour troop agreements they had made with the Mongols. Speedy Mongol correction in the form of a punitive invasion forced the Tangut to send troops to serve with Mukhali in the east but this arrangement collapsed once again in 1223 amid mutual recriminations. The Xi Xia were then finally driven by the Mongols' depredations to parley with their old foe, the Jin. Negotiations ended in the autumn of 1223 with a peace accord, no doubt forced through by mutual fear of the Mongols and by Jin's need to obtain horses from the Tangut breeding grounds.

The Jin had attempted to secure peace with the Mongols as early as 1220, when envoys were sent far to the west where Chinggis was campaigning against the Khwarazm shah of Persia.[13] However, the offer of recognising the khan as an older brother of the Jin emperor was rejected by Chinggis, and the Jin emperor refused to be 'demoted' to king of Henan. Peace negotiations with the Mongols had therefore ended in 1222. Having secured a pragmatic peace with one set of previously inveterate enemies, the Xi Xia, in 1223, the Jin looked now to secure peace with the Song. It was as if China was going to unify, however tardily, in the face of the Mongol onslaught. The last 'true' Jin emperor, Aizong, came to the throne in 1224 and his much-reduced empire made peace with Song in the same year, on the basis of Jin giving up its claim for tribute and on an equality of titles between the two emperors. In amongst all this chaos and action the Song emperor, Ningzong, passed quietly away on 17 September 1224. He had been an emperor very much in the background of his own reign; the minister Shi Miyuan had run the country, and the last act he carried out for the dying emperor was to write an edict elevating a new heir to the throne. Ningzong's children had all died young and one adopted son, Zhao Hong, who was the heir expectant, was replaced by another adoptee, Zhao Yun, almost at the last moment. The succession and enthronement of Zhao Yun as Emperor Lizong went without a hitch despite the odd character of his accession, and the whole affair made the Song state appear as calm as the eye of the storm that was tearing through every other part of China.

Chinggis Khan repaid Xi Xia for its peacemaking with Jin by the near-obliteration of their army in 1226 in a series of battles, one of which was fought upon the frozen waters of the Yellow River, and by a siege of their capital, Zhongxing, in 1227. The siege dragged on, but the liquidation of the Xi Xia state was essentially completed by the time of Chinggis's death in August 1227.

Jin obtained some respite from the Mongols following the death of the khan, as a regency under Chinggis's wife attempted to settle the succession issue. This was tricky because, despite some undoubted influence on Mongol polity by Chinese imperial customs,[14] Turco-Mongolic custom had always been for a 'patrimonial share-out' of a successful father's lands and wealth. The apparent solution to this was that Chinggis's son, Ogedei, was created khagan, or khan of khans, and his brothers were all made khans in their own right. In practice this meant that Ogedei was a *primus inter pares* and that his writ did not run too far geographically in an empire that already reached to southern Russia and would soon solidify those gains and expand further into the Middle East. His election was also held up for some two years because of an ongoing opposition to his election and animosity from his brother Tolui. Ogedei managed finally to quell all the overt opposition to his reign but the fact that the 'great khan' had only limited power over the 'junior' khans and that this authority was diminished with each subsequent reign would become more and more apparent as the Mongol empire reached its end.

Ogedei was in a position to recommence the war on Jin in 1230 and from the pool of fifteen- to sixty-year-old males that the Mongol nation made available to him he formed a personal bodyguard of ten thousand men and deployed armies of thirty-nine thousand men in the west and centre under his truculent younger brother Tolui and sixty-two thousand more in the east under his own command. The armies also included Chinese engineers who had defected from the Jin, along with their gunpowder weapons. The Mongol armies met near the Yellow River during the winter of 1231, where, under the command of Subetei, probably Chinggis's most trusted lieutenant, the army crossed the fords despite the stout defence of some thirty thousand Jin troops. Subetei's outriders made it to the walls of Kaifeng by February 1232. The Song court had refused passage through Sichuan to the Mongols of Tolui's western army, but the Mongols journeyed through the province anyway and there was no Song response to the incursion.

A demand for the surrender of the capital was refused by the Jin court and a siege began in April. Further negotiations ended in July when two Jin officers murdered the Mongols' envoy along with thirty men of his entourage. This apparent act of madness on the part of the Jin officers is more easily understood against the backdrop of Kaifeng's misery and chaos in the summer of 1232. Disease and famine are of course natural sequelae to any war, but the total collapse of governance and recriminations within the court, with summary executions commonly following a few days after any man's promotion, were the street theatre of the dying city. The music accompanying the city to its grave was made by the 'thunder crash' bombs of both sides and by the fire-lance rockets of the Jin engineers. Arguably, the Jin's superiority in technology was the only thing that kept the Mongols from rapidly capturing the city. The fire-lance rocketeers would certainly have had an effect on Mongol cavalry, with their long reinforced paper pipes spewing flames over 3 metres long.[15]

February 1233 saw the Jin emperor flee the doomed city for Henan, where he holed up in Caizhou (modern Runan). Kaifeng was left under the control of several generals, and General Xu Li took overall command in May by virtue of his elimination of any dissenting official or general. He then offered the city to Subetei. His act may have constrained the Mongols in their sacking of the city and the massacre that ensued was at least limited to only the male members of one clan. Xu Li was, however, a victim of the Mongol victory as he was murdered by a fellow Jin officer.

Then, in the summer of 1233, rumours spread to the Song court of a Jin plan to cut through the Song border and form a route of escape for Aizong to Sichuan. However, when the Jin crossed the border they were rapidly defeated by General Meng Gong, and the Song counterattack effectively cut the Jin forces at Caizhou off from any hope of relief. The Song army was now fully in control of southern

Henan. The confidence this gave the Song meant that Jin emissaries seeking a pact were sent home, without even the courtesy of an audience being extended to them.

Aizong sent more desperate missives to the Song court, begging for at the least supplies, and at the best armed support against the Mongols who were closing on Caizhou by December 1233, but the Song were by this time already plotting with his enemies for the destruction of Jin.[16] Aizong committed suicide and handed the reins of power, worn out though they were, to a distant relative, Mo Di.

The siege of Caizhou saw the entire populace of the region crowded into the city, for fear of the Mongols, and famine quickly ensued. The Song supplied the Mongol army with grain and no Jin relief army would come to the new capital's aid, as all strategy had broken down and the armies of the Jin were still defending patches of land across the now dead empire. The rainy season was also in full flow and floods slowed those forces that did respond to the Jin emperor's pleas. In September 1233 the Song had begun retaking their former prefectures from the Jin and their massing on the border of a large army also drew Jin forces away from the war for the heartland.

Before his death Aizong had attempted to buoy his troops defending the southern border with these words:

> The fact that the Tatars unleash their forces and often win battles is because of their northern style and because they use the tricks of the Chinese. It is very difficult to fight against them. As to the Song, they are really not our match! They are weak and not martial, just like women. If I had three thousand armoured soldiers, we could march into Chiang and Huai provinces. Take courage[17]

The Jin then defeated the Song at the battle of Changtu Tian and this Song failure must have made it obvious to the Mongols that the Song state was defended by an army that was, despite its size and sophistication, at times, a paper tiger.

By this time, cannibalism had broken out in Caizhou, and the Song, under General Meng Gong, joined the Mongols in besieging the city in November 1233 with ten thousand men. They breached one wall, but were driven out. Then, on 8 January 1234, the Mongols broke the banks of the Lien River and Song engineers diverted the Ju River away from Caizhou. This effectively denuded Caizhou of its western and southern defences and by 20 January the Mongols were in the western part of the city. Mo Di was killed in house-to-house fighting as the Mongols stormed Caizhou on 9 February 1234. A large body of Jin soldiers, loyal to the last, had desperately tried to defend him and perished with him. General Meng Gong seized the Jin imperial seals and part of Aizong's burned body as proof of the end of the dynasty, and Song garrisons were placed in southern Henan.

The Song had now outlasted two enemy dynasties, the Liao and the Jin, though they themselves had defeated neither and had even failed once against the armies of the dying Jin. Now they faced another invader from the north, one with which they had made common cause with in the last few months of Jin's demise. A Chinese proverb that predates the Song dynasty tells us, 'When the lips are gone, the teeth soon become cold.' The Jin were gone and Song now faced the Mongols alone.

~ 3 ~

All Under Heaven

Song's Long War Begins

War is not a thing to be trifled with.

He Yenxi, Song dynasty commentator on, and collator of, Sunzi's Art of War[1]

Extolling the virtues of emotional intelligence may be a distinctly twenty-first-century phenomenon, but some management of passion at the Song court as they deliberated on how to deal with the collapse of Jin and their new Mongol neighbours might very well have saved the dynasty from committing the series of grave errors that brought them into a war they could not win. It seems likely that the Song court was entirely emotionally-driven in its strategy to meet the new geopolitical situation in northern China, and it has been suggested that immediate subordination to the Mongols and the taking of a position of inferiority to the new masters of northern China, as the Song had to the Jin, would have served the Song's immediate interests better.[2]

The argument for such an arrangement was probably never heard at the Song court in 1234, but it is also difficult to see how such an arrangement could have saved the Song in the longer term. It might have delayed the Mongol descent into southern China because, as was argued above, the Mongols had, in many ways, made a serious error in their invasion and occupation of northern China and by their act had essentially destroyed the ethos that underpinned their steppe empire. As later events would show, the tension between the life and actions of a nomad and the obligations of being a settled ruler of a state was a Gordian knot that the Mongols never managed to cut. I have written elsewhere[3] that the response of the leaders of the Mongol empire to this tension was continual expansion and rapine – in simple terms allowing the dogs of war to slip and wreck neighbouring states rather than have them tearing your own apart. The later doomed campaigns of Qubilai against Japan and Indonesia are evidence of this approach and the short life of the Yuan Dynasty, torn apart by rebellion and by its own supporters, is proof of the failure of the Mongol polity and its inability to address this core issue. The Mongol creed of creating an empire of *tianxia* or 'all under heaven' was in fact not born of rational policy but of fear of what would happen if the expansion stopped. The Mongols were, in truth, as emotionally driven as the Song.[4]

Given the above argument, it therefore seems inevitable that the Mongols would have invaded Song at some point and, as we will see, the Song court essentially failed to create a strategy that could defeat the Mongols in either the short or medium term. Song therefore blundered into a war with the Mongols without a clear plan of how to conclude it. The Song court's chief failure was to maintain a blind indifference to their greatest assets and to what had carried them through the two previous contests they had endured against steppe empires in northern China: they had political stability and the ability to mobilise vast economic resources. At this juncture the Mongols had neither. The Song therefore failed to play the long game that Sunzi would have applauded and that would have seen the Mongol polity collapse for lack of success in breaching the Huai–Yangzi line and from an inability to expand and plunder.

The Song court blindly ran towards the opportunity offered with the collapse of Jin, as they had after the demise of Liao, of recapturing former Song lands and three of the old Song capitals: Kaifeng, Yingtian and Luoyang. Court intrigue and power politics also played their part in the ensuing policy debacle, as the generals who had defeated Li Quan, the Shandong bandit, agitated for the re-liberation of the old capitals of Song and an immediate invasion of Henan. The subsequent campaign was so badly organised that it did not even reach its final objective of Luoyang. Ten thousand men reached Kaifeng in July 1234, followed by a further fifty thousand in reinforcements, but this second group was then ambushed on the way to Luoyang and destroyed. Song had therefore suffered its first defeat of the Mongol war. Furthermore, the Song had also effectively poisoned relations with Ogedei Khan beyond all hope of repair when in fact the Mongols had, up to this moment, been scrupulous in completing their part of the 1233 agreements made with the Song to dismember Jin and share out the spoils. Even the Song army's failures and Song's inability to meet its part of the bargain during the mopping-up of the Jin had not soured relations. Whether the Song court also acted out of a total distrust for Mongol fidelity[5] is hard to say, but by undertaking an unprovoked act of war they had lost both the moral high ground[6] and, perhaps more practically, through their blundering early campaign, any momentum in the war.

They had, of course, also either underestimated the strength of the Mongol army or grossly overestimated the capabilities of their own. As discussed earlier, the Song army had improved from its nadir of the eleventh century and a 'gunpowder evolution'[7] had taken place, with rockets capable of firing arrows and larger missiles being deployed for city defence. Further developments in personal military equipment in this period are difficult to assess due to the fact that much of it was formed from *mingguang* or low-carbon steel, which has rusted to nothing. Therefore, much of the archaeological theory of Chinese arms is based on the assumption that not much changed from when weapons were made of bronze, of which we do have extant examples. However, we do know that infantry were protected by lamellar armour, and language has offered us a few clues about other armaments. It seems likely that in the Song period two types of sword existed: the *jian*, a straight slender double-edged tapering blade sword, and the *dao* for cavalry men, a sturdy single-edged sabre with a slight curvature. These words have been retained in the modern Chinese language to differentiate these distinct shapes in both swords and long cooking knives. The long confrontation with the Jin had also led to the demise of fanciful weapons such as the *ji*, a multiple-blade long-handled weapon. Heavy axes, halberds and long spears were used instead as the infantry was expected to present a mass of points to the enemy cavalry and not to swing or slash.

The crossbow remained the queen of weapons and it was mass produced in state armouries. The design dated from 1068, when the emperor had rewarded the winner of a state-sponsored competition to improve on the current standard issue model. The weapons available in 1234 would have been made from mulberry wood and brass and been capable of piercing a tree at over 100 metres. Song crossbowmen could keep up a continuous fire by deploying in three ranks, and the use of repeating crossbows, which had begun in the eleventh century, was also becoming common by this time. A text dating from 1259 discusses a box magazine on a crossbow which was operated by a lever. Such complex machinery could only be produced from within a highly developed small-arms industry, and the *Gongnuyuan* or Bow and Crossbow Institute set a pattern standard which was then copied by small workshops all over the state. Such was the quality of these weapons that long-range crossbows could be used by snipers for assassinations, as with the killing of the Kitan general, Xiao Talin, in 1003. Grouping crossbows together on wooden frames to intensify their onslaught had been common in China since the Qin Dynasty (221–206 BC) and the Song had increased the effective range of such mounted bows from around 700 to 1,000 metres. This was achieved primarily by the employment of mechanical winches.

The role of cavalry in the army was small; this was a prime reason for the failure of the Song's first excursion across the Huai in the Mongol war. The steppe peoples had always been cautious over the sale of horses to the southern Chinese and had virtually maintained a system of sanctions on the sale of this strategic asset. This said, armoured horses or *makai* existed in the Song army, although we can be certain that their effectiveness among the rice fields and irrigation channels of the south was limited. The Song also worked hard to produce and maintain a light cavalry force armed with halberds and fire-lances, chiefly through the constant manipulation of the price of tea. The eventual failure of this policy will be discussed later as the Song failed to meet the challenge of the Mongol cavalry forces.

The above interference in the tea market, albeit disastrous to the tea merchants, shows clearly that, although the Song army often failed, the logistics system underpinning it and the state's ability to maintain a war economy over a protracted period was both hugely impressive and distinctly modern. The Song had broken with Tang traditions and had embraced a cash economy and a technological drive that had enabled the Song military, despite repeated blunders and the fanatical application to the war of their Mongol foe, to maintain the contest for over forty years.

The Song Dynasty was, in many ways, an intellectual golden age for China and this was reflected not only in higher culture but also in the application of science to even mundanities such as training for specific functions within the army, physical education and drilling for troops. All the military attributes required of the troops were tested and quantified and role-specificity was ensured. 'Special forces' of hand-picked men were used for night missions, and unarmed combat training was given to palace guards. A Song Dynasty text also prescribed *jueli* or games of strength for troops and this included wrestling matches or *xiangpu*, This contest is a possible precursor of the Japanese sport of Sumo.[8] The directorate of weapons did its part by giving awards for technological innovations and through supervision of armament manufacture for both quantity and quality.

In this last period of the Song the writer Chang Yu described a level of command and control that was also impressive. Five-man units could be deployed five deep in sections and in 'companies'. It is likely that each of these *wu* contained two spearmen and three crossbowmen. The crossbowmen drew protection from the halberds or spears and could be deployed to the front of the line to present their weapons en masse, which increased the shock of their fire. Chang Yu wrote, 'when they shoot nothing stands in front of them,' and that even cavalry charges could be defeated by their fusillade. This system relied on a disciplined drill of each crossbowman advancing behind a large shield to shoot and then retiring to reload.

Chang Yu also tells us of the higher divisions within the army, with two of these five-man units making up a section. Five sections made for a *dui* of fifty men. These units were the interconnected blocks out of which an army unit of three thousand two hundred men was formed. In Chang Yu's words:

> Each is subordinate to the superior and controls the inferior. Each is properly trained. Thus one may manage a host of a million men just as one would a few . . . officers and men are ordered to advance or retreat by observing the flags and banners, and to move up or stop by signals of bells and drums. Thus shall the valiant not advance alone, nor shall the coward flee.[9]

The armies were vast by world standards; no contemporary European or Middle Eastern commander would ever have been able to raise armies of the size seen in eastern Asia in this period. Therefore the movement of masses, so difficult in the medieval period in all theatres, was essential to the Song's commander. Tang treatises, amended in the Song period, tell us that:

> At the end of the fourth sounding of the horn, the men of all the *dui* simultaneously draw in their spears and kneel on the ground. Their eyes watch the great yellow standard of the commander-in-chief, their ears listen for the sound of the drum. The yellow flag points forward, and the drum begins to beat; they shout in unison, 'Wu-hu! Wu-hu!' and move forward to the centre line . . . when they hear the gong sound, they must stop the shouting and fall back, carrying their spears on their shoulders.[10]

Sunzi tells us that 'gongs, drums, pennants, and flags are the means to unify the men's ears and eyes,' and military officer training focused on battlefield deployment and specialised technical knowledge, for, as we have seen, Chinese warfare was very technology loaded. Indeed, a constant theme in the military classics is that the commander is not placed in the thick of the action, but rather conducts the war from afar; 'to command the troops and direct their blades, this is the role of the commander, to wield a single sword is not'.[11]

It seems likely, however, that 'higher strategy' above control of the battlefield, of the kind that Sunzi's treatise was generally directed towards, was not the fodder of generals, but rather of the civilian literati at court. The disconnect between the *Shumiyuan* or Bureau of Military Affairs, which was responsible for setting armies in motion, and the generals, who were only responsible for leading the armies in the field, is obvious here. What this split between staff and field command meant in reality was that even when the Song court devised a strategy that was appropriate, the execution of the plan was so poor that it often made the plan itself look reckless.[12]

In 1234 this disconnect can be seen in the way that a minority of civilian officials in the central court were able to gain support for their decision on the Luoyang expedition, through the support of military men who had, in fact, not had to face the Mongols or the Jin in Henan. As discussed above, the generals who had fought Li Quan in Shandong and the fertile land of the east Yangzi basin advocated for war, whilst those who knew the hard lands of the northwest described how it was currently impossible to feed the south without even considering the extra strain of taking on the north, and that even if the north could be taken, defending it would provide the Song state with so many difficulties that they were likely to overwhelm it. General Meng Gong, who knew better than most the perils of the region and the Mongols' capabilities, was particularly vocal in his opposition to a campaign that could bring a Pyrrhic victory at best, but he was not listened to and the 'eastern party' carried the court to war.

Another example that shows very clearly the impact of the absence of an effective Song body equating to the modern-day concept of chiefs of staff was, in fact, the very same campaign against the Song's erstwhile ally, the Shandong bandit, Li Quan, that had so inflated the egos of the eastern generals and the Song court. As discussed earlier, by 1227 Song court intriguing had driven Li Quan into the arms of the Mongols, but he continued to act with his own best interests at heart. His 'fire-lance soldiers' were the best flamethrower troops in China and Li Quan added to their number and his own power with the recruitment of men from Song lands and through the building of a navy. By 1230 he had an army of thirty thousand well-trained men and may have been planning to invade Song lands. The Song appeased him with supplies whilst acting to eradicate his clan; his brother, a son and a concubine of his were all killed in internecine fighting in Shandong that included Song troops who switched sides, Song governors who played their own strategies and who acted above all in their own interest, and Mongol commanders, who must have been bewildered by the chaos they had stirred up in Shandong. As discussed above, it is entirely possible that two contradictory Song strategies were in play here – one aimed at subverting the bandit to the Song cause and one aimed at his extirpation. As late as 1230 when Li Quan was besieging the major Song city of Yangzhou, the Song court was still piling honours and offices upon him, even as their field commanders called for action against the bandit.

Eventually the Song were forced to respond by Li Quan's obvious declaration of war on their state. The Song army performed magnificently on this occasion and Li Quan was killed in battle in February 1231. This rapid victory was then the unfortunate catalyst for the eastern generals to call for a campaign to reclaim the old Song lands, and this call was rapidly and blindly taken up by the civilian court. Both the eastern generals and the court had, however, failed to account for the fact that the Mongol backers of Li Quan had been busy mopping up fragmented Jin armies during the successful Song offensive against the bandit. The court should have noted how badly the Song army had fared against the Jin cavalry every time it crossed into the flat plains beyond the Huai River line, and the similarity between the Jin and the Mongols' style of warfare should have driven the lesson home, but, as we have seen, like the eastern generals, the court had convinced itself that the former Song empire might be made whole again. The mantra of reclaiming the lost sixteen provinces continued to hold the Song court captive. The term 'wooden-headedness' would seem the most appropriate way of expressing this phenomenon.[13]

As we have seen, Song court officials studied Sunzi, but without practical experience or the desire or ability to read the ground on which they expected their plans to be carried out, such study was redundant and dangerous. The central chapters of Sunzi extol again and again the fact that, 'the one who excels at warfare first establishes himself in a position where he cannot be defeated while not losing [any opportunity] to defeat the enemy. For this reason, the victorious army first realises the conditions for victory.' The Song court could not do this as it was too far from the front, and mutual antipathy excluded any chance of consultation between field generals and bureau officials. Even when discussions did take place the court only listened for good news. There was, therefore, no one who saw the whole picture, and this disconnect between the field and the court caused the blunder of provoking the Mongols into war in 1234. Li Quan's legacy was also not effectively ended by the Song; his wife led what remained of the army back to Shandong and the Mongols recognised her son, Li Tan, as ruler there in 1233. However, this arrangement would later cause the Mongols more problems than it would the Song.

The Song's Luoyang expedition of 1234, on its march towards Kaifeng, passed through wasted and burned countryside and through cities that had become veritable ghost towns. Twenty years of war had reduced the old Jin lands to ashes and Kaifeng was able to offer nothing to the Song army in the way of provisions. The Mongols had broken the banks of the Yellow River and flooded the land all about, ruining crops and destroying all hope of the next harvest too. The miserable statistic of a drop in Chinese population from over one hundred million in the Jin and Song lands to under sixty million in 1393 had its origins in this early period of Mongol domination.[14]

Furthermore, whilst Ogedei is recorded as being a 'mild' ruler by Mongol standards, he still unleashed a rapacious tax farmer named Abd al-Rahman upon the former lands of Jin, whose professed Muslim faith did not restrain him from charging very un-Islamic 100 per cent rates of interest on loans and attempting to milk northern China dry.[15] In this period, and probably because of such policies, there was a huge volume of refugees fleeing the north for Song lands, which brought the provinces of Hubei and Shandong to a third of their former population level. It has also been suggested that an argument continued for some time at the Mongol court on the feasibility and merits of the mass extermination of the northern Chinese. Eventually this argument failed against the hypothesis that medieval treasuries were, by and large, filled by the efforts of peasants. This does not seem particularly stunning logic, but apparently to the Mongols it was.[16] If the Song court thought that the city of Kaifeng would be able to reprovision its army as it headed north, it was to be very much disappointed.

Three-quarters of the Song army refused to move on to Luoyang, and those that did were so poorly provisioned that they added little to the smaller force that had already 'liberated' Luoyang. In truth, there was not much of Luoyang left to liberate. Most of its population was already dead and those that remained were starving to death. The troops were forced to eat their own horses in order to survive and yet the army moved on to capture other apparently deserted cities. Then the Mongols struck from hideaways in each of these northern ghost towns. They ambushed the Song infantry and sent the entire Song army into a headlong and ill-disciplined retreat that cost many more troops their lives than the encounters with the Mongols had.

In Hangzhou there were recriminations, as the commissioner-in-chief for the central border region, who had been a vocal opponent of the war, was blamed for withholding supplies from the expeditionary force, but in truth the difficulties in operating in the wrecked and famine-struck north with an army of sixty thousand men would have been beyond the capabilities of any logistics train that could have been put in place. The ten thousand men sent to Luoyang were incapable of defeating the Mongols but could be fed, the sixty thousand sent to Kaifeng were a large enough force to cause the Mongols some concerns, but were too difficult to provision in the field.

The poor showing of the Song army probably encouraged the Mongols to take their time in responding to the Song affront, and even when they did so, no armies were immediately dispatched but rather a single envoy, Wang Chi, was sent to the Song court to admonish the emperor for his rash actions. Operations in southern Russia and mopping up after the invasion of Korea seem to have been higher priorities, initially, for Ogedei than the Song were. He was also distracted by internal affairs as the shift to empire strained ever harder at Mongol family rule and senior princes and aristocrats showed more and more independence. Ogedei may also have been concerned over the poor showing of the Mongol navy in the Korean campaign. The khan would have known that any assault across the Huai was likely to be a severe challenge given the Song's riverine naval power.

Then, in the summer of 1235, the Mongol hammer fell. Ogedei dispatched three armies into the central border region and into Sichuan. Frontier fortresses were rapidly captured, but it is likely that the change in terrain and climate encountered in Sichuan was enough at this juncture to cause the Mongols to think twice about penetrating any further into the region. On the central front they expelled the Song armies from all the areas the Song had captured the year before during the collapse of Jin, but then on entering Song 'proper' they concentrated on *chevachees* and on transporting spoils back to the northern lands rather than on retaining territory.

The spring of 1236 saw more attacks across the Han River. A mutiny of Song troops at Xiangyang distracted the military and civil commands and the Mongols advanced some 200 kilometres into Song territory. The uprising at Xiangyang was suppressed by late summer, but Mongol attacks continued on the central front and, in the west, a massive army of Mongols, Tangut and Jurchen horsemen struck deep into Sichuan. Senior Song commanders were killed in the ensuing destruction and the Song armies in the region simply disintegrated under the onslaught. Tens of thousands of soldiers and civilians were slaughtered, and by November the Mongols were 500 kilometres inside Song territory. Then the army leader, Kuchu, the son and heir of Ogedei, was killed and the western Mongol army abruptly withdrew from the engagement and from the territory they had captured.

The Mongol central army, however, continued to press on the Huai River front, and it seems likely that large numbers of Song troops were rapidly redeployed to this region from the Sichuan front. Certainly, during battles fought on the Sichuan front during the summer of 1236 Song troops were outnumbered ten to one.

Despite massive civilian and army deaths, the Song line held both in Sichuan and on the Huai front. General Meng Gong was credited with saving the state from greater ruin by his leadership during the autumn of 1236, and as the Mongols withdrew towards the end of the year the Song reclaimed their lost land with the exception of Xiangyang, which only returned to their possession in 1238.

The Mongols came again in the autumn of 1237. They made progress in the central Huai region and briefly seized Fuzhou, but General Meng Gong repelled them before they could move onto the regional capital of Jiangling. The Song army, under General Meng Gong's direction, then stabilised the line and began digging in and preparing a stubborn defence of the river, as it had, again and again, against the Jin following initial defeats. The war was moving towards a stalemate and by 1238 the Mongols had evacuated most of the territory they had gained the year before and had also sent envoys to the Song court.

The Mongol envoys offered peace and made a demand for silk and silver that exactly matched what the Jin had extorted from the Song as tribute in previous times. The Song court, perhaps impressed by its own army's obstinacy in the face of vast Mongol forces, refused, and then sent its own envoys to the Mongol court to offer a peace based on equality and not junior partnership. Perhaps the Song knew of the Mongols' concurrent entanglements in Russia – they were struggling to subdue Moscow – and of Ogedei's near-permanent inebriation. Certainly, it was a matter of public knowledge that the khan's brother, Chagatai, had given Ogedei an ultimatum that he must only drink a certain number of cups of fermented mare's milk per day and that the khan had agreed once he had purchased a truly gigantic cup to take his liquor from.

The Song army repaid the trust its government had placed in it at the end of 1238, as a large Mongol army was redeployed from Korea and sent against Luzhou in the east and another of equal size was dispatched against Kuaizhou in the west. Both of these armies were repulsed by the garrisons of Kuaizhou and Luzhou. The numbers of troops garrisoned in both these cities was undoubtedly small, but the Song army had become skilled in the defence of such places during their long wars with the Jin. Much of our information about Song static defences comes from the dynasty's encyclopedia compilers. Elaborate details about the types of weaponry that could be used in siege warfare are given in 'The Comprehensive Essentials of the Artillery', 'The Tiger Seal Manual' and 'The Record of the Defence of the Walled City'. Much of these texts is devoted to the deployment of large-scale projectile machines with long-range capabilities kept safe from incoming fire by fortress walls.[17]

The trebuchet had a long lineage in China before the Song, but the *huopao*, or fire-bomb catapult, was a Song innovation. These devices had done enormous damage to the Jin armies at the siege of Kaifeng in 1126, and throughout the Song dynasty the imperial ordinance industry mass-produced them. Jingzhou was just one of the many factory towns, and it produced two thousand trebuchets per month between 1253 and 1258. We can be assured then that both the cities attacked in 1238 were well supplied with both trebuchets and bombs.

The bombs were diverse in their design, but not in their quality, as the process had become highly standardised early in the dynasty. Generally these were incendiary or explosive grenades made from bamboo, with fuses to be lit before they were flung from the trebuchet. Explosive packed with metal or porcelain fragments inside the grenade made for a very deadly anti-personnel artillery. The type of explosive varied depending on the need. The '*Wujing Zongyao*' or 'Essentials of the Military Arts' produced under the Song in *c.*1044 gives the first gunpowder formula known in history. The composition of the powder – sulphur, saltpetre, massicot, dry lacquer and hemp roots – could be altered and added to, so as to produce 'poison smoke balls' (with added arsenic and wolfsbane) or manipulated in terms of its nitrate content to produce either incendiary or explosive effects.[18] The thunder-crash bombs used by the Jin against the Mongols at Beijing were of this second type, and the *Jinshi* or imperial history of the Jin records how, when they were ignited, there was a flash of fire – the thunder-like sound could be heard over a hundred li away – and a vast area would be incinerated. Mongol soldiers were torn to pieces by them and no trace of the victims could be found.

By the time the Jin had obtained this weapon, however, ingenious Song artisans had moved on to the production of high-nitrate gunpowder cased in metal, the *tiehuopao*, which had therefore both a higher grade of explosive and due to its casing an even greater potential for damage from its fragmentation. The Mongols assaulting Luzhou would then have faced iron-bombs thrown great distances by counterweight trebuchets[19] and Song infantry well-armed with a variety of personal firearms. The fire-lance has already been discussed above, but Song troops also had smaller hand-held weapons such as the *huotong* or fire-tube, which was a kind of early pistol with the flame-shooting tube mounted on a short wooden handle. This weapon could be loaded with sand, which would fire out to blind, burn and confuse the enemy. It seems likely, too, that the Song's research and development departments within the imperial ordnance industry had also been able to create hand-held deadly weapons capable of firing objects such as bits of broken metal and pottery with sharp edges.[20]

The vital supply of these weapons and their ammunition was overseen by an elaborate bureaucracy that started with the chamberlain for the palace revenues, descended to the director of imperial manufactories, then to the directorate of imperial workshops and the directorate for armaments. The directorate of imperial workshops monitored the production of weapons and ammunition, whilst the directorate for armaments was specifically tasked with the procurement of raw materials and the supervision and creation of workshops in the provinces. Standardisation of design and quality was a vital part of this process, as the workshops used were often small and semi-independent and were dotted all over the state, usually near the border to allow for easy transport to the front for their products. The manuals guiding manufacturers contained over one hundred chapters of references describing materials that could be used for manufacturing weapons, over seventy chapters on tools and parts, four chapters on repairs and twenty-one chapters on miscellaneous items.

There was an effort to keep these powerful weapons out of the hands of the Song's enemies, but it is evident that this failed as the Jin commonly deployed gunpowder weapons, and by 1233 the Mongols were employing basic incendiaries in their destruction of the cities of Jin China. The leaking of technology to the enemy was not surprising, given that maintaining the vast supplies required civilian artisans who, although technically forbidden to manufacture weapons, were enlisted in the war effort since imperial workshops alone could not possibly meet the demand. These private factories were tightly regulated and delivery to the imperial arsenal had to be made within thirty days. This was in order to avoid stockpiles being secretly shipped to the enemy. Certain 'top-secret' weapons were never to be produced by civilians but technology leaks were impossible to control, and by the mid-1250s the Mongols had even obtained winch-crossbows, capable of firing arrows in a near-constant stream, and naphtha-throwing trebuchets. Prior to their acquisition of 'Greek fire', it seems that the Mongols had resorted to taking the fat off the people they killed, melting it and throwing it onto houses to incinerate them.[21]

Song defences needed to be strong, as the army was at a huge numerical disadvantage,[22] and yet it managed to beat the Mongols off in 1238 with relatively small losses. Part of the developing Song approach to the Mongol war in this period was to concentrate on maintaining command of the rivers that served both as barriers to the Mongols and as arteries for supplying fortresses and cities with men and munitions. It might be suggested that the Song 'system' of reacting to Mongol assaults, and of not moving out of a defensive mode, surrendered the initiative to the Mongols, but given the previous Song disasters during offensives and the fact that 'outliving' the enemy had worked twice before, the policy does not seem that foolhardy. Furthermore, there may well have been intelligence available to the Song on the increasingly serious problems erupting within the Mongol political system as Ogedei's health failed under an onslaught of alcohol. Certainly the continued peace envoys sent from the Mongol court before 1240 would have encouraged the view that, whilst the Mongols might be dominant in the field, they were politically fragile.

Ogedei died at the close of 1241; it seems that simultaneous hunting and drinking may have been his undoing.[23] His widow, Toregene, maintained a regency whilst the succession was fought over. The patrimonial share-out was again the root of the problem as it had been at Ogedei's succession, but the Mongols had also failed to develop an institution worth the name to counter its destabilising effects, and the *quriltai*, a meeting of all the tribes, was hardly up to the task of deciding the fate of an empire. A five-year interregnum, of which civil war commonly seemed the most likely result, therefore afforded the Song a measure of peace, although their act of imprisoning an entire seventy-man Mongol peace delegation because they were found to be 'overly arrogant' may have been considered as pushing the limits of diplomatic recklessness. The Song used the respite to replenish their armies and recover lost territory, but sporadic fighting still erupted along the border and at times the Mongols penetrated quite deeply into Sichuan and began the first of many raids along the eastern front, even raiding close to the mouth of the Yangzi.

In 1246 Ogedei's son, Guyuk, ascended the throne, but was almost immediately challenged for it by Batu, the khan of southern Russia. Again the Song were afforded a modicum of peace as Guyuk was now more preoccupied with enemies within his own family then with his adversary to the south. He rode to the west with an army but died, probably of an alcohol-related illness, just outside Samarqand. More succession squabbles dominated Mongol activity for the next three years and the near-extermination of all cattle and horses in northern China by a severe drought also ensured the Mongol war machine was not deployed against Song again until 1251.

The Song worked hard in this period to strengthen the west, an area of proven vulnerability, despite their limited troop reserves. General Meng Gong took up the central border and Sichuan command in 1242. The *baojia* system was reinvigorated as an attempt to cover up for the fact that, despite being a million-man army, the Song line was stretched thin. The border was incredibly long and the Mongols' mobile form of warfare meant that they could hit almost anywhere. This had been the undoing of the Jin as they had persistently dispatched armies to the last place the Mongols had struck, only to be attacked at another point. Reprisal attacks against the Mongols were also not an option for the Song commanders as the enemy had no base worth the name near the Song border.

The Mongol interregnum came to an end in a fairly bloody coup and purges of the families of Ogedei and Chagatai by the Toluid branch of the family led by Mongke, Qubilai, Ariq Boke and Hulegu.[24] The Toluids' rise to the top of the pile also involved an agreement, with Batu Khan in order to garner his support, that the Toluids would not to interfere in Batu's Russian empire. Mongke Khagan was formally elected to the throne of Chinggis in 1251. The centralisation of power and finance into one khagan's hands after years of internal dissent meant the restart of conquest. Campaigns were planned for Mongol generals in both Korea and western Asia, but the khan of khans would personally lead the war against Song China.

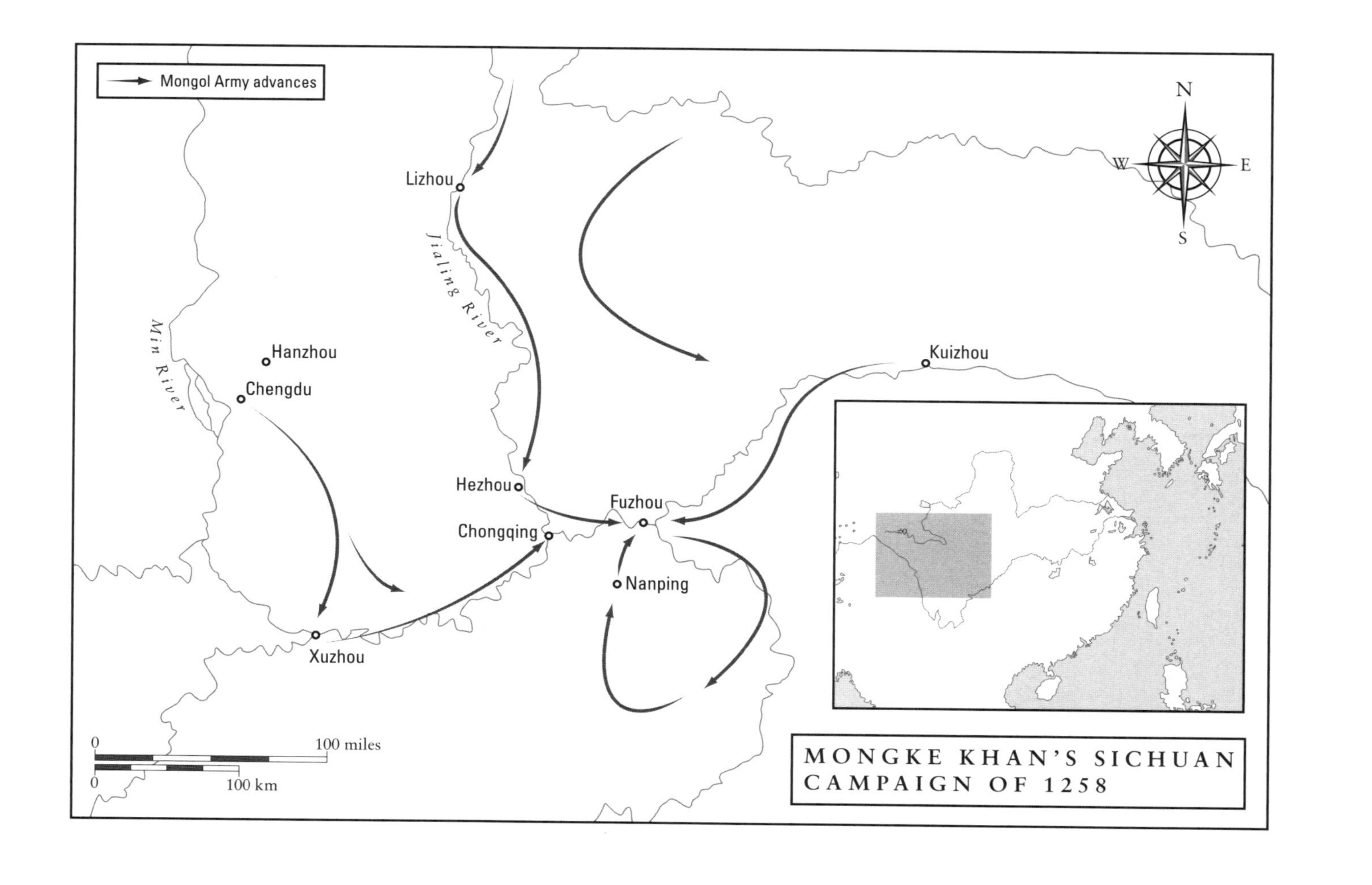
MONGKE KHAN'S SICHUAN CAMPAIGN OF 1258
Mongol Army advances
N
W
E
S
Lizhou
Jialing River
Min River
Hanzhou
Chengdu
Hezhou
Chongqing
Fuzhou
Kuizhou
Nanping
Xuzhou
0
100 miles
0
100 km

~ 4 ~

Feeding the Beast

Song Resistance on the Yangzi and Huai and the End of the Mongol World Empire

> The southern soil is low lying and damp, and the summer months are steamy and hot
> This is precisely the season that torrential rains are frequent and the vegetation is dense and deep.
> Sicknesses will surely arise . . . moreover the enemy will make strict preparations in advance
> He will certainly make his walls strong and defend them stoutly.
> If you encamp the army to assault them, provisions will not be supplied
> And if you divide your troops to pillage, you will have nothing left with which to counter your enemy.
>
> *Cui Hao, statesman of the Wei Dynasty (386–557 AD)*[1]

In stark contrast to their rapid success in most of Eurasia, the Mongols were fought to a near-standstill in southern China by the Song; the reasons for this are easy to identify. The Song defence was tenacious and stolid, the terrain suited the defender, the climate did not favour men from the northern steppe and the Song's navy made the Yangzi and Huai rivers into almost unbreachable barriers.

Mongke's brother, Qubilai, had been granted northern China as his appanage when the Toluid branch of the Chinggisid family divided up the eastern empire between themselves. He was charged in 1251 by Mongke with the task of reducing the Dali kingdom (modern Yunnan) to the southwest of Song as a prelude to a massive flanking manoeuvre which would allow the Mongols to push into Song lands well behind Sichuan and far west of the major river fronts. Qubilai was given two out of every ten men in the empire and spent several years showing all his considerable organisational talents and struggling with the logistics of maintaining an army in the mountains and gorges of southern China before reducing the petty kingdoms in the region in 1255. However, he did not then carry out the second part of the grand strategy and he did not advance into Song lands. Perhaps what Qubilai had already endured in terms of climate and terrain made him think twice about continuing with the Yunnan route into Song territory.

Mongke began making plans in 1256, but only commenced his full campaign in 1258. Song had been at peace for fifteen years by this time and the death of its two most talented generals, Meng Gong in 1246 and Yu Jie in 1253, placed it at a further disadvantage in the coming war. Despite these losses the Song court had at least read the Mongols' intentions correctly and began moving one hundred thousand troops from the northeast to Sichuan in early 1257. The troops arrived just in time as a full-scale Mongol invasion began. Ninety Mongol tumens – in theory some nine hundred thousand men – were committed to the offensive by Mongke, but these tumens were probably at about two-thirds strength, so around six hundred thousand troops began the invasion of southern China. About one in twenty of these troops were Han Chinese, and artisans were also press-ganged into the Mongol army for their engineering skills.

There were no major river crossings in western Sichuan to negotiate, so the campaign was initially successful and by early 1258 six Sichuan prefectures had capitulated to the invaders. Other raids by two smaller armies in the east tied down Song troops, and much of the western plain of Sichuan was soon under Mongol control. Mongke took a personal role in the Sichuan invasion at the end of 1258 and brought another forty thousand men with him. Hanzhou was surrounded and the Mongols then moved north to assault Lizhou. By now ten provinces of Sichuan and the cities of Chengdu and Tongchuan had been swallowed up in the Mongol advance and the collapse of the entire western front seemed likely, until the Mongols reached the city of Hezhou in the heart of Sichuan in March 1259.

The Mongols laid siege to Hezhou and its population of one hundred and fifty thousand. Its defence was led by General Wang Jian. The general had very few troops at his disposal, but the heroism of the city's population was enough to stop the Mongol advance dead. A five-month siege then ensued, which did far more harm to the Mongols than it damaged the doughty defenders of Hezhou. A Song relief army under General Lu Wenti was also deployed to the defence of Hezhou and it harassed the besieging Mongols, whilst the government of Sichuan was evacuated to Diaoyucheng in the east. Mongol attempts to decapitate the government of the western Song lands were stymied by this move and they were now effectively bogged down. They were then pounded by heavy summer rains. An epidemic of 'camp sickness' soon followed and the khagan was killed. We have been given a choice of deaths for Mongke by the writers of the period: he may have been killed by a Song arrow or a well-aimed catapult missile or by the disease that was spreading through his camp. Whatever the case, his death in early August was enough to put paid to the campaign, despite the march into Song lands of another Mongol army under General Uriangkadai from Yunnan. In truth, all the Mongol armies that had been deployed were struggling by this point, either with the mountains and the gorges of the Yangzi in the west and the wide rivers in central Song territory or against dogged Song defence. It seems unlikely that Mongke had ever read Sunzi, but if he had, he would have found the following instructive:

> Country in which there are precipitous cliffs with torrents running between, deep natural hollows, confined places, tangled thickets, quagmires and crevasses, should be left with all possible speed and not approached.
>
> While we keep away from such places, we should get the enemy to approach them; while we face them we should let the enemy have them on his rear.[2]

Qubilai was now in command of the central front on the Yangzi in Hubei and crossed the river at Ezhou, but was then held up in besieging the city. The Mongols could not gather any degree of speed in their assaults, simply because the Song's strategic fortresses forced them either to take longer routes in order to avoid the risk of counterattack or to spend time attempting to reduce them. Song troops also began a campaign of guerrilla warfare against their unusually static foes. Qubilai's troops were reduced to small-scale raids in Hubei, and the question of the succession to Mongke now also hung over the invaders. Qubilai was reluctant to abandon the siege of Ezhou, and the breaching of the Yangzi front must have had a huge psychological impact on both his own troops and on the Song defenders, but letters from his wife describing an increasing possibility of civil war in Mongolia and of threats against his lands there from his brother Ariq Boke were enough to make him look to disengage from the invasion.

The Song chief minister Jia Sidao had been sent from Hangzhou to Ezhou to direct its defence. His reputation in history is not a good one; he was recorded generally as idling, self-seeking and self-promoting. Of course the tendency in all Chinese dynastic histories is to look for the 'one bad minister' that can explain away the fall of a dynasty, but when Jia Sidao offered Qubilai a deal to partition China along the same lines within which the Jin and Song dynasties had operated he was acting rationally and with the best interests of his country at heart. As we have seen above, all attempts by the Song to operate north of the Yangzi had always thrown the state into a greater state of jeopardy and the Yangzi had shown itself, again and again, to be a formidable barrier to northern invaders. Initially, Qubilai refused the offer, stating that his crossing of the Yangzi made such an agreement redundant, but he would soon discover just how exposed his position was on the 'wrong side' of the river and far from the machinations of Ariq Boke in Mongolia. Furthermore, whilst Qubilai had received reinforcements from the Yunnan front these were outnumbered by the quantity of Song troops released from the forces that had been facing Mongke. Therefore the situation, by virtue of its stalemated condition and by the continued massing of yet more Song troops as Ezhou's siege was breached by the Song river navy, favoured Jia Sidao. In the end, showing an astute recognition of the political and military situation that he faced, Qubilai offered Jia Sidao a soft deal that would allow Qubilai to withdraw from Ezhou and return to the Mongol capital of Qaraqorum to form a *quriltai* to decide on the succession to the dead khan. This was undoubtedly fortunate for Jia Sidao but fateful for the Song. Two hundred thousand taels of silver and two-hundred bolts of silk were paid to Qubilai and a rapidly written pact of non-aggression was sealed.[3]

The problem was that the Mongols' precipitate flight north to attend to the deadly internal divisions in their ruling house inflated Jia Sidao's reputation to such an extent that even he fell victim to his own propaganda. The pact of non-aggression was almost immediately broken by the Song when they attacked the rear of the Mongol column of Uriangkadai's retreating army, which had been effectively isolated in Yunnan after the Song's reoccupation of Sichuan. When the Song army, under Jia Sidao, quickly dislodged the last remaining Mongols in the central region, the minister was very much the first man of government.

Both Qubilai and Ariq Boke held *quriltai* in May 1260 in Mongolia. Both meetings were technically illegitimate as neither included all the members of the ruling clique. Ariq Boke's was attended by what might be conveniently termed the 'wilder' steppe elements of the Mongol junta – the Chagatai, Batu and Qaidu branches of the family – whilst Qubilai attracted to his standard most of the senior generals, many of whom had fought with him in the last China campaign.

Civil war, as so often with divided houses, was the almost immediate sequel to the two *quriltai*, and the fact that Qubilai could mobilise the resources of northern China for his war against Ariq Boke was the decisive factor in the conflict that dragged on until 1263.[4] Even when Ariq Boke had been captured and then died, possibly poisoned by his brother, his influence continued with the 'true' steppe-living Mongols, and both the Qaidu and Chagataid clans would continue to be antagonistic to Qubilai. They viewed Qubilai as having become Sinicised, and in many ways they were correct. Qubilai relied heavily on his northern Chinese lands and subjects for both his war against the Song and the confrontation with his brother. His involvement with Chinese government even went as far as using Chinese systems of 'fair' taxation, Chinese administrators and Chinese levies. The *heijun* or Black Army of Han Chinese troops had been started by the Mongols as early as 1235 and was renamed the *xinjun* or New Army in 1241, when it achieved a strength of some ninety-five thousand men. By the time of Qubilai's reign it even had Chinese officers with hereditary rights to titles, and it was only when Shandong unsuccessfully rebelled against the Mongols in 1262 and Chinese army officers joined the fight against their Mongol overlords that the *xinjun* was put back under close Mongol supervision.

Ariq Boke lost the Mongol civil war because Qubilai could marry the mobility of steppe cavalry together with the supply systems and ability to hold land and garrison cities of a sedentary state's army. The world of Mongol warfare and, by virtue of that, Mongol politics, had been effectively changed and had been Sinicised. The Mongol world empire or the idea of 'all under heaven' had also disintegrated and the war with Song would begin to look more and more like a Chinese civil war of north versus south.

Jia Sidao thought that he saw an opportunity with Qubilai's evacuation of Song lands. When he was offered a second peace accord by Qubilai that had to all intents and purposes the same terms that had been agreed with both the Liao and Jin, he haughtily refused it and staked his political reputation on belligerent opposition to the Mongols. Qubilai's envoy, Hao Jing, a former Jin general, was imprisoned on charges and some writers of the time suggested that Jia Sidao took this unusual action in order to silence the envoy, who knew too much about *sub rosa* negotiations that the minister had been engaged in with the Mongols to secure himself a place in any new Mongol administration of a conquered south China. It is just as likely, however, that the envoy was imprisoned for the insult that his message from Qaraqorum implied. The Mongol word for peace, *il*, is decidedly double-edged. It does not simply mean the cessation of hostilities, but rather complete submission to Mongol rule. This was, needless to say, unacceptable to a dynasty that had outlasted two previous barbarian enemies and had just seen another depart its lands empty-handed.[5]

It has also been suggested[6] that Hao Jing's advice to Qubilai that he should make a 'false' peace with Song to allow him to finish the war with Ariq Boke and then return to the field to conquer the south had been discovered by Jia Sidao and that, in preventing Hao Jing's return, Jia Sidao stopped Qubilai from learning that his 'grand plan' had been discovered. This, however, seems an unlikely reason for holding the envoy, given that neither Jia Sidao or Qubilai, two seasoned politicians, would have had any illusions over the true intent of any offered peace accord.

Jia Sidao's policy of belligerence would also have not seemed to be particularly reckless in the early 1260s. Qubilai's war with Ariq Boke required him to leave much of the administration completely to his Chinese bureaucrats, and it seems that Qubilai had become so trusting of his Chinese bureaucrats that he did not even retain hostages against their good behaviour at the 'standard' Mongol rate of 2 per cent of the population.[7] In terms of the leftover petty 'bandit kings' such as Li Tan, the son of Li Quan, Qubilai's administrators were given the simple instruction to, 'apply Han law to Han officials'. This would not be an easy task as Li Tan, just like his father, was very much his own man. He ran both black market and legitimate trade across the Song–Mongol border in Shandong and he only really took the Mongols' side in any conflict with the Song if it suited his own ends. Petty rulers often do well when great powers are at war and Li Tan also consistently acted to undermine any peace negotiations between Song and the Mongols. He had cooperated with Mongke in campaigns against the Song and had often dispatched his navy to raid Song coastal towns. He took silver and gold from Qubilai in 1260 to finance raids on the Song but, despite this, he also commonly enticed Jia Sidao's government with protestations of loyalty to encourage them in the belief that Shandong could be regained by the Song.

In February 1262 Li Tan offered Shandong to the Song and this time he may very well have been serious. He had certainly over-extended himself and when Qubilai, largely because of his problems in Mongolia, had declared himself emperor of China, Li Tan had challenged the claim, no doubt hoping for a popular uprising in his name. It never came and so he turned quickly to the Song as Qubilai dispatched armies to destroy the upstart. By August it was all over and Li Tan attempted suicide. He was caught, however, before he could carry out the deed, and was instead trampled to death by horses whilst tied in a sack. In a way he was fortunate: the ancient method of killing traitors in China was the *wumafenshi*, literally meaning 'five horses, pieces of meat'. In this very visceral warning to others the prisoner was pulled apart by five horses that were chained to his members and head. Li Tan's execution was also a bizarre form of compliment, as the direct shedding of a prince's blood was against Mongol principles.[8]

Qubilai's faith in Chinese officials was shaken by the Li Tan incident and his Chinese troops soon enough found Mongol officers being placed over them. A system of dual administration was introduced at province level, with Chinese officials being monitored by foreign staff who were not uncommonly drawn from the Islamic lands. There may have been inspiration for this in the ancient Chinese system of the 'tiger tally', where the army of a region could not be mobilised until both the troop commander and the governor of the region came together and matched up their two halves of a tiger figurine.[9]

What Li Tan's rebellion, with his calling upon the Song, also signified for Qubilai was that he could never be confidently assured of Chinese loyalty and maintain an air of legitimacy as northern China's ruler whilst the Song imperial line continued. He claimed to be emperor of China but he knew that, even if the Jin had achieved at least a modicum of legitimacy in the eyes of their Han subjects, a Mongol monarch was almost certainly beyond the pale for most Chinese. It is noticeable that Qubilai did not take a Chinese dynastic title for his reign at this point; he would have known that at least partial conquest of the Song's lands or the Song's acceptance of an inferior position to his regime following defeat in the field would be required before he could reasonably make this move.

Qubilai knew that he could tackle and defeat the Song army in the open field, but the campaign of 1259 among the mountains and forests of Sichuan had been a failure not only because of the death of Mongke and the reported swarms of locusts that had plagued the region, but also because of the terrain. Another option to open up the Song line was to breach the rivers in the central region, as Qubilai had in fact done in 1260, but he would have known that his siege of Ezhou would probably not have been successful in the long run, even without his precipitate return to Mongolia. Getting across the river with one army was a great achievement, but Song resistance had actually hardened the further the Mongols had pushed east, and without complete control of the river no army's survival in Song territory could be guaranteed. Song control over the Yangzi also meant that their supply lines were effectively shortened, whilst Qubilai's would be stretched to the limit. Qubilai's essential problem, then, was that the Song navy outclassed his own both in terms of numbers and in sophistication.

China's merchant and military navies were poorly developed prior to the Song dynasty. Muslim merchants plied China's trade routes and the nation's regional defence was supplied by small locally based flotillas. The Song were literally forced to take to the sea by the defeats they suffered at the hands of northern invaders starting with the Liao, and the subsequent breakdown of land-based trade via the famous Silk Route. The reforms of Wang Anshi described earlier also encouraged educational, economic and military initiatives to embrace the new reality of the Song with their reduced lands and limited opportunities in the north of China. Fiscally exhausting wars with the Liao and Jin also, in some ways, compelled the Song to go to sea to seek revenue beyond 'traditional' channels. The encouragement and then taxation of mercantile trade was the financial saviour of Song after the loss of the north to the Jin in 1127. Of course, motivating merchants to sail to and from Song ports was one thing, but the protection of these trade routes required a state navy and coastal defences. Failure of an amphibious expedition in 1077 against the Vietnamese, in which merchant vessels from Fujian had been co-opted for government use, had spurred the government into a large-scale shipbuilding programme that saw six hundred large vessels and six hundred smaller patrol boats and transports built, and this was the platform on which the Song built China's first seagoing naval force.

War with Jin brought the need for river defence, and the Song minister Li Kang created two squadrons to patrol the Yangzi and 'static' patrols for each province that straddled the river. Experienced seamen were recruited into the new 'Wave-riding Tower-ship Force' and they were all trained in the particular tactics required for the deployment of incendiary weapons. All seafaring merchant fleet men were enlisted in the reserve for both this force and the sea navy.

The shipbuilding programme produced, in the main, a type of vessel known as the 'mullet ship'. These vessels had flat decks for the mounting of trebuchets and siege crossbows, a beam of 3 metres and length of 15 metres. Stability of the vessels was a must, as a common method of destroying the enemy was to use the *paigan*, a 15-metre boom bearing a huge spike that would be dropped into the enemy ship's deck to pin it, while fire was deployed to burn it or boarding parties were dispatched to kill its crew. Such parties would include the fifteen marines carried in each ship.

Districts that were unable to submit sufficient funds to the programme for building new ships were allowed to contribute ships in a form of lend-lease agreement. The rapid expansion of the navy in the first quarter of the twelfth century that this investment produced required the creation of a unified command system. The vast length of the Huai and Yangzi rivers meant that two officers were dedicated to this region and two more to the care of the coast. An investigating censor for the defence of the river and an investigating censor for coastal defences were appointed and military commissioners for both divisions were also assigned. After the initial set-up of these commands was completed the censors' posts were dissolved.

The Yangzi defence line had squadrons patrolling the river from Jingzhou in Hubei to Pingjiang at the mouth of the river and also had a headquarters at Nanjing. Three classes of ships are recorded as part of the Song navy, both for river and sea use. First-class ships had a beam of over 8 metres and a crew of over forty. Second-class ships were between 7 and 8 metres wide and were crewed by thirty-six men, whilst third-class ships, those with a beam of under 7 metres, had a crew of twenty-six men.

Every ship had thick arrow screens and iron rams, though the opportunity for ramming, even on the widest parts of the Yangzi, must have been limited and the lack of a significant keel would mean that the ship would be less likely to stay 'on line' after any collision.

Each ship carried sufficient equipment to extinguish fires aboard and the emphasis was on weaponry that could set the enemy ablaze. A strong emphasis was placed on fire because Chinese boats and ships of this period were virtually unsinkable, having several bulkheads and compartments capable of being sealed off if they were breached by ramming or by projectiles. The construction of these ships was impressive, with transoms fixed to stemposts and sternposts, and double-planked hulls that were in fact tripled at the turn of the bilge. All planking was fastened with iron clamps and spikes.

Nothing like these vessels could be found in Europe or the Middle East in this period. Whilst the Song were operating vessels of over 65 metres in length, the rest of the world had ships of only half that length, and the rudder that allowed for tight control during river warfare on the Yangzi was also not present on any other contemporary vessel. Writings from 795 indicate that even in this early period in China there were six types of warship, of which the largest were tower-ships with three-storey superstructures supporting catapults and trebuchets for firing molten iron, stone and fire. The defence against fire was generally to sheathe the ships in felt or leather, but there is evidence of heavier armour, including rhino hide, being applied to Song vessels.[10] The hull of a ship recently recovered by archaeologists in Quangzhou was small according to the sizes given in the 795 texts (a ship capable of carrying chariots and with an unbelievable beam of over 300 metres is described in one text), but it carried all the other features of larger vessels, with some twelve bulkheads separating it into distinct compartments, a hull clearly built for rough seas and ports and openings for crossbows and lances.[11]

Smaller vessels included combat-junks, which were sail and oar-powered, some of which had castles mounted amidships. There were also 'sea hawks', which were fully rigged craft built for combat on the open sea, and 'flying barques', which were multi-oared and designed to carry marines quickly into boarding actions.[12] Even in much earlier periods than the Song there is evidence of a further variety of design, with large catamarans and small craft carrying 'castles' at their stern being recorded.

The Song navy had performed well against the Jin in the twelfth century, at one point even rescuing the Song emperor as the Jin neared Hangzhou and spiriting him away to sea. A retreating Jin army had also been trapped by the navy and sprayed with fire from piston-powered flamethrowers for three months on the wrong side of the river. Minister Chang Yi summed up the navy's performance very neatly when he said, 'China now must now regard the sea and rivers as her Great Wall and substitute warships for watchtowers.'[13]

A naval arms race with the Jin had ensued in the 1130s and had required new initiatives by the Song government. An edict of 1132 required that all ships with a beam of over 4 metres should be commandeered for military use one year in every three. The Jin were at a disadvantage in this contest because the northern Chinese were not accustomed to naval warfare and the small, shallow-draught vessels that navigated the Yellow River were not of a suitable design for the powerful and fast-flowing Yangzi.[14]

The Jin army's mobilisation in the late 1150s for a massive attack on Song spurred the Hangzhou government to even greater lengths, and six huge war vessels with 10-metre wide top decks were built and *haiqiu* or whales, giant seagoing merchant vessels, were requisitioned for the coming war.

As the Jin assault unfolded in 1161, a Song fleet of 120 ships stopped the Jin attack on Haizhou in Jiangsu province dead and burned its supporting fleet of ships into the waters of the Yangzi. Then, armoured paddle-wheel warships powered by human muscle via treadmills surprised the Jin army as it was in the act of boarding ships to cross the river. Catapult-fired lime and sulphur bombs that exploded when they hit the water filled the air with fumes and blinded the Jin troops and sailors and allowed the paddle-boats to close for boarding. Thousands of Jin troops and their horses were drowned in the action. The Song fleet then sailed out to meet the seagoing Jin fleet off Shandong. The Jin fleet was surprised whilst it was still sailing in line formation and was rapidly destroyed through fire and boardings before it could take up a battle formation off the coast of Qingdao. The Jin admiral, Zheng Jia, described how the Song fleet 'suddenly appeared and finding us unready they hurled incendiary gunpowder projectiles onto our ships'.

Having lost virtually all his ships, and by extension also the control of the Yellow Sea, to the Song, Zheng Jia committed suicide by jumping into the sea.

The main Jin army attempted to cross the Yangzi in Anhui province and was able to build a pontoon bridge across the river, but the deployment of *haiqiu* ships on 25 November soon put paid to the Jin's hopes, and their bridge was destroyed by Song fire-bombs. Another attempt to cross the river two days later was also killed off by bombs, rockets, fire-rafts and naphtha. In December, another attempt was made but by now the Song commander, Yu Yunwen, had the support of one hundred *haiqiu*, numerous war galleys and smaller paddle-wheel boats. When the Jin commander tried to force his troops across the river they swiftly mutinied and killed him.

The Jin, despite these disasters – perhaps because of them – continued to try to compete in terms of sea power, and in response to this renewed challenge the Song court, in 1170, brought all coastal fleets under direct imperial control. The shrewd Emperor Xiaozong expanded the navy further and also invested in coastal defence. In 1170 a traveller on the Yangzi described seven hundred vessels being on manoeuvres. Equally impressive was the complement of seven and a half thousand men garrisoning Xiupu and guarding the mouth of the river. Xiupu became the largest of a series of naval bases and defended the port of Huating, modern Shanghai.

If Qubilai had had to face the navy of Xiaozong, it seems unlikely that he would ever have been able to breach the 'new Great Wall', but from the beginning of the thirteenth century the Song navy had gone into a decline. With twenty active squadrons and fifty-two thousand men in the navy in 1237 the number of ships had actually increased, but meddling by the Song court after it assumed direct control of the fleet meant that ships and men were often deployed to other duties, including the shipping of rice. Pay was also withheld for protracted periods and the morale of the navy sank as vessels were not replaced and the efforts of its officers and men were not cherished as they had been in the past. In 1239, the duke of Xu, at the Song government's behest, inspected the coastal defences and found only one in ten men ready and fit enough for combat. Of the others he recorded that:

> The rest of the men were weary, dispirited, deaf, moronic, emaciated, short, and frail. Look at them and one can imagine what the men [in the other naval bases] are like. They cannot ride the waves and thrust with their spears. This is the result of thirty years of neglect [of the navy]. They cannot be used for combat and yet they cannot be demobilized. They can only be employed to pitch tents and carry flags in the camps of South China.[15]

The duke also discovered that many officers connived with pirates and some were actively involved in piracy themselves. This corrosion of the service must have been fairly advanced because Duke Xu arranged a general amnesty in an attempt to rehabilitate rather than punish the wrongdoers; thanks to the diligent duke, things improved again for a few years. His report of 1256, however, showed a further decay in every part of the navy. At one base there should have been six thousand active troops, but three thousand had been deployed elsewhere, five hundred were on long-term sick lists and four hundred more were artisans rather than front-line troops. The ships were in little better condition, with some too old and rotten to be seaworthy and others listed as being in active service, but in fact long sunk or taken by pirates.

The government bureaucracy compounded these problems by continuing to demand ships from owners whose vessels had been lost in storms or captured by pirates. Bankruptcy was often the only alternative for a ship-owner hounded by imperial officers and instances of the sale of wives and children and of suicide among merchants are recorded with great frequency in this period. The wise duke of Xu attempted to rectify this destructive system with the introduction of the 'voluntary shipping system', by which ship-owners would club together to build ships and turn over half of the volume produced to the government. The other vessels produced would be retained by the owners for joint use in trade. This seems, at first glance, to be a pretty rough deal for the merchants to have engaged in, but the duke recorded that ship-owners realised they were dependent on the state for protection and it was the corruption and ineptitude of bureaucrats that they abhorred rather than the sacrifice of their ships for the defence of the realm and of the trade routes they depended on.

In 1265, at Diaoyu in Sichuan, the Mongols defeated a Song fleet, possibly through the use of fireships. The river battles fought on the Yangzi in Sichuan were fought in relatively tight spaces, with little chance for manoeuvre. It may be that the Mongols had the advantage of the current and that the Song ships were chained together in an attempt to maintain their formation in the fast-flowing river. The current was commonly a deciding factor in such engagements. Whatever the case, Qubilai's fleet captured 146 Song ships and with this success the khan had managed something that the Jin had never been able to do: to inflict a significant defeat on the Song navy. Qubilai certainly had better ships at his disposal than the Jin emperor had ever had; this was because he patronised the merchant class in a way that no ruler had done before and allowed both Chinese and foreign ship-owners opportunities that had also never been granted before in China. There was no immediate mass desertion of ship-owners in Song lands to the Mongols in this period, but Qubilai's initiatives gave him the chance to compete with the Song in this vital strategic area, and the well-crafted naval policies he introduced would eventually become decisive in the long war of slow destruction upon which he was about to embark.

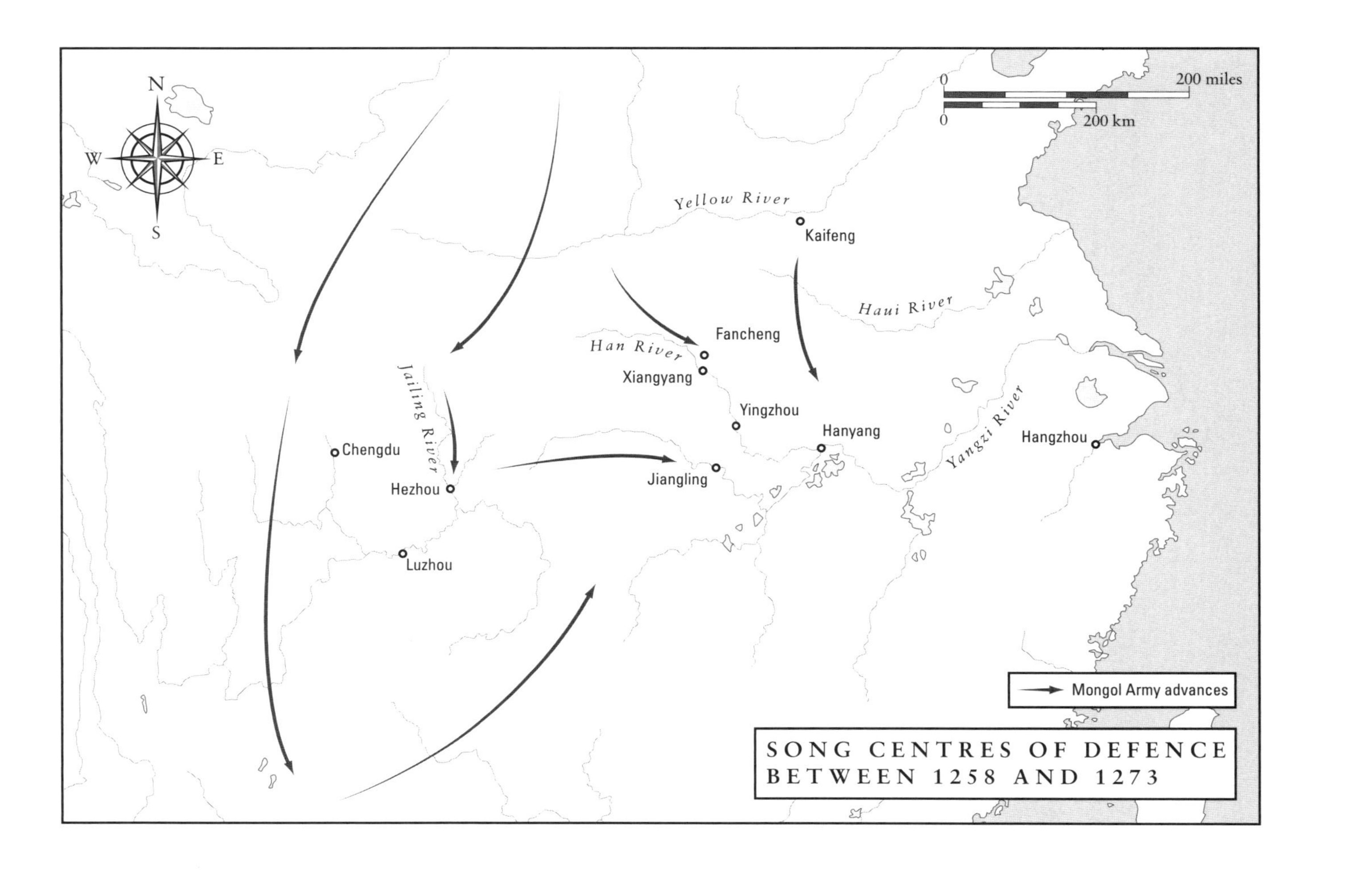
N
W
E
S
0
200 miles
0
200 km
Yellow River
Kaifeng
Haui River
Han River
Fancheng
Xiangyang
Yingzhou
Hanyang
Jailing River
Chengdu
Hezhou
Luzhou
Jiangling
Yangzi River
Hangzhou
Mongol Army advances
SONG CENTRES OF DEFENCE
BETWEEN 1258 AND 1273

~ 5 ~

Rumours of a War

Court Politics and the War of Attrition

The General shares heat and cold, labour and suffering, hunger and satiety with the men. Therefore when the masses of the three armies hear the sound of the drum they are happy and when they hear the sound of the gong they are angry.

When attacking a high wall or crossing a deep lake, under a hail of arrows and stones the officers will compete to be the first to scale the wall.

When the naked blades clash, the officers will compete to be the first to go forward.

It is not because they like death and take pleasure in being wounded, but because the General knows their feelings of heat and cold hunger and satiety and clearly displays his knowledge of their labour and suffering.

The Tai Kong, c.1100 BC[1]

The Song Emperor Lizong died in 1264. He had reigned since 1225 and had been a compassionate ruler, even founding a child benevolence and free medical service to care for Hangzhou's orphans and poor. He was unlucky in the series of floods, droughts, locust swarms and earthquakes that plagued his reign year after year from 1239 to 1264 and in the wars with Jin and the Mongols that had flared hot and cold and which required a million-man army to be maintained by the state. The famine of 1240 must have seemed particularly unpropitious as ordinary citizens were kidnapped from the streets of Hangzhou to be served up later in the marketplace as meat for cooking. Hangzhou also burned seven times during Lizong's time on the throne, perhaps because it was simply overcrowded with refugees from the war-ravaged north and from the natural disasters striking every part of China.

To make matters worse, by the end of Lizong's reign the yearly revenue surpluses accrued by Xiaozong were a distant memory. The sixty-five million strings of cash that Xiaozong's government had raised annually had been halved, as the provinces retained more and more revenue for local defence while local bureaucrats skimmed a cut from all returns. The 'stretching' of the war across the entire border with the north by the Mongols made this problem decidedly acute in Lizong's reign, and after 1234 there are no records of Sichuan remitting any funds whatsoever to the central government. The enormous damage done to the agricultural infrastructure of the border regions by the Mongols and the killing or flight of so many of its inhabitants further destroyed the state's agrarian economy and revenue base. Then, in 1259, the renewed Mongol offensive actually saw revenue flowing in the opposite direction as the central government emptied the treasury to pay regional commanders and to refortify the border. Requiring soldiers to till fields and villagers to adopt the *baojia* system did little to reduce the drain on the central treasury. As the government scrambled to find new sources of revenue it employed more and more bureaucrats and was effectively becoming a victim of fiscal entropy as the clerks and accountants began to cost more than they actually gathered for the state. Hyperinflation soon struck the economy and the populace, as the government turned to money printing to meet its requirements for liquidity. There was a twenty-five-fold reduction in the value of paper money due to this quantitative easing, and notes nominally worth in excess of a billion strings of copper were seen. The government exhausted its gold, silk and silver reserves, in theory maintained to back the currency, to make payments for war expenses.

Domestic unrest was the natural sequel to this economic misery and banditry became such a serious problem that in 1234 the central government mobilised thousands of crack troops and tens of thousands of militia to put it down. Suppressing the bandits of the southeast took four years and culminated in the execution of the exotically named Three-spear Chen, who had terrorised Jiangxi province before his capture. Complete quelling of the banditry that had erupted all over the state required the government to offer a general amnesty to all bandits who agreed to lay down their arms.

Song was, however, strong enough to survive all of the above tribulations and maintain the war against the Mongols. The real failing of Lizong was not, in fact, his handling of the economy but rather his handling of his officials. Loyalty is a laudable trait in any ruler, but misplaced trust and deliberate disregard of the faults of ministers are habits that emperors would be better to dispense with. Lizong, particularly in his final years, was too easily swayed by the opinions of his ministers and did not, unlike Xiaozong, work hard to uncover the truth that lay in the country beyond the court's cloistered atmosphere. To be fair, however, Lizong was certainly a better emperor than his successors would be. They secluded themselves almost completely from the trials of the state and it was possible, at least until his later years, to speak truth to power with Lizong. He advanced men to positions even when they were critical of him, but he failed to control dissent among his ministers and his failure to place his hand firmly on the rudder of the ship of state was a key reason for the Song's dismal policy decisions from the 1240s through to 1264. At no point was there a cohesive plan to bring the Mongol war to an end through negotiation, following either a limited victory or the achievement of stalemate. Times of peace were not used to prepare for war, and war was undertaken without any defined objective. The fourteenth-century writer Liu Ji was almost certainly thinking of the failures of the Song when he wrote, 'The rule is "even if the land is at peace, to forget about warfare leads to collapse".'[2]

Lizong's obsession with female companions was the main reason why he left the running of the state to overly powerful ministers. In later years this became a virtual addiction, and he moved from high-born ladies through Taoist nuns to street prostitutes. This was odd, given the political renaissance of the neo-Confucianism of *daoxue*, which had been persecuted in the 1190s but which Lizong had strongly patronised, even ensuring its inclusion in the curriculum of the Imperial University. This may, of course, have been simple window dressing if it was the case that the emperor was ashamed of his own licentiousness, but even that seems unlikely as he was surrounded by sycophancy in his inner court. As discussed earlier, Xiaozong had developed a strong inner court of favourites in order to counter-balance overly powerful outer court officials. Unfortunately, by Lizong's time this retinue was dominated by eunuchs such as Dong Songchen, whose only interests lay in corrupting the emperor further, in isolating the throne from the world in order that he should be the only conduit to imperial power and in accruing bribes for favours. His particular talents seem to have been the gathering together of street girls for the emperor's pleasure and the forced requisition of land upon which to build pleasure palaces for the emperor. It was commonly agreed that the emperor's licentiousness was just one symptom of a failing dynasty that heaven was turning away from. The natural disasters that continually struck the state, and the Mongol scourge, were taken as evidence of heaven's growing disapproval of its representative on earth.

Despite all these problems, it is a fact that the Song bureaucratic system still managed to produce some ministers with a degree of acumen and ability, and even the worst of the senior ministers were at least only one part of a court where alternative opinions could be heard and sought. Shi Songzhi negotiated the anti-Jin pact with the Mongols and commanded the final offensives against the Jin. He also had the wisdom to oppose the ill-fated Luoyang expedition of 1234. He denied the Mongols any progress in the 1230s and 1240s through his organising of the Song's stubborn defence of the river line, and his management of the huge problem of refugees fleeing the north was both imaginative and revenue saving. Each new arriving clan was allotted land near the border at low rents and recruited into the *baojia* system. In other areas of economic policy, however, Shi Songzhi was weak, and the state's rampant inflation effectively buried any savings he managed to make in the defence budget.

From 1256 minister Cheng Yuanfeng managed the state as the Mongol war intensified. He strengthened the border defences and increased the army's size by one hundred thousand men, but failed to put together a cogent strategy for using these men or for paying for them. He stepped down from power in the spring of 1258 and, as we have seen, the Song armies were caught largely unawares by Mongke's assaults of 1259 in Sichuan, though the chief responsibility for this must lie at the feet of Cheng Yuanfeng's successor, Ding Dachuan.

Ding Dachuan ignored the build-up of Mongol forces in the west and then, when the Mongol army was pushing through Sichuan, he imposed a ban on all discussion of the situation. Whether this edict was designed simply to stifle debate over his inept handling of the conflict or to arrest any erosion of morale is largely academic. Rumours proved far more damaging than the truth, and morale of the troops was corroded as much by the perceived inactivity of the court as by the successes of the Mongols. As Sunzi stated, quoting Wu Chi: 'The troops must have confidence in the orders of their seniors. The orders of their superiors is the source whence discipline is born.'[3]

Ding Dachuan's experience of war was negligible and he was finally abandoned by the emperor in November 1259 amid news of the retreats from Sichuan.

Ding Dachuan's removal from office brought Jia Sidao to the helm. He was the brother of a former consort of the emperor, but also came to the office with an impressive record of government appointments and exposure to military affairs. His father had been a distinguished commander and Jia had been civil and military commissioner in the central Song territories. He was also well-regarded by many of his contemporaries and it seems likely that he was innately talented but flawed by an arrogance of the sort that Ding Dachuan had also suffered from. Jia Sidao had first been introduced to the emperor when he was associate administrator at the Bureau of Military Affairs in 1254. He and the emperor, presumably in part because of the charms of his sister and a shared interest in carnality, immediately became close, and the emperor showed his inherent tendency towards blind loyalty in abundance in the case of Jia Sidao.

Almost the first act of minister Jia Sidao in 1259 was to quash any idea of evacuating the capital from Hangzhou to Mingzhou (modern Ningbo) and to take direct control of the front facing Qubilai at Ezhou. Qubilai's retirement from the siege, as discussed earlier, and Jia Sidao's stand on the court remaining at Hangzhou gave the minister an immediate reputation at court as a stout defender of his country. He appears to have revelled in the role somewhat excessively and arrogantly, and this may well account for many of his later failings as a commander-in-chief.

The withdrawal of the Mongols from Song territory gave Jia Sidao a little time, at least, to try to rectify the mess that the war economy had become. He first attempted to reform the 'harmonious grain' levy. This tax was paid in grain and was procured from all farmers by the state to feed the army. Jia Sidao abolished the levy, which was in practice virtually impossible to collect from powerful landlords, who claimed all sorts of complicated exemptions. The announcement was, of course, warmly received, but Jia Sidao then followed it with a further edict that seized for the state one-third of all holdings in excess of 240 hectares. This was then later extended to all landholdings of over 120 hectares. Compensation was given, but in the form of paper currency, which of course was losing value every day in the face of the state's hyperinflation. Equally worthless were the tax remission certificates or certificates conferring official status on the owner. Many landlords were paid as little as 5 per cent of the value of their land. The state became the largest landowner in the empire and the supply of grain for the army was thus, in theory, secured.

Jia Sidao was going against his own class with his actions, and this was unusual for a scholar-official in the Song dynasty. During the Song period the gap between rich and poor widened enormously as more and more land came into the hands of rich government bigwigs. It was brave of Jia Sidao to attempt to reverse this trend, but he negated any moral lesson that this might have relayed to his countrymen when he and the emperor continued to live richly and frivolously. Stories about the splendours of the private home and ancestral temple that Lizong had built for Jia Sidao at the empire's expense fuelled the ordinary people's antipathy to the minster and the derision of the men of the court on whose support he might one day have to rely. He also offended the great political body of the Imperial University student community when he had the faces of protesting students tattooed as if they were common criminals. There was no immediate response to the provocation but there would later be a severe backlash against the minister from this vocal political group.

As previously discussed, Jia Sidao had further inflamed the scholar-officials of the court with his high-handed approach to the Mongols' peace envoys and his imprisonment of their envoy, Hao Jing, in 1260 without recourse to the emperor or court. At this juncture the Mongols still maintained an army in Yunnan and their threat, despite the brewing civil war between Qubilai and Ariq Boke, was far from removed.

Jia Sidao was undoubtedly unlucky in the February 1262 Li Tan affair which he had personally managed, and his decision not to involve the Song state directly in the war was certainly the correct one. If Li Tan had maintained an army of the size that his father, Li Quan, had attracted to his standards, then – given Qubilai's distraction in Mongolia – he might have been able to secede successfully. Li Tan's forces, however, numbered only twenty thousand rag-tag men, and if Jia Sidao had wished to take advantage of Li Tan's rebellion, he would have had to commit a large number of men to the Shandong region. As we have seen, the Song were defending a fantastically long border against the Mongols and the commitment of such numbers would have denuded other areas of the defensive line. Jia Sidao was therefore a double loser in the rebellion: he could not afford to involve the state in the Shandong war, and Li Tan's defeat and death meant that directly controlled Mongol lands now abutted the Song border in yet another location, thus stretching the Song army to an even greater extreme.

Emperor Lizong died unexpectedly on 14 November 1264 and he was succeeded by his nephew Duzong without incident. For Jia Sidao it was business as usual as he had firm command of the new emperor. He had been the young man's tutor before his elevation to heir and had worked hard to ensure that Lizong adopted his student as heir. This said, the ongoing Mongol threat – which, with the eradication of Li Tan's 'state' in Shandong and Qubilai's settling of his steppe affairs, looked likely only to increase – called for an experienced hand and, as we have seen, Jia Sidao had extensive experience in a number of military commission roles. Jia Sidao certainly invested heavily to improve the physical defences of the fortress of Xiangyang and this showed enormous foresight, for this was exactly the point where the Mongols would strike. The 1259 expedition had proven to the

Mongols that, as a route into the Song heartland, Sichuan was a non-starter and getting across the river further east, with the Song navy patrolling it, was equally hazardous. Jia Sidao and Qubilai obviously both realised that Xiangyang and its 'twin city' of Fancheng were the key to the Mongols breaching the Song defence line. The cities were situated in Hubei on the Han River, which ran north to south, and joined the Yangzi just to the east of the cities. The Han was an obvious arterial route into the Yangzi River line if the Mongols could take it. The two cities would also be key elements in any Song counterattacks following a Mongol advance in Hubei and could disrupt the Mongols' supply lines during any push south, as they jutted out into the north from the Song defence lines and were the most important forward posts of it. They were, therefore, not only a source of strength to the Song, but also potentially their weakest point. If they fell, the enemy could advance swiftly down the Han River valley and into the Song heartland; Song would fall.

Jia Sidao also poured money into the environs of Xiangyang and into Sichuan. Overdue payments to demoralised troops were made and special awards given to troops on the border. The Song finally looked as if they were truly preparing for the war that they had in fact been fighting for many years now. Soldiers tilled the land and every defensive wall was repaired. Palisades and low wall defences along all the rivers were also attended to and the grain stores were replenished. The troops could, in theory, expect just over 1 litre of grain per day as a ration, though in the past the Song military bureaucracy had rarely met this target. Men were recruited into the army and Jia Sidao followed the edict of a century before when he had willow trees planted all along the river to impede Mongol cavalry. Hangzhou also had its walls repaired and strengthened.

For his part, Qubilai was, after the Li Tan incident, suspicious of the Chinese inside his empire, but he in fact had little choice other than to continue using both their institutions and their manpower. He had by now realised that Yunnan was useless as a staging post for an invasion. The Mongols had also subjugated northern Vietnam and lay in strength along both the Song's western and northern borders, but they had not broken through and seemed unlikely to do so on the eastern front. Sichuan was also too heavily fortified and well defended to be taken. Xiangyang was essentially Qubilai's only choice of battlefield. The battle for it and Fancheng would also involve an attempt to attract to Qubilai's banner members of one particular Song family, the Lu clan. This clan controlled most of the Song defence line in central China and had been a family of generals over several generations. The need to attract powerful families such as the Lu was one reason for the *volte face* in policy towards Qubilai's Chinese troops and his northern Chinese subjects in the second half of the 1260s.

Qubilai would later take a dynastic name for his reign and the 'Great Yuan' would be brought into existence in 1271 as the dynasty that *should* rule all of China, a position that was conveniently 'backdated' to include all the khans back to Chinggis. As we have seen, however, he also made the claim to be the universal ruler of China, though without a dynastic title, in 1262. The reason for this has also been briefly discussed above in relation to Qubilai's Mongolian problems and his war with his brother, but it must also be remembered that war against Song required engineers, shipbuilders and seasoned sailors experienced in navigating the rivers of central China. Qubilai needed a sophisticated war machine to take on Song. In short, Qubilai was almost entirely dependent on China for all the war resources he required for victory over the Song. He could never again hope to rely on the Mongolian steppes to supply his army's needs, as the Mongol world empire was now largely a fiction and the steppe simply could not supply what he needed. Indeed, Han soldiers in his army now outnumbered Mongols five to one; at this point, in fact, it is more convenient and very much more accurate to label Qubilai's forces as the 'northern army' rather than use the designation 'Mongol'. This largely reflected the fact that the Mongols needed the technical expertise of the Chinese and that they lacked experience of naval warfare. Seventy thousand men were recruited from territories lying along the Yangzi both to crew Qubilai's new navy and to construct the required vessels. Provisions for the new campaign were gathered from the north but also through raids on Song territory. These raids also seem to have been large-scale 'press-ganging' operations. Mongol armies attacked cities and counties along the Han River and took large numbers of prisoners to act as oarsmen and also seized ships.

Qubilai's Sinicisation was inevitable given the changing nature of his army. He needed therefore to shift from conqueror to ruler to appeal to his Chinese subjects of the north and to his northern army. In order to attract the Lu clan and the other influential clans of the Song lands to his banner he needed to appear as a moderate Chinese-style emperor. These were the reasons for Qubilai's adoption of a policy of *zhongtong* or moderate rule from which his subjects could expect lower taxes, succour for the poor, reverence for Chinese ancestral gods and respect for traditional Chinese ways.

The fact that the Lu clan was so powerful in Sichuan and in the west was partly historical but also born of more recent court politics. As stated earlier, it had been an important military household for several generations, but Jia Sidao further extended its political influence through pacts with it that helped him maintain his status as the first man at court. The military build-up Jia Sidao instigated around Xiangyang and in Sichuan was certainly sensible but it also solidified his position as first minister as a fearful capital and court looked to him, as the 'victor' of 1260, to defeat the Mongols. Jia Sidao even went to the length of getting General Lu Wende to falsify a report of Mongol incursions and to generate rumours of an impending invasion in 1264 as part of a power play for further extensions of his authority. He had resigned all his offices in protest at sniping from other men at court and had been begged to return, with extra honours being offered as a sweetener, by the very frightened emperor.

Jia Sidao set a trend with such actions, and by the mid-1260s the court was rotten with this kind of intrigue. Lu Wende joined in the plots with aplomb, so now the military of the western defences were also caught up in the murky acts of courtiers. Lu Wende certainly had experience of such things; in 1261 when the Lu clan had felt threatened by the Liu clan, another military household, he had denounced General Liu Zheng for misuse of funds. Liu Zheng was undoubtedly innocent of the groundless charges but, expecting no justice, he had fled to the court of Qubilai with his entire army.

Liu Zheng was welcomed by the Mongols, who realised that he knew far more of the weaknesses of the Song defence system than they could ever hope to discover. He became the key adviser to Qubilai for the southern campaign and almost completely changed the Mongol approach to the war. The Mongol tactics of fast-moving cavalry living off the lands or moving with vast herds of cattle was valueless in the south, and there was little hope of a breakthrough when the Song were prepared for defence in depth, with the rivers as a front line and armies drawn up behind it. Liu Zheng therefore rejected the 'classic' pronged attack that Mongke had tried in Sichuan previously and proposed instead focusing on one point of the Song line. He must have seen that this would be logistically easier to maintain and therefore more sustainable in the long run. Also, although the Mongols, were quickly catching up, they were still weaker than the Song in their navy. Concentrating all their efforts on one location meant that they could bring all the ships they had there and effectively block the Song's greater numbers from gaining an advantage in any confrontation.

Liu Zheng must have recognised that attacking the twin cities of Xiangyang and Fancheng, heavily fortified and defended as they were, would effectively draw the Mongols into a war of attrition. The Mongols had certainly already planned to attack the twin cities before Liu Zheng's defection, but it was his influence that decided Qubilai on making them the almost sole focus of his efforts, despite the obvious difficulties of deploying troops for an assault on them when the river running through much of the ground near their fortifications was too deep to wade in summer and too choked with sandbars during the winter to allow for easy navigation, even for small 'landing craft'. The Song had done well in the past in such grinding contests, but Liu Zheng knew that the Song had to defend Xiangyang and Fancheng or lose the war and that the Mongols, with their well-known bravery that bordered on disregard for life, would be prepared to take an almost obscene casualty rate rather than turn away from the contest. Perhaps Liu Zheng simply felt that it was possible to bleed Song dry, just as Von Falkenhayn, the German general, postulated that Verdun would bleed France white in 1916.

In late 1267, the Mongols formed a ring around Xiangyang's 6-kilometre square of defensive walls and around Fancheng. Forts were constructed by the Mongols and passage of the river was contested by their fleet, in order to deny the Song the chance to create a naval supply line and because their own troops would need

1. *(above and below)* The famous Song general Yue Fei. Yue Fei fought the Jin invaders to a standstill on the Yangzi River line but was later betrayed and poisoned by the Song court as part of a peace pact with the Jin. His legendary words, 'give me back my country' which are written above his tomb in Hangzhou became a rallying call for liberation from the next wave of invaders from the north – the Mongols. *Author.*

2. Zhu Yuanzhang, the ex-monk and destitute peasant whose Red Turban armies brought the Yuan dynasty to an end. He took the throne name of Hongwu and founded the Ming Dynasty in 1370.

3. Wen Tianxiang was fortunate not to be arrested and tried as a spy by the Song governor of Yangzhou. He fled to the Song stronghold after escaping from the Mongols and following the fall of Hangzhou. He and his twelve followers then made their way to Fuzhou to join the fugitive Song court. *Author.*

4. Statues of Wen Tianxiang in Hong Kong. Wen Tianxiang remained loyal to the Song Dynasty even after its fall, and was the last chief minister of the Hangzhou court. After his capture by the Mongols he refused to serve their dynasty and was executed by Qubilai. *Author.*

5. The bamboo forests, rivers and highlands of Sichuan were a huge advantage to the Song defenders as they denied the Mongols their greatest asset, the opportunity to unleash their horse archers to wreak havoc across every part of the Song state. The war very quickly turned into one of attrition.

6. Zhu Yuanzhang's greatest rival for control of southern China was Chen Youliang. Chen Youliang's fleet made an attempt on Nanjing in 1360. The key to Chen Youliang's plan was to take possession of its water gates, but the assault was repulsed and Chen Youliang's fleet and army suffered a huge defeat among the islands of the Yangzi.

7. (*left*) Chang Yuchun was an early companion of Zhu Yuanzhang. He expelled the Mongols from Shanxi and Shaanxi after the Ming army had taken Beijing and was both the most aggressive and one of the greatest of the Ming's generals.

8. (*above*) The Beijing opera masks for Li Tingzhi, a heroic Song general, and Bayan, Qubilai's greatest field marshal. Opera was a popular diversion during the Yuan period and was often used as a vehicle for subversive political commentary of Mongol rule.

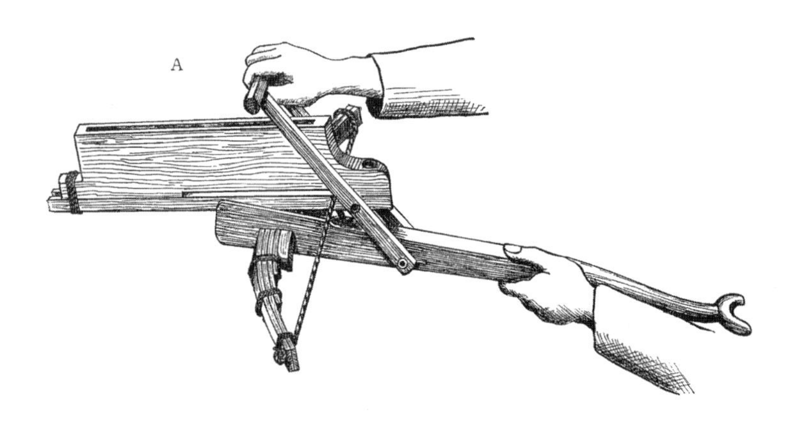

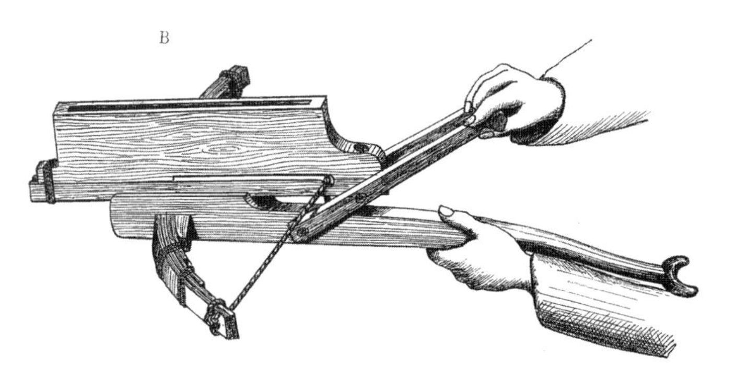

9. Song infantry were supplied with the very best in technology and whilst the repeating crossbow had only a limited range it could lay down a rapid rate of fire and was of enormous value in the defence of fortified places.

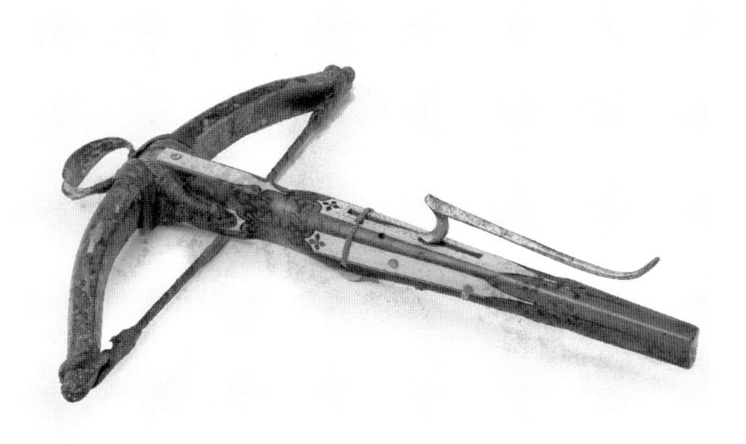

10. Mass production of crossbows was one of the Song state's major achievements. The huge expansion of the army that took place during Song's long war with the Mongols required an easily reproducible model to supply the new infantry forces, though specialist long-range weapons for snipers were also produced.

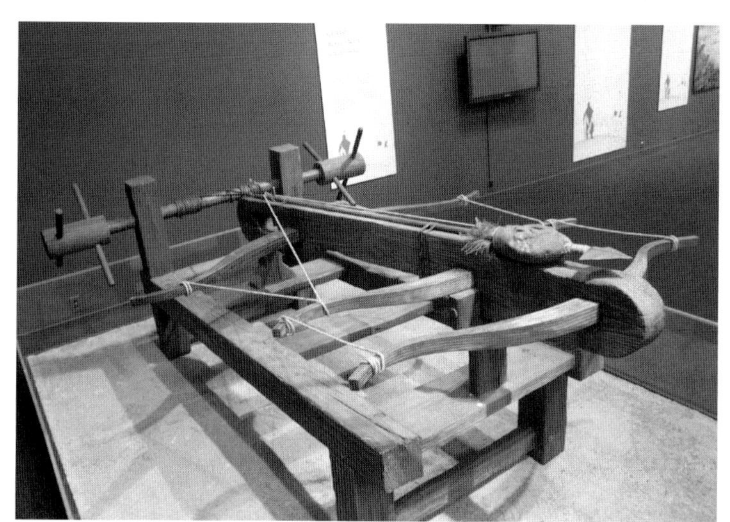

11. The Song armaments industry worked under conditions of extreme secrecy to prevent leakage of new technology to their Mongol enemies, but inevitably weapon prototypes did fall into the hands of the khans' generals. This Mongol crossbow is designed to fire 'quarrels', large bolts capable of knocking down palisades and even light fortification.

12. Bactrian camels were one of the key components of the vast Mongol logistics system during the khans' conquest of northern China.

13. Two paintings from the hand of Emperor Huizong of the Song Dynasty. Expressions of high culture such as this were the hallmark of the sophisticated Song court. Emperor Huizong was, however, responsible for one of the greatest political blunders of the Song government when he formed an alliance with the Jin against the Liao. The Song soon lost northern China to their erstwhile ally.

14. The construction of the Great Wall under the Ming Dynasty was a direct result of the scars that the Mongol invasion and occupation left on the Chinese psyche.

15. The design of this Chinese war junk of the nineteenth century would have been unchanged for centuries. The high stern could be used for deploying troops onto city walls during amphibious operations on the Yangzi River.

16. Beijing's gates and walls were no defence against Chinggis Khan's hordes. His Mongol troopers slaughtered tens of thousands of people as they stormed the city in 1215.

17. Walls inside Beijing were built to separate the 'Tatar' and Chinese sections of the city after the Ming Dynasty's taking of the city as a capital. The trauma of the long Mongol war excited xenophobia in China, and caused the country to turn in on itself. Modernity, in many ways, therefore passed the Chinese by until the advent of European aggression in the nineteenth century.

18. These transport junks are carrying US army supplies in 1901. The Yangzi River was the key to the logistics of the Song defence of southern China and in particular Xiangyang, and was also a vital artery of supply for the Ming armies as they conquered the region from the Mongol Yuan and southern Chinese warlords.

19. A Song cavalry squadron. The troopers look impressive in their livery but in fact the Song had very limited cavalry forces and relied heavily on their infantry for the defence of their empire. Their Turko-Mongolic foes, the Kitan, Jurchen and Mongol, consistently outclassed them in cavalry and the Song could never hope to project military power into the plains of northern China.

20. A Yuan Dynasty painting by Zhao Yong of a man on horseback. Though he is not wearing armour and the peaceful nature of the picture is obvious, it is notable that the rider still carries his composite bow. The Mongol troopers of the thirteenth century were inseparable from steed and bow; by the fourteenth century, however, much of their martial quality had dissipated.

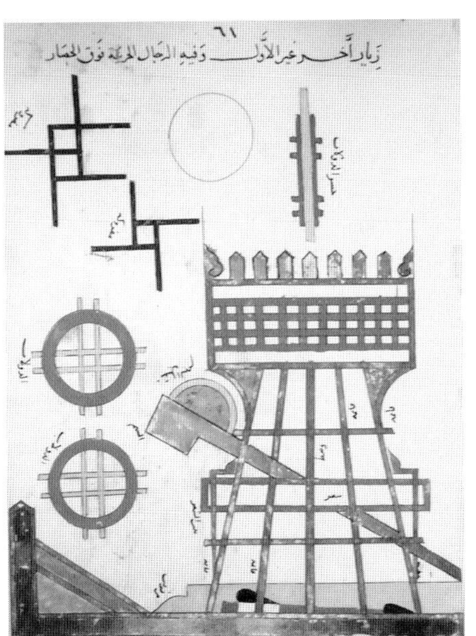

21. *(above)* A Yuan Dynasty painting by Zhao Mengfu. The rider is mounted on a steppe pony but wears the garb of a Chinese aristocrat. The Song resistance to the Mongol onslaught, lasting nearly fifty years, forced the Mongols to take on Chinese characteristics in order both to complete the subjugation of China and to rule their new possession.

22. *(left)* An Arabic text describing the counterweight trebuchet. The deployment of these devices at the siege of Xiangyang by the Mongols finally brought the fortress-city to surrender after five years of resistance. They came east with their Persian engineers in 1272. *Sharjah Museum of Islamic Civilisation.*

23. Yangzhou was a key defence point on the Yangzi and remained fiercely resistant to the Mongols even after Hangzhou had fallen.

24. A Song dynasty archer. Chinese archers carried the same type of composite bow that the Mongols used.

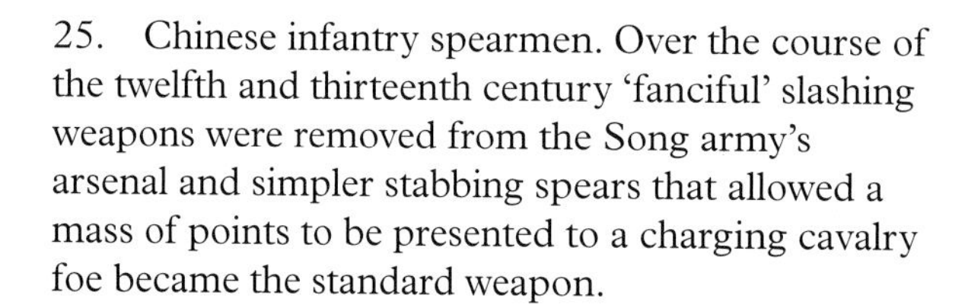

25. Chinese infantry spearmen. Over the course of the twelfth and thirteenth century 'fanciful' slashing weapons were removed from the Song army's arsenal and simpler stabbing spears that allowed a mass of points to be presented to a charging cavalry foe became the standard weapon.

26. A Japanese woodblock print by Utagawa Kuniyoshi portraying Yang Lin, a hero from the Ming Dynasty novel known in the West as 'The Water Margin'. The novel was probably first written down by the Yuan period writer Shi Naian, and though it was set in the Song period it was very much a criticism of Mongol rule. It was later melded with legends of the Song general Yue Fei by the Ming Dynasty writer Qian Cai to create a tale of resistance to foreign invaders.

27. A Yuan cannon. It would be incorrect to speak of a gunpowder revolution in China but there was certainly a long and continuing evolution of these weapons starting with the bamboo flamethrowers of the Song Dynasty and ending with cast cannon.

28. A Song Dynasty painting by Fu Ming. The warrior is obviously Central Asian in origin, and in the employ of the Song state. Even after the Ming Dynasty's expulsion of the Mongols from China, cavalry from the steppes beyond the Great Wall were still retained by the Chinese emperors.

29. A Song dynasty painting of the herding of horses by Li Gong. Despite strenuous efforts to procure horses from Central Asia and the near ruination of the Sichuan tea industry by the government's efforts to fund this enterprise, the Song could never hope to match their Mongol enemy in cavalry.

30. A Chinese army officer; the dress and weapons illustrate perfectly the blending of Turko-Mongolic warriors and Chinese military men that occurred during the period of the Mongol wars.

31. A rider lassoing a horse. The role of cavalry in the Mongol invasions of China and the Islamic world cannot be overemphasised. The Ming Dynasty retained Mongol cavalry and the importance of the horse has been a constant in Chinese military history. Ming Dynasty. Ink and colour on silk. *Freer Gallery.*

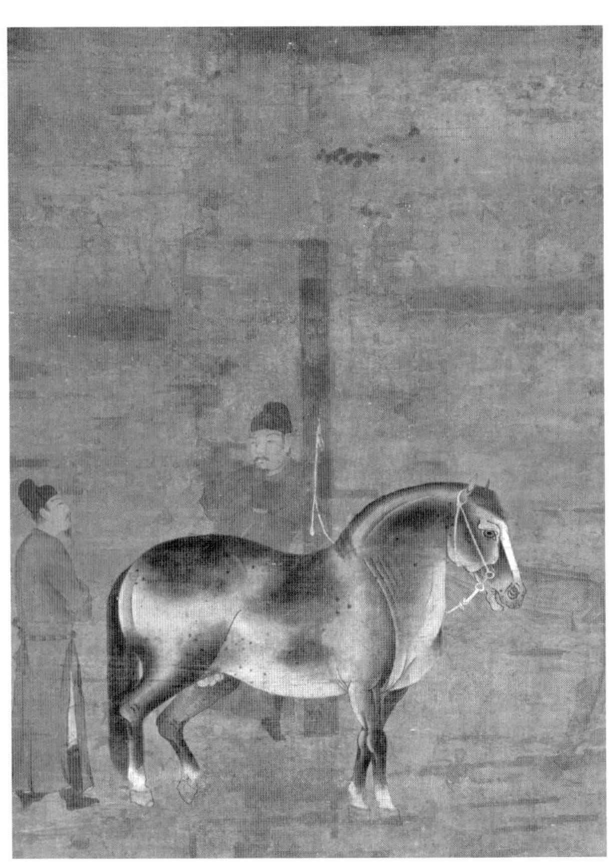

32. Evaluating a horse. The Song maintained bureaus on their north-western border for the importation of horses and breeding grounds within the Song state for warhorses but the dynasty completely failed to match the Mongols in the key area of cavalry. Ming Dynasty. Ink and colour on silk. *Freer Gallery.*

33. Tartar horsemen: the riders' Turko-Mongolic features are obvious in this picture. The Song Dynasty faced three distinct waves of northern invaders: the Kitan, the Jurchen and the Mongols. Yuan Dynasty. Ink and gold on paper. *Freer Gallery.*

to be able to assault Xiangyang from the south if they were to have any hope of success. The initial Song response was to strengthen further the 7-metre-high stone walls of the city and to try to attempt to deny the Mongols any control over any part of the Han River. The Mongol commander, Aju, countered the naval threat of the Song by deploying a further five thousand boats and supported this with stone-built observation towers and the construction of more forts along the riverbank. He still faced a huge challenge in assaulting the city, however, simply because three sides of Xiangyang's circuit of walls faced mountains, whilst the fourth faced the river. The city also boasted an encircling and permanent 90-metre-wide deep-water moat, fed by the river, and its pontoon bridge connection to Fancheng ensured that the cities could give each other mutual support during any attack. Xiangyang also had three gates that opened directly onto the river, so the chances of a Mongol landing party being able to leave their boats and breach the walls were very slim. Back in 1257, during an unsuccessful campaign against the city, Mongol cavalry had forced a gate on the land side of the fortress-city, but had then been caught between two layers of walls and slaughtered by its Song defenders.

Aju began a close blockade of Fancheng in 1268 and by 1269, with the siege already two years old, Lu Wende must have realised that the Mongols were not going to turn away from their investment of his cities. The Song had not, however, been idle during this time. Relief forces had pushed through Mongol lines to bring provisions to the trapped garrison, and Mongol attempts to build more fortifications, effectively to cut off Hezhou, had been thwarted. Limited counteroffensives were also launched in the west and east against Mongol-held cities. Chengdu and Luzhou were assaulted and attacks were also launched in Jiangxi. Chengdu had been held by the Mongols since 1258, and the 1270 Song attempt to take it back failed dismally. A further attempt on the city in 1273 regained it for Song for the briefest of periods but it returned, soon after, to permanent Mongol control and would become the staging post for further expansion in Sichuan towards the end of the war. The Song had more success with Luzhou. It had fallen to the Mongols twice in the early 1260s, but had been recovered both times and was returned once more to Song control after the 1269 campaign.

The problem was that, whilst the Mongols raided on a large scale and their *chevachees* gained them both booty and many thousands of prisoners, the Song were effectively only retaking their own territory. They were either incapable or unwilling to take the war to the Mongols in the north and so it was Song lands, the most fertile and productive lands of their empire, that were left untilled. They were now also losing another precious commodity, that of manpower. The situation became so desperate in 1270 that when Lu Wende called for more men for a planned counteroffensive to be launched from Xiangyang the Hangzhou court sent him the equivalent of a Children's Crusade. By this time, vast numbers of children were being pressed into service in every region's army. Every 'man' over fifteen was now liable for service and later in the dynasty the prefect of Jiangling reported that at least 20 per cent of his army was either underage or too elderly to be serving. Non-Han recruits were also drafted from the southern provinces and by the mid-1270s any pretence of control over the military by the civil arm was lost as survival and simply maintaining armies in the field became the only goals of the government.

Most of these disasters still lay in the future as Lu Wende prepared his counter to the Mongols in 1270. He was one of the few Song generals who had been consistently successful against the Mongols. In 1237, he had fought along with his brother and cousin on the Sichuan and Huainan fronts against the Mongols, and his clan had become prominent through his exploits and military prowess. He fought against Mongke in 1259 at Hezhou and then led the fleet that relieved Chongqing up the Yangzi, and also drove a Mongol army from Fuzhou. During Qubilai's siege of Ezhou Lu Wende's son defended its sister city of Hanyang. Lu Wende also broke through the Mongol lines to reinforce Ezhou. Lu Wende had allowed all the glory of this repulse of Qubilai to go to Jia Sidao, and when Jia Sidao gained total control of the court the Lu clan was richly rewarded by the minister.

It was therefore a major blow to the dynasty when Lu Wende died before he could launch his attack in 1270. Equally unfortunate was the fact that whilst Lu Wende had been very much Jia Sidao's man, he was also a trusted individual even among Jia's enemies at court. In some ways his status as a military man meant that he was no direct threat to the scholar-officials since no army general could be a senior minister. His untimely death stirred up the opposition against Jia Sidao in Hangzhou, and the entire court was now more unsure than ever about the Lu clan's loyalty to the Song Dynasty.

Lu Wende's younger brother, Lu Wenhuan, took up the command at Xiangyang, and Jia Sidao appointed a new civil military commissioner to the region. He had wanted to take the post himself, but was prevented from doing so by court factions who feared that the minister, whom they considered to be totally untrustworthy, would make a pact with both the Lu clan and with the Mongols for a peace that would put Jia Sidao at the head of a southern Chinese vassal state. Under pressure from his opponents and also personally prevented by the emperor from leaving Hangzhou, Jia Sidao eventually appointed Li Tingzhi to the post.

In many ways this was an odd choice, as Li Tingzhi was, despite being a subordinate to Jia Sidao, one of his most vocal critics. It is possible that Jia Sidao hoped to remove Li Tingzhi from court and then to undermine Li Tingzhi's position through his Lu family connections. Jia Sidao's underhand manoeuvring rapidly created a situation at Xiangyang where Lu Wenhuan often defied the man who was effectively his superior, and where Li Tingzhi could not effectively manage the larger strategy of the region he had been sent to govern. The fragmentation of military policy that resulted from this meant that Li Tingzhi could do little more than occasionally break the Mongol siege and resupply the twin cities. Furthermore, having had Li Tingzhi foisted upon it as its overseer, the Lu clan also began to suspect that it was now not trusted by the Song court. It could, of course, also look to the past and to the example of the fate of Yue Fei to see how things were likely to end. The Mongols certainly played on the Lu clan's fears after the appointment of Li Tingzhi and attempted to coax Lu Wenhuan into changing sides. However, for the time being, the Lu clan stood firm with the Song cause.

The Song offensive of October 1270 was a small disaster, with one thousand men lost. 1271 saw the deployment of over a hundred thousand men for a single Song naval manoeuvre, but three thousand more men were lost, and the cities still could not be relieved. Elsewhere Mongol raids continued and required the presence of Song armies on the Yangzi and Huai fronts well away from Xiangyang. The Mongol tactic of 'pulling' the Song armies first one way and then another never allowed the Song to build a coherent policy for defence, and it soon became obvious that the Song had totally lost the initiative in the war. Indeed, it is notable that after the fall of Xiangyang and even after that of Hangzhou there were still large but dispersed and ill-used Song armies in the field. During the entire time that Xiangyang was besieged, barely a single Song counterattack at any other point along the front was conducted and almost every engagement was won by the northern armies.

In 1271 Xiangyang's supplies were running dangerously low and by the summer of 1272 the Mongols had tightened the siege. By this point Jia Sidao's failure to secure any kind of diplomatic solution in 1270 when, arguably, Qubilai might have listened, was looking more and more like a disastrous lapse of judgement. Student riots calling for the expulsion of the Mongols from former Song lands and against the continued command of Jia Sidao became more frequent in this period, and indicate just how weakened the court had become in terms of its ability to control the state and public opinion. Every member of the 'establishment' realised that Jia Sidao's failure to act in 1270 had left the Song with a bleak set of options. Either they defeated the Mongols at Xiangyang or the state would fall. As discussed above, in 1271 Qubilai claimed the Mandate of Heaven as the great Yuan emperor of all China, and that this required the total eradication of the Song dynasty was implicit in the announcement.

Meanwhile, the Song navy was still running the blockade and supplying the twin cities, but the high cost in lives and materiel this required made it increasingly obvious that such heroics were unsustainable. More men were also assigned to the campaign to defend the cities, and at one juncture even the commander of the palace guard, Fan Wenhu, was seen at the front. At this point, it also seems likely that the Song were suffering higher casualties from disease and famine than their enemies, as the northern soldiers were sitting further back from the cities and concentrating on starving them out, rather than directly attacking them.

By the end of 1272, the Mongol commanders wanted to move to force an outcome at the twin city front, but Qubilai showed incredible political acumen when he set out his aims for the campaign – he wanted Xiangyang and Fancheng but he also wanted Lu Wenhuan as an associate for the campaign that would follow. He realised that gaining the loyalty of the most powerful military clan in the Song state would mean that the advance on Hangzhou would be eased by mass desertions from the Song armies. Qubilai therefore offered both high positions and large financial rewards to Lu Wenhuan and his relatives, but still Lu Wenhuan's loyalty held.

As the long siege of Xiangyang and Fancheng dragged on, two traditional tales of Jia Sidao illustrate very concisely the inner Song court's attitude towards the miseries of the cities at this time. At the height of the siege an official aide, sent to give a message to minister Jia Sidao, found him in his pleasant villa in the Geling Hills near Hangzhou, watching crickets fighting. Jia Sidao had written a treatise on the art of training fighting crickets to champion status and this among other distractions – such as the collecting of art and antiques to fill his famed villa, 'the Garden of Clustered Fragrances' – appeared to be of more interest to the minister than the fate of the last bulwarks that stood between the Mongols and Hangzhou.

Traditionally the messenger is said to have simply asked Jia Sidao, 'is this an important affair of state?' The minister's wilful disregard for reality evident in this tale is made even more clear in a contemporary conversation recorded between the first minister of the state and the emperor.

Emperor Duzong:	I have heard that Xiangyang has been under siege by the Mongols for several years now. What should be done?
Jia Sidao:	The Mongols were beaten back years ago. Where did his majesty get that kind of news?
Emperor Duzong:	I just heard it from a maid in-waiting.

It was recorded that Jia Sidao found the maid and had her summarily executed on trumped-up charges.

Perhaps Jia Sidao really had an expectation that the Song would eventually win the war of attrition that was being fought far beyond the peaceful walls of the capital and palace, or perhaps he was just deluding himself, as indeed most of the court seemed to be. Jia Sidao, with his love of fine civilised things and his attempt to create a heavenly condition on earth, was, in fact, entirely representative of the attitudes of late Song scholar-ministers. But abodes of peace, such as the ones described in his journal, 'Random Excerpts from the Hall where One Enjoys Life' can only survive when the abode of war is kept far from them. In early 1273 the Mongols, who at this time thought only of war and had no notion of the uses and value of peace, had brought men from the western lands of their empire to the Han River. These men would change the dynamics of the siege of the twin cities completely and with that bring war to the Song heartland. Heaven was about to be truly inverted.

~ 6 ~

A Chinese Civil War?

The Fall of Fancheng and Xiangyang

The art of war is of vital importance to the state.
It is a matter of life and death, a road either to safety or to ruin.
Hence it is a subject of inquiry which can on no account be neglected.

Sunzi, The Art of War[1]

Xiangyang and Fancheng were prepared for an assault by bombardment. Their moats kept the enemy at a distance beyond which trebuchets would be both ineffective and inaccurate, and netting screens made from rice stalks fashioned into ropes 10 centimetres thick and some 10 metres in length were festooned over the cities' buildings in order to dampen any impact a projectile might make. Thick clay was also laid over every part of the city's walls to the same end. The northern army's artillery assaults, conducted over the length of the siege, had therefore little effect on both the garrison and the city folk's morale or on the physical defences of the city. The garrison could also hit back with its own catapults and other hurling machines. It derived a height advantage from the positions atop the cities' walls and towers where the devices were mounted over the ground-set machines of the northern army. It could therefore achieve a greater range than the enemy, and, as we noted earlier, the science of Chinese defence and the Song's armaments industry would have ensured that a huge number of engines were in place in both Xiangyang and Fancheng.

Any advantage the defenders held disappeared, however, in early 1273 with the introduction by the Mongols of the *huihuipao* or counterweight trebuchet to the siege. The writer Zheng Sixiao (1206–83) gives us a tantalisingly short description of these machines, saying that they derived from Muslim countries and were more destructive than ordinary *pao*. He describes how their framework of huge logs was driven into the ground, that the rocks shot from them were several metres thick, and that when these missiles fell to earth they would bury themselves in the ground to a depth of more than 1 metre.

This description is less than satisfactory, to say the least, and the evidence for the revolutionary impact of the 'new' super-weapon is based less on documentary evidence of its construction and more on the way it completely changed the campaign for Xiangyang. A little more evidence on its origins can be gained from a study of its use in another theatre of war at the other end of Asia. The counterweight trebuchet was used extensively by the Mamluk dynasty of Egypt and Syria in the Mamluks' final destruction of the Crusader states of the Levant. The Mamluks brought the largest counterweight trebuchet ever known to have been built, 'al-Mansura' or 'the victorious' to the walls of Acre in 1291 to complete their annihilation of the last Latin settlement in Palestine, and they had been using the device from the 1270s, to great effect, against their Christian foe's virtually impregnable castles and fortified cities. In fact, the Franks' nemesis may very well have been their own invention, as the Muslims called the original design *al-Franj*.[2] Even then the long and truly international story of the *huihuipao* and its development is not finished. The progenitor of the Frank trebuchet, or at least its underpinning technology, may very well have evolved in China as early as the Warring States period (475–221 BC) and spread across the Islamic world with the Turkish migrations from east to west of the eighth century AD. The development of trebuchets of a simpler design by the Avars, and which were then used by them against the Byzantines in the pre-Islamic period, is also traceable.[3] From Byzantium the entry of this machinery into Europe's armies would have been a relatively simple transmission. If this was the case, then the return of the technology to China along with two Persian engineers, Ismail and Ala al-Din, in 1272 carries a certain degree of irony, and the *Pax Mongolica* had effectively acted as a conduit for military zeitgeist to flow from west to east.[4]

The Persians gave a demonstration of their devices to Qubilai that year and fired 100-kilogram rocks through the air and punched holes in fortifications that were several feet in diameter. The two engineers were, of course, Muslims, and the Chinese word for Islam, *hui*, gave the machine its name, the *huihuipao*.

Twenty of the fearful machines were deployed in early 1273 to the walls of Fancheng and began hurling 300-kilogram stones at its walls. There were evidently variations in design, as the writer Zheng Sixiao recorded that 'the largest [trebuchets] had their framework set above a hole in the ground.'[5] This is very similar to the way a European siege engine would be set up. Others were not dug-in in this way.

Fancheng was first to suffer since Xiangyang, as noted above, was both dependent on its twin city for flank defence and was too large to be assaulted without the destruction of its satellite being undertaken first. Furthermore, and as mentioned earlier, Qubilai also had the defection of the Lu clan to his cause as a strategic goal of the campaign. A demonstration upon the 'little sister' of what would be Xiangyang's fate might very well bring Lu Wenhuan over to the Yuan cause.

In late 1272, the Yuan had intensified their assaults on Fancheng and concentrated on gaining control of the waters of the Han River that ran past the city, in order to stop the flow of reinforcements from Xiangyang. Then, in February 1273, the Yuan began their counterweight trebuchet bombardment of the smaller city and simultaneously worked to destroy the pontoon bridge between the two bastions. The bridge was constructed from two lines of wooden piles driven into the riverbed, connected by heavy chains, with boats slung between them supporting the platform above. Protection was given by a permanent naval squadron. An attack on Fancheng via the land route gave cover to a second operation, during which engineers used saws to cut the piles and axes to break the chains of the bridge. Incendiaries were also applied to burn the bridge. The Song naval guard was defeated and thirty of its ships were captured. The northern navy's deployment of fireships in this engagement burned much of the Song squadron into the river.

Fancheng was now isolated and the northern army made an all-out assault from every side upon the city. Liu Zheng personally led his troops from the south, and they broke through and burned the palisade wall that defended the city along the river. His engineers then prepared platforms for the new trebuchets under the cover of a Song defensive rampart which had been cut to sit deeper than the surrounding ground in order to thwart infantry attacks, but which now unfortunately provided cover for the enemy as the trebuchet pits were dug. The Song garrison laid down a withering arrow and stone barrage, and made repeated sallies, but were unable to dislodge Liu Zheng's intrepid men.

The Song navy then rejoined the fray and attempted to push the northern forces from the riverfront, but the Yuan navy again deployed fireships and a perfect wind carried the blazing vessels on their destructive mission. Another one hundred Song ships were lost. Two days of fighting saw Yuan forces well established on the riverbank, despite high casualties and the disruption of a great snowfall during the action. Liu Zheng's men used the remaining material from the Song palisade to fill the moat ahead of them and prepared for an assault on the city's second defence wall, the last before the city walls proper. Their first attempt was repulsed by a missile and arrow barrage from the city wall, but at dawn the next day they took this second wall. The discipline and heroism of Liu Zheng's Chinese soldiers, fighting under Yuan banners, is attested by the fact that they then scaled and claimed the high city walls despite a continued desperate resistance by the defenders.

Elsewhere, other Yuan assaults were meeting with similar successes. Fancheng's moat had been filled in many sectors and the city's walls had been breached. The cost in men was huge for the Yuan, and most of the commanders engaged in the assault were wounded. Song commanders were equally heroic and the invaders had to take each street and each house bloodily, and against the most stubborn resistance; many Song commanders' defence ended only with their death. The blood-letting and brutal hand-to-hand fighting was accompanied by the whine of Mongol whistling arrows, the ancient equivalent of tracer fire, and by the continued crash of giant stones as the counterweight trebuchets turned buildings within Fancheng's walls into sand. With the final collapse of large sections of the landside walls, Yuan Mongol cavalry was then deployed to finish the job.

The city fell within a few days, with many Song commanders throwing themselves into burning buildings to commit suicide and to avoid the shame of capture. By the end of February the city was under the control of the northern army. The new Yuan concepts of *zhongtong* were conveniently forgotten as a ruthless Mongol slaughter then ensued. The entire population was put to the sword and some twenty thousand bodies were then stacked up outside the city's walls, ostensibly to cow the garrison of Xiangyang. The mound of death was reportedly of a size sufficient to dwarf Fancheng's now ruined but still impressively high walls.

If the barbaric act's aim was to impress upon Lu Wenhuan the hopelessness of his position, then it may have been successful. The fact that the general had already endured six years of siege with no hope of rescue and had now lost a major component of his defences was probably more significant, however. The 'test shots' of the counterweight trebuchets now being applied to Xiangyang and the general's knowledge that the Song court's suspicions of him were likely to be growing exponentially would also have influenced Lu Wenhuan far more than the view of the charnel house that Fancheng had been turned into. The situation was obviously now hopeless unless the Song government could make an instant response. Lu Wenhuan therefore sent a messenger to the Song court requesting immediate reinforcements, and his desperate note made it past the Yuan forts and outposts and reached Hangzhou, but no assistance was ever sent. Meanwhile, a stone bridge inside the city was destroyed by a trebuchet missile. This caused chaos among the garrison and civilians and they attempted to open the city's gates and flee. The Yuan commanders' ultimatum to Lu Wenhuan, that if the city did not surrender it would meet the same fate as its twin city, also became common knowledge. The northern army's *huihuipao* then began to demolish the drum tower and turrets of the city walls one by one as a frank demonstration of its ability to wreak on Xiangyang the same havoc that Fancheng had endured.

Lu Wenhuan surrendered the city on 14 March 1273, and it seems likely that a precipitating factor in his decision to do so was that Qubilai removed Liu Zheng from Xiangyang's siege and away to Huaixi. It was unlikely that Lu Wenhuan would contemplate surrendering to Liu Zheng, as he viewed him both as his personal political enemy and as a turncoat. Throughout the siege, and now at its conclusion, Qubilai's management of the Lu clan showed the sort of deft political touch that had completely eluded the Song court throughout the crisis. Qubilai consistently read the political auspices accurately, whilst the Song court did not.

The attacking northern army also performed bravely and efficiently during the siege and at its conclusion, but the defence of Xiangyang became untenable largely because of the Song court's ineptitude in defending this key point of resistance. Liu Zheng and the Yuan commanders' limited strategy and the fact that they could only see one way through the Song defence line is proof enough in itself that had the Song court managed the support of Xiangyang better then the Mongol assault on Song would have petered out. A similar situation was faced at the other end of Asia, by the Mamluks of Egypt and Syria, who fought the Mongol armies for over fifty years along the northern Euphrates. They consistently defeated them in the field and at the fortress city of al-Bira and outlasted the Mongol state of Persia by nearly two centuries. As an historian of the Mongol empire has noted, the Persian Ilkhanate collapsed in 1335 without showing any particular signs of decline,[6] and political fragility was a consistent presence in every Mongol state. Song might have been forced to become a Mongol tributary state or to endure an 'inferior position' and to pay annual tribute as it had to the Jin, but the losses the Yuan incurred in the reduction of Fancheng are proof of the fact that taking Xiangyang against a united and organised Song resistance would have been beyond Qubilai's army, even with its new military technologies and the undoubted skill and bravery of its officers and soldiers. If the Song court had managed the defence of Xiangyang with more skill, the Song state might very well have outlasted its enemy. Court faction-making dating from the death of Lu Wende, and the subsequent political inertia it engendered – only broken by Jia Sidao's disastrous decision to send Li Tingzhi to the region – effectively sealed the dynasty's fate in the spring of 1273.

Other members of the Lu clan had fought to the death in Fancheng but it seems that Lu Wenhuan's ire was now entirely turned upon the Song and not the Yuan. He could have simply retired from the war but instead he actively participated in the conquest of Song. His breach with Hangzhou was therefore complete, and this was certainly related to the fact that his chief advocate, Jia Sidao, had lost much, though not all, of his authority with the loss of Xiangyang. Oddly enough, the Song court continued to keep up a quixotic correspondence with Lu Wenhuan, asking him to intercede with the Mongols to maintain the imperial family, even as Song lands were swallowed up by Qubilai's armies and Lu Wenhuan's own troops advanced with them.

Three months after the fall of Xiangyang, in the summer of 1274, Qubilai postponed a planned campaign against Japan in order to free up more resources, particularly warships and naval transports, for a campaign to take the Han River valley and to move from there down the Yangzi to Hangzhou. General Aju was joined by General Bayan, also an experienced commander and trusted lieutenant of the Khan. Aju had complained to Qubilai early in the campaign against Xiangyang and Fancheng that his Mongol troopers would be of little use in the coming engagement and that he needed more Han infantry. As outlined earlier, by this time the Yuan army had changed its nature considerably to become predominantly Chinese in terms of its troop base, if not its leadership, and Aju's request reflects the fact that getting across the river would rely more heavily on infantry, engineering and on the Yuan navy than on steppe cavalry. The Song navy's ability to supply Xiangyang and Fancheng for five years during the long campaign over those cities would have made it plain to the Yuan that their traditional mode of warfare would be of limited value in the next part of the campaign. Ogedei Khan had been advised by Yelu Chucai that 'though the empire was conquered from horseback, it cannot be ruled from horseback,'[7] but southern China could not even be conquered from horseback alone. Of course the Mongol cavalry would still have a role to play in Qubilai's Song endgame once the river valleys were opened up and the Yangzi and Huai lines were breached. The Han infantry was supported by Jurchen and Mongol troopers and *semuren*, non-Mongol Central Asian horsemen who were usually Muslim Turks, but the fact remains that the majority of the men of the northern army were now Han Chinese involved in what was now effectively a Chinese civil war. As if to add a sardonic twist to this situation, the Song historian Xu Maguang tells us of Mongol defectors fighting in the front ranks of the Song army. When these men were captured by the Yuan armies they were simply re-incorporated into the army of the north.

Qubilai consequently strengthened Aju's forces with twenty thousand Chinese infantry. The Yuan seem to have had an almost miraculous supply of men to apply to the campaign, and equally astounding was Qubilai's reduction of the 'ship gap' between his navy and that of the Song. The panic induced in the Song state by the naval report of 1256 had, oddly enough, actually assisted the Mongols in catching up with the Song in terms of numbers of vessels available for war service. The subsequent forced, and clumsily undertaken, registration of vessels under the Song flag has been discussed earlier, with private owners being compelled to rotate ships through government service and to enrol in a system of shipbuilding that was expected to turn over three out of every six ships to the government. The heavy hand of Song bureaucracy made these already onerous requirements even more arduous and turned many already discontented ship-owners into implacable opponents of the state. Against this, the Mongols' easy trade terms and low tariffs made taking service under the khan a more attractive option than remaining under the emperor's jurisdiction. This was especially the case as Song's economic woes increased. Qubilai showed enormous wisdom in his policy towards merchants, and essentially created the Yuan navy from the Song merchant fleet. Indeed, under the Song, Yuan and early Ming dynasties, Chinese seaborne commerce and warfare flourished and China was, in this period, the strongest maritime state in the world. Arguably, the Yuan had been forced to take to the water because the war with Song forced them to do so, and the naval war was essentially an all-Chinese affair. As we will see, there would have been no further progress in Qubilai's war with Song without a powerful Chinese navy being at the khan's disposal for the Han, Huai and Yangzi river campaigns. The Mongols were essentially mounted archers and therefore unlikely to be pleased by the thought of going to sea or sailing on China's great waterways.

It was unfortunate for China, and of immense significance for the future of the world, that the vast achievement of Song and Yuan in this area was so sharply curtailed by the Ming emperors after the journeys of Admiral Zheng He.[8]

Lu Wenhuan led the way for the Yuan army and convinced all the members of his clan to surrender themselves and their forces. The domino effect this had on some other generals and their 'personal' armies was also certainly significant, but mass desertions from the armies did not occur and disintegration of the state did not immediately become apparent.

Song now stood like a swaying and aged warrior, bloodied and exhausted, but with an instinct for resistance still intact. This presented the Mongol Yuan with a huge problem. If they were to succeed as China's only legitimate rulers then Song needed to be extinguished with the minimum amount of damage done to the lands and people of southern China, and the easiest way to do this was to 'decapitate' the dynasty. A rapid campaign that would sweep down upon Hangzhou was envisaged, but beaten and bloodied though Song was, the one blow that would take the dynasty from the contest continued to elude Qubilai for years to come. The old warrior simply refused to lay down his weapons and would hand only the most hollow of victories to Qubilai and the Yuan armies.

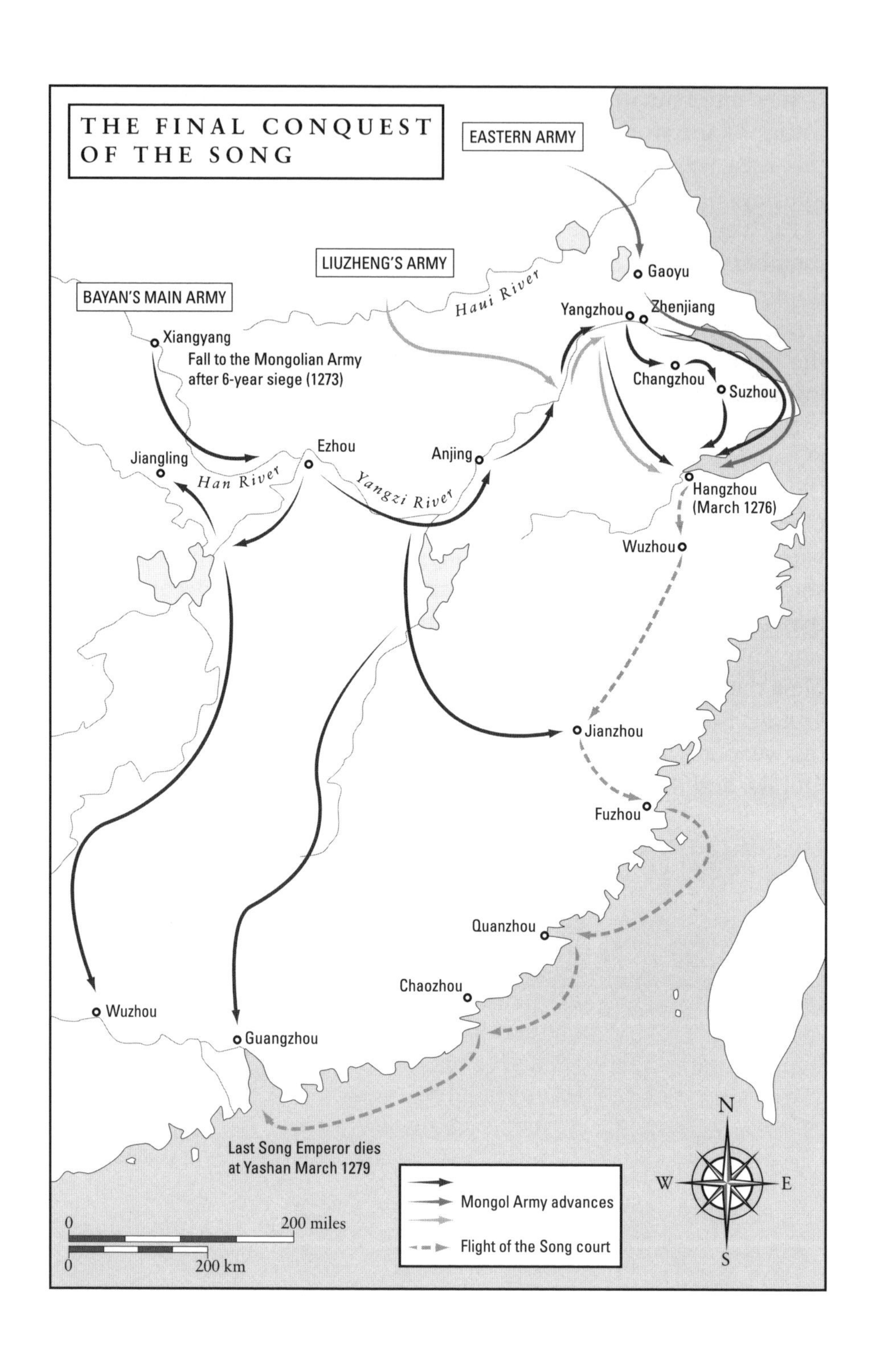
THE FINAL CONQUEST OF THE SONG
EASTERN ARMY
LIUZHENG'S ARMY
BAYAN'S MAIN ARMY
Gaoyu
Haui River
Yangzhou
Zhenjiang
Xiangyang
Fall to the Mongolian Army after 6-year siege (1273)
Changzhou
Suzhou
Ezhou
Anjing
Jiangling
Han River
Yangzi River
Hangzhou (March 1276)
Wuzhou
Jianzhou
Fuzhou
Quanzhou
Chaozhou
Wuzhou
Guangzhou
Last Song Emperor dies at Yashan March 1279
Mongol Army advances
Flight of the Song court
0
200 miles
0
200 km
N
W
E
S

~ 7 ~

Horses on Heaven's Wide Plain

The Loss of Hangzhou and the Flight of the Song Court

精忠报国

To the defence of my country.

Words reportedly tattooed across the upper back of the Song General Yue Fei

Song still had some seven hundred thousand men in the field and probably as many as one thousand warships on the Yangzi and Han rivers. What these forces lacked was leadership and direction as the court had collapsed into chaos and thought only of its own safety. And yet the machinery of Song governance still operated and resistance came from loyal generals, junior officials and from citizen-soldiers, even after the Yuan's capture of the 'last' Song emperor.

The Yuan's first objective was to clear the Han River and to place their forces in the Yangzi River valley. The autumn of 1274 saw generals Aju and Bayan at the Song defence line on the lower Han at Yingzhou. This was composed of two strong fortresses which maintained a chain-barrier across the river, and a garrison of perhaps as many as one hundred thousand men. The Yuan fleet available to Bayan and Aju was impressive, and numbered some eight hundred warships with about five thousand smaller transports, but Bayan decided to bypass the forts on the Han completely. Given the defections that Lu Wenhuan's presence in the Yuan army was likely to effect among Song generals if the campaign picked up momentum, and the fact of the Song leadership's apparent paralysis, Bayan probably wanted, at all costs, to avoid another long siege like Xiangyang. The Yuan certainly made initial forays against Yingzhou during the summer but Song military investment in the area had been substantial, and the northern armies faced formidable resistance. The fortress-cities on either bank were constructed of stone walls, and General Zhang Shijie had refused to surrender. Yuan attacks from the river and from the landward side of the fortresses were all repelled.

Further attempts on Yingzhou were therefore abandoned and the Yuan army moved on, leaving the city unsubdued in its rear. It was, however, an involved, laborious and time-consuming process to carry boats and ships on bamboo carrying frames around the obstruction. The main column averaged only 20 kilometres a day and the Yangzi was not reached until the spring of 1275. General Zhang Shijie had therefore gained the Hangzhou government some time in which to reorganise. The Yuan army's progress was further retarded by other loyal Song commanders who continued to harry the slow-moving column all the way on its journey, and even mounted one major attack against it despite the presence of two flanking columns of ten thousand Yuan troopers and infantrymen.

Unfortunately, the time gained by the commanders at the front was frittered away by the partisan scholar-officials of Hangzhou, who formed numerous strategies for their own internal squabbles but failed to form any to counter the enemy outside the walls of the court. The crisis in the court was deepened by the untimely death of Emperor Duzong, in the summer of 1274. An apparently chronic infection rapidly worsened with poor medical care and carried the emperor off at the age of thirty-four. His doctor was immediately banished and Duzong was succeeded by his four-year-old son, as there was no time to place an adopted older son on the throne. The child, Zhao Xian, was rapidly enthroned and named Emperor Gongzong, but the Song had not been ruled by an infant for nearly two centuries and even then the child had 'reigned' during a time of peace. Gongzong was the titular emperor but the reins of power were now effectively handed over to the Dowager Empress Xie, the widow of Lizong.

During January 1275, the Yuan army of Bayan moved on the fortress of Yang Lo and the cities of Hanyang and Ezhou, where Qubilai's campaign of 1259–60 had come to an end. Yang Lo was protected by an impressive Song fleet, so during a diversionary attack on the fortress the Yuan sent light boats across the river upstream of their position and Aju was able both to establish a position on the south bank of the river and to construct a pontoon bridge to allow for a two-pronged attack on the fortress and its defence fleet.

From the sources available it is impossible to reconstruct the river battle that then ensued. It is certain, however, that the Song fleet suffered heavy losses; perhaps as many as three thousand vessels were lost and, given the fragmentary evidence of the large-scale deployment by the Yuan of incendiaries and *huihuipao* trebuchets, it is to be wondered whether a rain of missiles from both riverbanks and the Yuan ships were enough to dispatch the Song fleet without the Yuan fleet having to close with their enemy and without the need to board Song vessels. The entire campaign from Xiangyang onwards seems to have been dominated by explosive missiles and mines. Contemporary writings describe how Yuan artillerymen such as Chang Chunzuo caused 'smoke and flames to fill the sky and the city to fall', and how when the Yuan met fierce resistance at a city in their 1277 campaign their explosives destroyed the entire city and buried all but two hundred and fifty of its defenders alive. It is heartening to learn that the Yuan commander, in this instance, allowed these doughty men to go free, and even provisioned them, but the destructive nature of this warfare was also evidenced in the siege of Zhangzhou in 1275. The Yuan applied *huihuipao* and siege crossbows day and night against the city, and their approach to Yangzhou was marked by the almost continuous thunder of explosives. Song chronicles of the period record that the bombardments only ceased when 'clouds covered the sky, a cold wind blew, and a shower of rain fell'. Cheng Xuxiao records the ongoing destruction of Song cities by the *huihuipao* and how, when their missiles struck temples, towers, and public halls, these buildings were simply broken into pieces. The Song had tried to copy and mass produce the *huihuipao* as early as 1273, and may even have produced prototypes that actually improved on the current design, but the imperial munitions factories, denuded of funds as they were and in areas now being overrun by the Yuan advance, could not, in fact, produce the volume required to match the Yuan in this or any other area of artillery and munitions.[1]

What was left of the Song fleet fled downriver and Yang Lo surrendered. Hangzhou was now only 560 kilometres distant and the Song court sent the first of a series of entreaties to Bayan for a peaceful conclusion to the contest. These were rejected out of hand as Bayan felt he could close the war without negotiation. The Yuan were beginning to draw benefit from the presence of Lu Wenhuan, as he brought several demoralised Song commanders and their armies that had been standing between Bayan and the Song capital over to the Yuan cause. This quickened the northern army's pace of advance, and the fact that the Yuan could now release their Mongol cavalry to a greater extent on both sides of the river and in the surrounding plains to forage and to terrorise entire districts into surrender added to the gathering momentum of the drive to Hangzhou.

As discussed earlier, in terms of cavalry the Song had never been able to match any of its northern adversaries from beyond the line that would later, under the Ming, become the Great Wall, and whilst this had led to the failure of so many campaigns north of the Yangzi–Han line it had not affected their ability to resist the Jin or Mongols to any great extent when their enemies had attempted to breach the Sichuan or Yangzi river fronts. Arguably, the Mongols' campaigns of 1259 and 1273 had been assisted to a great extent by their ability to strike in unexpected zones and thereby to pull the Song army out of position or to exploit weakness in the line, but generally the war in Sichuan and along the Yangzi had quickly deteriorated into a plodding affair, with the Song infantry exploiting fortification and the lie of the land effectively to prevent any war of movement breaking out. The Yangzi line was now, however, breached, and the Song's weakness in cavalry was very much exposed. The Song writer Zhao Hong wrote of the Mongols' exceptionally skilled use of cavalry tactics:

> As soon as the scouting screen of a Mongol army made contact with the enemy, the main body extended in front over as great a distance as possible so as to overlap the flanks of the hostile force. On closer contact and the approach of action, skirmishers went forward, and scouts were called upon to bring in reports about local topography, lines of communication, and the strength and disposition of the opposing troops.[2]

These tactics were now fully deployed against the Song and distracted and wrong-footed every attempt by Song commanders to counter the Yuan drive to Hangzhou. The Song had nothing to parry this fast-moving style of warfare because, even when they controlled northern China, they had never solved the thorny problem of adequately supplying their army with enough horses to produce a true cavalry force. This had been a major failing of the early period of the dynasty, and had, in some ways, brought them to the crisis of 1275. If they had provided their armies with the striking power and range that warhorses would have given it, then military objectives such as the prefectures lost to Liao and the northern lands lost to Jin might have been recovered. The failure of the Song to recover lost territory, particularly in the northeast, had constituted a serious threat to the regime's border security as the natural barriers of mountains in that region were lost. The Yellow River plain below these peaks was ideal land for the northern barbarian armies to operate on, and even the Song's retention of highlands in the northwest could not provide security for the state since the valley passes of Jingzhou and Yuanzhou gave access to northern invaders.

The Song response to this problem was to set defence lines on natural barriers such as rivers, and use a nodal defence system based on heavily walled cities. The problem was that they then faced the challenge that Frederick the Great so succinctly described many centuries later when he said to his generals, 'the art of defending fortified places consists in putting off the moment of their reduction.' What Frederick meant, of course, was that fortification could never be the total solution to security because offensive action was required to relieve such places and to defeat the enemy before the fortress fell. The Song government therefore had to create effective offensive elements to connect its defensive outposts and fortresses at its borders. Once mobilised – a process that took about three days – the Song field army was a fairly impressive force, but its northern enemies commonly struck with speed at multiple points. Only cavalry could operate with the speed required to maintain both communication between, and relief of, the Song fortified cities. Unfortunately, from the first formation of the Liao state the Song had been denied access to the lands that offered sufficient quantities of good-quality warhorses.

The Tang empire, during its apogee, had been able to maintain over seven hundred thousand horses, but the Song cavalry never numbered more than five hundred thousand even during the period when the north of China was controlled by the dynasty. Certainly the dynasty made strident efforts to meet this strategic shortfall and the *mazheng* or horse agency attempted not only to procure horses, but also to ensure that they were well pastured and trained. The dynasty also tried to achieve autarchy in terms of supplies of horses but, despite the creation of the office of supervisor of herds being created in 995, the extensive provision of government-controlled pasturage and of veterinary institutes that conducted research into techniques to improve both pastureland and the reproduction of the horses, there was still a large dependence on foreign importation of animals. Native horses from most regions of the Song state, such as Fujian and Hunan, were too small to be used as warhorses. The perceived value of northern horses successfully reared in southern climes in this period is evident in the fact that a roll of silk would be awarded to the pasture clerk for every foal born on land under his jurisdiction and that he would lose a month's salary if the death rate among animals under his care exceeded 10 per cent.[3]

The eleventh-century military reforms of Wang Anshi attempted to develop domestic programmes for the provision of horses and linked their pasturage to the *baojia* or military communities that he devised, but his fall from office essentially killed any expansion of the imperial pasturage system, and reliance on importation rather than rearing of foreign horses became the dominant theme. Therefore military missions from the Left and Right Flying Dragon Commissioners, whose remit was to oversee directly the administrative matters related to the procurement and maintenance of warhorses, were frequently sent to the border regions to purchase horses from Turco-Mongolic traders. The Bureau of Horse Grading also established numerous horse trading posts in the border regions where horses could be appraised, purchased and graded for their allocation to the imperial stables. Chinese civilians were forbidden to buy horses for private use from foreign traders for fear that demand would drive up the market price and undermine government tenders. Of course, civilian horse trade still continued despite this restriction, and later laws on the right of the Song government to forcibly procure suitable horses from the populace for war service are evidence of this.

At its height this system brought about thirty-nine thousand horses per year into the Song state and a horse of the first grade cost one thousand strings of cash. Payment for them was made in coin but also in tea and silk and redeemable vouchers. The generation and transmission of huge funds to the borderlands was a major bureaucratic and fiscal task, as was the paying of salaries to distant horse grading officials and the provisioning of fodder for winter feed.

Inflationary pressures due to the depreciation of the Song currency and high war expenditures eroded the imperial stabling and pasturage system during the eleventh century, but the system was also not found to be particularly effective in maintaining the battle-readiness of mounts. Perhaps the switch from northern plains to southern climes had a softening effect on the imported and previously hardy steppe ponies.[4]

The loss of the north to the Jin in 1126 and the movement of the imperial capital to Hangzhou drove the Song to take up a riverine defence policy, and, as we have seen, they consequently concentrated much of their revenue on naval development. The imperial horse procurement system suffered from official neglect during this period and also attempted to switch its foreign suppliers away from its enemies and towards the areas of Yunnan, Guizhou and Guangxi. The horses obtained in these regions were, however, far inferior to the horses of the northern steppes. The Office of the Herd and its domestic breeding programmes were closed as Song's economic problems really began to bite, and much of the apparatus that had existed for horse procurement was subsumed in the Bureau of Equipment, which at this juncture had far more interest in crossbows and incendiaries than it did in equine stock. Small-scale pasturage was still maintained around the Yangzi in the mid-twelfth century, but much land was lost to human agricultural needs and through both legitimate and corrupt means to the estates of scholar-officials.

The government's attempt to remedy this deteriorating situation was to move to a system similar to that which it had introduced to meet the naval crisis of the 1250s. They effectively farmed out their horse problem to independent militiamen. In this arrangement, private pasturage was used by a state-owned horse, and if horses died or became lame whilst under the care of militiamen then a financial penalty was incurred. The state, through this system, effectively moved a great deal of its pasturage problem onto the shoulders of private individuals who had, unfortunately for them, also been caught up in the *baojia* 'national service' system. This programme later evolved into a system whereby militiamen were effectively given a state horse to care for and it also included the outright purchase and upkeep of a warhorse by well-to-do locals. Property levels of three thousand strings of cash for city dwellers and of five thousand strings of cash for country gentlemen were set as the minimum level of wealth that would incur an obligation to purchase and care for a state horse. Wealthy families with higher property levels and personal worth were, of course, expected to maintain more horses, but whether this was the case in practice is hard to decide from the information available to us.

Amalgamating two apparently quite disparate bureaus into the Superintendence Office for Tea and Horses was an initiative dating from the 1090s. The impetus for this move seems to have been born out of simple financial expediency and the hope that the vigorous internal and external trade in tea and the government's direct taxation of the trade as well as its involvement in the industry as a major vendor of the beverage would bring sufficient profits to make the mass importation of horses affordable for the state. It was hoped that the system would stimulate entrepreneurship but in fact it suffered from the need to maintain, at all times, a delicate balance in the amount of tea sold. If too little tea was sold, then too little revenue could be garnered for the purchase of horses. Equally, if the volume of tea sold was high, then the market price would drop and relatively speaking the tea industry would be losing revenue on its product, and the price of horses would remain hard to attain. Direct trading of tea for horses with Tibetan traders was also a part of this strategy. Sichuan tea was purchased by the government at a fixed price and bartered for warhorses. It has been argued that Sichuan's tea industry was effectively destroyed by this process[5] and that the Song dynasty gained very little in terms of horses from the process. The two government aims were essentially antagonistic to each other. A drop in the price of tea effectively made the bartering for horses cheaper for the government but any drop in the price of tea adversely affected government revenues drawn from taxes on tea. This catch-22 situation continued until the end of the dynasty in one form or another and was made profoundly worse by the Mongol khans' order that no horse from their lands should ever be sold to the Song state.[6] In the last quarter of the thirteenth century, when the Song needed a cavalry force to counter the flying raids of the Yuan, there was none to be found.

The dowager empress made more peace overtures to the Yuan army commanders, but also appealed to the peoples of the Song lands, claiming that the three hundred years of virtuous rule that the dynasty had delivered deserved the loyalty of its people now that its throne was teetering. Reportedly two hundred thousand men heeded the call to the banners, but an army and navy of one hundred thousand men had already left Hangzhou for the front under Jia Sidao in February. The minister obviously felt that one more roll of the die might see him through his present political difficulties and his campaign is indicative of the fact that among his contemporaries Jia Sidao's name could not have been as blackened by the disasters of 1273 and 1274 as later writers would have us believe. If this was truly the case he would not have been entrusted with such a large army nor would it have followed him. Jia Sidao aimed to block Bayan's advance in Anhui province near Tinglong at Tingjiazhou and to drive the Mongols back across the Yangzi and Han rivers.

Jia Sidao poured almost the last of the treasury's money into the venture and, given the collapse in morale that had occurred since the fall of Xiangyang, this was probably a pretty reasonable gambit. He lavished 2,800 kilograms of gold, 14,200 kilograms of silver and ten million strings of cash on the campaign to furnish it with the necessary ships and it is certain that the Song, in this one battle, significantly outnumbered their foe in both men and in war junks. Jia Sidao attacked at Jiangzhou on the north-western tip of Poyang Lake, which had recently fallen to the northern army, but the Yuan counterthrust under the personal direction of Bayan and Aju came against General Sun Huchen, Jia Sidao's lieutenant, near Tingjiazhou. Jia Sidao had given Sun Huchen some five thousand ships, many from the fleet that had escaped from the debacle at Yang Lo, to support his army and obviously hoped that the hilly terrain and the wide Yangzi River that the Song forces were positioned on would stymie the Mongol cavalry and give his ships room to manoeuvre.

The battle at Tingjiazhou was a disaster. Two thousand Song ships were lost before the rest of the fleet turned tail and sailed away. Worse still was the fact that these boats were not even sunk or crippled, but rather handed over intact to the enemy by their crews. Hangzhou now lay open and vulnerable without an organised army between it and the advancing Yuan forces. Jia Sidao fled from his positions 40 kilometres from Tingjiazhou at Wuhu with the remainder of his forces to Yangzhou. He wrote from there to the court, suggesting the evacuation of Hangzhou and the removal of the emperor to Ningbo.

Jia Sidao's letter seems to have done even more damage to his position at court than the crushing defeat he had just incurred. The counsellor Chen Yizhong immediately called for Jia Sidao's death for propagating defeatism. Jia Sidao's next, and last, act as chief minister would only have increased Chen Yizhong's anger. He sent a peace envoy to Bayan. Hao Jing, whom Jia Sidao had kept imprisoned for fifteen years, was also released. The peace offer was, however, ridiculously paltry given the current military position. It amounted to a small payment of tribute for the Yuan army's complete withdrawal from Song territory and was rejected out of hand by Bayan.

Jia Sidao was quickly and quietly relieved of command by an order from Hangzhou and arrested. The former chief minister was saved from the immediate execution his rivals wished by the personal intervention of Dowager Empress Xie. Empress Xie no doubt recognised the fact that though Jia Sidao had been reckless in his judgement during the war he had served the dynasty for a considerable period and during the worst of times. She also perhaps realised that such a move would make obvious the collapse of order within the government and rob the Song of virtually the only weapon they had left – the loyalty of the rank and file of the armies and of the population. She did not, therefore, sacrifice him to his enemies but it was certainly politically expedient to banish him, as the empress then made a further appeal for a truce, and asked Lu Wenhuan to act as an interlocutor with the Mongol generals. Jia Sidao was effectively blamed for everything that had occurred between the Song emperors he had served and the khans. The appeal once again fell on deaf ears; the extinction of Song was the only thing the Yuan desired from their campaign now.

When they looked for justification for Jia Sidao's execution his political enemies went back again to the imprisonment of Qubilai's emissary Hao Jing by Jia Sidao as the *casus belli* that had brought the Song to its current wretched condition, but in fact Qubilai had never, in so many years, ever pressed for the return of Hao Jing. Jia Sidao's accusers looked to blame him for starting the war through this act but the long Mongol assault on Song was not driven by such small events or even by Song's aggressive acts against the khan, such as the Luoyang campaign, but rather as a response to the dissolution of the Mongol world empire in 1260 and Qubilai's subsequent need for legitimacy as a Chinese emperor. Qubilai sent Hao Jing to talk of peace in 1260 because he was distracted by the brewing war with his brother Ariq Boke. In 1269 he again made pacific gestures, but at the same time that he sent proclamations of security to the Song people his troops were pushing further into the Han River valley. The proclamation of *zhongtong* was a similar ploy, designed to reduce the Song people's desire to fight the invaders. In 1272, when Li Tingzhi sent emissaries to discuss possible terms for a peaceful resolution to the Yuan–Song contest, the envoy was denied entry to Yuan territory and, as we have seen, Qubilai was uninterested in hearing any peace overtures during the siege of Xiangyang or after the city's fall.

No action of Jia Sidao's could, indeed, have altered the fact that the Mongols were set on the destruction of the Song Dynasty. His chief failure was his political machinations and the kind of basic blunders that the Song court had made so many of in the past. He placed too much reliance on his political clients, the Lu clan, and he undermined the defence of Xiangyang through his tardy responses to the appeals of its defenders. His appointment of Li Tingzhi, the enemy of the Lu clan, as military commissioner in the Xiangyang region effectively paralysed the Song's wider response in the strategic theatre around Xiangyang as the city buckled under the Yuan onslaught. This said, after 1270 Jia Sidao was in fact semi-retired and only attended court once every ten days. Other officials must have been involved in a policy that lasted many years and consisted, for long periods of time, of the Song government just sitting on its hands.

Jia Sidao was assassinated six months after he was banished, and the property of his family was confiscated by the state. He was killed on the way to exile in Zhangzhou by the officer commanding his escort. It is hard to determine exactly from whom the order for his murder came.

Bayan and Aju's army was only one of three unleashed upon the Song by Qubilai in 1275. Their Chinese comrade in arms, General Liu Zheng, commanded an army that pushed down south on the Yangzi front near Wuhu and linked up there with the army of Bayan. Further to the east another force swept down past Suzhou, and by the autumn of 1275 the Yuan, in a Sherman-like drive, had reached the sea. During a battle on the coast, at Guazhou, they captured seven hundred and eighty seagoing ships from the Song and at Huating they seized another three hundred merchant ships. Pirates and smugglers also took the opportunity to join the Yuan navy at this juncture, and this added another five hundred ships to Qubilai's forces. This new Yuan armada then sailed down the coast, supporting the eastern army's march, and positioned itself to the east of Hangzhou, ready to take part in the cutting-off of the Song capital from all outside help.

By the spring of 1275, then, the Song had been pushed back on the Yangzi front and had lost Ezhou, Huangzhou, Jiangzhou and Anqing. After the disaster at Tingjiazhou almost all the important cities along the Huai had also rapidly surrendered.

Bayan pushed through past the city of Nanjing in April 1275 and, whilst no Song army worth the name contested the field with him, the growing resistance of each small walled city and an increase in the volume of small-scale militia attacks and guerrilla raids on the Yuan army slowed his progress a little. Envoys sent to Hangzhou by General Bayan were also ambushed and killed by irregulars before they could deliver their demands for submission to the beleaguered Song court. Resistance in the Song heartland was beginning to stiffen and also manifested itself in a refusal to serve the invaders by petty Song bureaucrats and by the suicide of many middle-ranking officials.

Summer saw this resistance begin to crystallise as the Yuan faced another challenge from the Mongolian steppe and their armies toiled in the hot southern Chinese summer.[7] The notion of Mongol world domination was, of course, by now long dead in practice, and the enduring resistance of the Song in China and the spirited opposition of the Mamluks in Syria were major causes for the fading of this endeavour, but Qubilai may still have envisaged using the resources of China – if Song could be defeated quickly enough – to reconquer Central Asia from his own relatives. Such plans were now, however, being jeopardised by Qaidu, the grandson of Ogedei who had stoked up the ashes of Ariq Boke's rebellion against Qubilai and the house of Tolui. He had become the de facto leader of a loose confederation of tribes of the Chagataid Horde out to the west of Mongolia proper, between modern Xinjiang and the Aral Sea. The significance of Qaidu's co-opting of the Chagataid Horde to his own anti-Qubilai strategy has to be viewed against other antagonisms among the descendants of Chinggis Khan. A long-standing conflict between the Mongol Golden Horde of southern Russia and the Persian Ilkhanate, which was ruled by descendants of Qubilai's brother, Hulegu, was now reaching a peak of intensity, with the Golden Horde allying with the Mamluk enemies of the Mongol Ilkhanate.[8] The Chagataids, for their part, and probably with the connivance of the khan of the Golden Horde, had fought one of the bloodiest battles of the long-running Mongol civil wars at Herat in July 1270 against the Persian Ilkhanate. Qaidu took full control of the Chagataid Horde in 1271 and his influence on Central Asian affairs became a real threat to Qubilai's Mongolian possessions by the mid-1270s. Bayan was recalled by Qubilai to advise on the geopolitical situation in the summer of 1275, and the advance on Hangzhou paused momentarily.

The halt in the Yuan army's momentum caused by Bayan's removal from the Song front had an immediate effect. Resistance to the invaders flared up all over the regions surrounding Hangzhou. Northern army gains were lost as Song loyalists retook Yangzhou, Zhangzhou and Suzhou in the east and Ezhou on the central front. This opposition to the Yuan was not as such directed by the Hangzhou court, but some elements of it were born of the individual passions and frustrations of men within the court. The fall of Jia Sidao had been engineered by elder statesmen, all of whom had served under Lizong; among the most powerful of these men was Jiang Wanli, who had proved his anti-Jia Sidao credentials back in 1269 when Jia Sidao had tendered his resignation to the Emperor Duzong in a carefully constructed ploy to increase his influence at court. Jiang Wanli even went as far as to drag the weeping emperor from his knees to prevent him from begging Jia Sidao to reconsider, before rebuking Jia Sidao over his behaviour.

Jiang Wanli found an ally in his opposition to Jia Sidao in Wang Yinglin, a senior counsellor to the throne and a professor at the military academy; both men had disagreed vehemently with Jia Sidao over the defence of Xiangyang. The two men had criticised the plans as being too conservative and lacking in commitment. These leaders guided the state after Jia Sidao's fall but other younger men, who had known nothing else but the Mongol war for the whole of their lives, looked to save the state by direct action. Of these angry young men the most important was Wen Tianxiang. He had graduated from the imperial university with top honours in 1256 and for his court-administered civil service exam he had written an essay on how to pull the country out of its present crises. He had been a protégé of Wang Yinglin, whom he had impressed with his encyclopedic knowledge of history and commitment to civic duty. Wen Tianxiang had, however, then struggled at court as his idealism and fervour collided with the intrigues of eunuchs and the conservatism of senior imperial advisers. He had stood with Jia Sidao over the latter's refusal to allow the court to evacuate Hangzhou in 1259, but against the newly powerful minister and his war policy in the 1260s. This opposition to Jia Sidao's rising star cost Wen Tianxiang and he soon found himself at the periphery of the empire and under censorial indictment. Despite his removal from the court environs Wen Tianxiang's continued and brave opposition to Jia Sidao's domestic politics and management of foreign affairs had made him a touchstone for the opposition to Jia Sidao. His former service as minister of war was remembered now in Song's darkest hour, and his proven skill in recruiting local men for regional armies and inspiring resistance in other parts of the empire was a talent that the court no doubt felt would be of value in pulling the fractured armies of the Song back together.

Wen Tianxiang was evidently a firebrand. He was one of the loudest voices to call for the execution of Jia Sidao and he apparently viewed all human weaknesses with a very cold eye. He had called for the introduction of the death penalty for dereliction of duty by military officers and for ministerial neglect of office even before the fall of Jia Sidao. The fact that such men were fighting a superior army and had been doing so, with little reward, for decades, and with little assistance from their state, offered no mitigation for their failure in Wen Tianxiang's mind. His stiff-necked ideal of loyalty, duty and service, whilst admirable in many ways, would also undermine much of his later attempt to form a credible resistance to the Yuan. This said, Wen Tianxiang, the then governor of Ganzhou and Zhang Shijie, the general defending Zhongxiang in Hubei, were almost the only high-ranking officials to be found among the many lowly officers of state and ordinary people who responded to Dowager Empress Xie's *qinwang*, or call to arms on behalf of the emperor. The desperate call was made in early 1275 for help in the defence of Hangzhou and the dynasty.

General Aju, in the absence of Bayan, concentrated on retaking Yangzhou and on quelling any Song guerrilla attacks within the conquered regions. The Song, in a poorly coordinated attack, attempted to retake Nanjing, but this only led to the loss of a further seven hundred war junks. The Song court offered a general amnesty to regional officials who had deserted in an attempt to win back more territory simply by repopulating the regions with Song households and by reinvigorating the *baojia* system. Very few officials returned, however, and the court swiftly swung from clemency to severity when, in May, it threatened capital punishment for all deserters.

Aju destroyed another significant Song fleet under the command of General Zhang Shijie through the deployment of fireships at Zhenjiang. The Song vessels were all large, unwieldy, seagoing ships and their lack of manoeuvrability was further hampered by the decision to chain them together. Whilst this shackling of vessel to vessel may have prevented desertions and defections, it made the mass of Song ships a large immobile target for the Yuan fireships and *huihuipao*. At least ten thousand Song sailors either drowned or were burned to death in the debacle. Aju also deployed Mongol cavalry on the shores of the river and was able to capture both the river port itself and some seven hundred seagoing ships, which further bolstered the Yuan's already large oceangoing fleet.

Zhang Shijie surprisingly avoided the blame for the disaster; perhaps there were just so few commanders of any worth left to the Song that any general still fighting was beyond rebuke. He and Li Tingzhi were assigned to the defence of Yangzhou as the Song attempted to hold the Yuan advance on the Yangzi. Aju made attempts on Yangzhou for much of the summer and threw everything he had at the city in the early autumn of 1275, but the city held out, as did Zhenzhou.

In December 1275 Bayan returned and organised the Yuan march on Hangzhou. The armies concentrated at Nanjing, and then Bayan's own army and that of Liu Zheng swung south towards the Song capital. The two armies then split again, with Liu Zheng's army marching to the south of Hangzhou. Bayan's forces took up a position to the north of the city after marching down the length of the Grand Canal via Changzhou and Suzhou to the east of the capital. The third army seems to have continued to track the coast and to keep contact with the fleet. As discussed earlier, this ability to 'timetable' armies to concentrate their forces at one spot at incredibly precise times despite the distances that separated them was one of the greatest skills of the best Mongol generals.

Changzhou was fired by the new but uncoordinated spirit of Song resistance that had begun in the summer. The city had received a reinforcement of five thousand infantry and its populace was also prepared to defend the city to the last man. Bayan sent ultimatums for surrender to the garrison and when they were not answered the Yuan army stormed the city. Mass slaughter ensued and a vast mound of bodies to match the death heap of Fancheng was built. As many as ten thousand men, women and children were butchered.

Perhaps the purpose of the carnage at Changzhou was to cow Hangzhou into surrender. It certainly caused chaos in the capital but it also created new problems for the Yuan. The fact that Song was one political entity should have made the Mongols' task of conquering southern China easier, because if the region had been politically fragmented then decapitating the regime, which was effectively the only way of claiming legitimacy over the whole country, would have been far more difficult. During their unification of China in the tenth century the first Song emperors had been obliged to eradicate multiple polities in the north of the country before being able to claim the Mandate of Heaven. Bayan, through his inability or reluctance to apply clemency to his battle for Changzhou, lost the opportunity to finish the Song Dynasty at the turn of 1275 and 1276. The brutality of the Yuan army and its leaders was the catalyst for the final desperate actions of the Song court. Two young princes, Zhao Xia, a four-year-old, and Zhao Bing, aged three, were spirited away from Hangzhou before its fall. The 'alternate' court that was created around them by Song loyalists would require the Mongols to chase these infants for a further three years and would ensure that loyalty to the 'old dynasty' would dog the Mongols' efforts to pacify the South until the end of their dynasty, and that southern rebellions would continue to be called in the name of the Song even after the Mongols' final destruction of this new Song line.

The massacre at Changzhou did work to the Yuan's advantage in the short term. It created a situation where even if Song commanders wanted to hold out against their enemies the townspeople of each small city would refuse to support the defenders and would look to capitulate as soon as possible. This fracturing of the partnership between the military command and the populace caused the whole of the Jiangyin command on the north bank of the Yangzi to slip from Song control at the end of 1275. Jiangyin's surrender re-established the Yuan's access to the Yellow Sea and their ability to strike at Hangzhou from the sea. With their hold over Lake Tai now also secured, the north of Hangzhou was open to attack, and by the end of 1275 Bayan's grip was tightening on the Song capital. There were still up to forty thousand regular troops and many more irregulars who had heeded the *qinwang* call of the empress available for the defence of the city. The question was: how well would the court ministers use these soldiers?

The chief minister of Song at this point was Chen Yizhong. Despite an impressive reputation for sagacity he had not joined Jiang Wanli and Wang Yinglin in immediate condemnation of Jia

Sidao. This was surprising, as back in 1273 Chen Yizhong had been a vocal critic of Jia Sidao over his lackadaisical attitude to the war and over the latter's pardoning of Fan Wenhu. Fan Wenhu was Jia Sidao's brother-in-law and had deserted Xiangyang even though he had been given command of the region surrounding the key fortress through Jia Sidao's influence. Chen Yizhong had demanded Fan Wenhu's execution, but Jia Sidao had shielded his relative from the court's wrath. In truth, Chen Yizhong's condemnation of Fan Wenhu was excessive and it is likely that the real intention of the demand was to damage Jia Sidao through his brother-in-law's disgrace. Fan Wenhu's army of one hundred thousand men had been decimated by Aju's forces in the summer of 1271 and he had nearly been killed himself. Fan Wenhu survived the Song court's wrath over Xiangyang but his subsequent loss of Anqing in early 1275 was the prologue to his brother-in-law's catastrophic defeat at Tingjiazhou.

Chen Yizhong now, though, acted with the kind of shiftlessness for which he had previously denounced Jia Sidao. There were still, even at this desperate hour, several Song field armies in existence in the field. These surviving armies, still with intact command structures, pose an interesting question for the historian as to whether Song could have survived a little longer with better central command. It seems unlikely that Hangzhou could have been defended, and the fall of capitals and with them their ruling dynasties, even if the state that the dynasty ruled was not militarily exhausted, is a common theme in China's medieval history. However, as the flight of the child princes Zhao Xia and Zhao Bin and the three-year campaign to extinguish the 'new' Song Dynasty that awaited the Yuan indicates, there was still a desire to fight among the Song's troops and commanders. Unfortunately no direction came from the government of Chen Yizhong. The Empress Xie summed up the rapid dissolution that was occurring at all levels of government in this period:

> Our dynasty for over three hundred years has treated scholar-officials with propriety. While the new successor [Zhao Xia] and I have met with assorted family hardships, you subjects both high and low have offered no proposals whatsoever for saving the empire. Within [the capital], officials forsake their commissions and vacate posts. Away [from the capital], responsible officers relinquish their seals and abandon cities.

> Censorial officers are incapable of investigating and indicting for me, and the two or three at the counsellor level cannot lead and direct the efforts of the whole. Superficially, they cooperate [with me], but one after the other they flee by night.[9]

Wen Tianxiang had been sent as prefect by Chen Yizhong to defend Suzhou, which had been recaptured in the Song's summer campaign, and was a major defence point on the lower Yangzi, but then the chief minister changed Wen Tianxiang's commission and sent him instead to defend the Dusong pass as Bayan was threatening to force his way through it to Hangzhou. The pass had however fallen to the Yuan by the time that Wen Tianxiang could bring his forces to the region, and then, before he could return to Suzhou's defence, it too was lost to Bayan's army. Wen Tianxiang and General Zhang Shijie then urged the central government to mass the remaining Song forces to resist the Yuan and to bring them to battle, but Chen Yizhong refused their demands. Bayan was by this point at Mount Gaoting, only 15 kilometres from the capital. Bayan demanded the Song's unconditional surrender but the court would offer little more than discussion over protocols of superiority between the Yuan and Song emperor.

As the Yuan armies made further advances and, in a three-pronged attack, drove into the suburbs of Hangzhou and made an amphibious landing on the north side of the city, ministers began to desert the dynasty and the dowager empress sent the official Song seals to Bayan as a token of her surrender. Marco Polo claims that the empress also sent a letter to Bayan extolling the beauties of Hangzhou in an attempt to prevent the Mongols from destroying the city. Whilst this is unlikely, and Marco's reporting of the Song–Yuan war should at all times be taken with a large pinch of salt, Hangzhou was certainly a prize that was worthy of being spared the horrors that had been inflicted by the Mongols on so many other great Asian cities. The region surrounding it, the Jiangnan, was and remains the richest and most fertile region in China. Hangzhou was also probably the largest city in the world at this time, with the possible exception of Constantinople, and the beauties of its pavilions, orange gardens and book markets were the inspiration for the, perhaps by now somewhat hackneyed, idiom that: 'Above there is Heaven, below Suzhou and Hangzhou.'

Leading members of the Song court now also began to desert, although Wang Yinglin, given his history of hostility to the Mongols, may have left the city as much in disgust at Chen Yizhong's ineffective response to Bayan's encircling of the city as in fear for his life. Wen Tianxiang called for the royal family to flee by boat and continue the war, but this was opposed by Chen Yizhong, who now seemed to be waiting for a miracle to save the dynasty as he offered nothing in negotiation to the Yuan, but also did nothing to counter their attempts to close the war.

Eventually Chen Yizhong did yield to pressure from Wen Tianxiang and proposed to the empress that she and the infant emperor leave Hangzhou, but he did not remain in the capital to engineer the move and instead fled to his native city of Wenzhou. It seems that fear of being sent on a mission to the Yuan camp and of being killed by either Song irregulars on his way there or by Mongol troopers on his arrival was the catalyst for his flight from the court in early February 1276. One of his final acts in the weeks before his desertion had been to have the commander of the palace guard, Han Zhen, beaten to death for attempting to force the court to abandon Hangzhou. Mutinies among the palace guard had followed, bombs were thrown at the palace by its own praetorians and many of the guard had then deserted to the northern army.

Chen Yizhong's craven desertion seems to have sickened General Zhang Shijie to such a degree that he now withdrew his troops from the defence of Hangzhou and took them out to sea on transports whilst vowing to continue the war. In truth there were very few other places his army could deploy to. Hunan and northern Jiangxi province were lost and Changsha fell after a five-month siege of appalling loss and misery. Thousands of the soldiers defending Changsha and its citizens committed suicide rather than face Yuan retribution for their obstinate resistance. The whole Yangzi River valley was now in Yuan hands. Hangzhou was doomed. Bayan insisted on negotiating only with Chen Yizhong, but the empress could only send Wen Tianxiang, virtually the only high official left in the capital with extensive military experience. The empress made Wen Tianxiang chief counsellor and general commander of the Song armies on 5 February 1276. A day later, along with Wu Qian, counsellor of the left, and Jia Yuqing, the prefect of Hangzhou, he travelled the short distance to Bayan's camp north of the city. It seems that the arbitration did not go well if traditional accounts are to be believed:

> 'Do you have good will towards my country or are you set on extinguishing the Song?'
>
> 'My Emperor is very clear; we are set to extinguish the Song'.
>
> 'In that case please immediately pull your troops back to Suzhou, if you insist on wiping the Song off the map, the people in the south and the Song army will fight you to the bitter end, and you will reap a bitter fruit.'

Bayan was angered by Wen Tianxiang's defiance and retained the new chief minister as a de facto hostage until the empress replaced Wen Tianxiang with the decidedly more mellow Jia Yuqing. The empress now wished to surrender and to obtain the best agreement possible. It was obvious that Wen Tianxiang was not going to achieve this task. By 17 February the formal surrender had been made and agreed to. Jia Sidao's brother-in-law, Fan Wenhu, who had deserted the Song after his failure at Anqing, led the Yuan armies into Hangzhou. Bayan evidently believed that this would reduce the likelihood of the Mongol troops running amok in the capital and he was correct. Hangzhou was not turned into a charnel house as Beijing, Fancheng and Changzhou had been, and the transition to Yuan control was incredibly orderly. The riches of the Song dynasty were collected together by the palace eunuchs and shipped north to the Yuan capital of Beijing. Bayan waited almost a month before making his ceremonial entrance into the city on 28 March.

It is recorded by Marco Polo that by 1279 Hangzhou was a lively bustling cultured place and its physical makeup does not appear to have suffered too much during the Yuan occupation of 1276. The human damage is rather more difficult to measure. Certainly there was no mass slaughter, as discussed above, but the immediate suicide of one hundred palace women, for fear of being raped and enslaved, and the later suicide of other women during their long forced journey to Beijing were only the beginnings of a quiet decimation of both men and women who could not envisage a future under Mongol Yuan rule. The suicides also extended into the intelligentsia and bureaucracy that had underpinned the Song, and it seems correct to view these deaths both as a statement of desperation but also as the only form of resistance left open to individuals such as Xu Yingbiao, who committed suicide along with his entire family rather than serve the Mongols. Self-strangulations occurred throughout every stratum of society and numerous higher officials opted to starve themselves to death rather than involve themselves with the new regime. Many of these suicides occurred after these officials had performed their last duties for the child emperor and empress, before the royal party departed for Beijing.

Wen Tianxiang was sent to Beijing as a prisoner along with Emperor Gongzong. At Zhenjiang, however, Wen Tianxiang and a few followers were able to escape from their guards and they took a small boat to Zhenzhou. Wen Tianxiang would continue to make trouble for Qubilai until the day of his death, and beyond. He had also been the chief engineer of the escape, on 8 February, just before Hangzhou's fall, of the two princes Zhao Xia and Zhao Bing. He had agitated, during the last weeks of the Hangzhou government for the boys to be appointed to regional posts in the far south as a diplomatic pretext for their departure, and a convoy carrying the infant princes and their mothers escorted by a small troop of guards slipped away under the cover of night. That Wen Tianxiang had endured considerable opposition from the rest of the court over his plan is evident from the fact that Empress Xie attempted to get the convoy to turn back to Hangzhou a few days after its departure.

Qubilai, through Bayan, had agreed during his final negotiations with the Song to ensure that there would be no destruction of the Zhao imperial family's altars. Furthermore the Zhao imperial family itself, the family that had ruled Song for its entire existence, was also to be preserved in order to ensure the maintenance of sacrifices to the Song's ancestors. This was vital to Qubilai as he needed the Song Dynasty to 'fit' the accepted norms of Chinese imperial history. If this did not take place then Qubilai's own Great Yuan could not be legitimised as the successor and inheritor of the Mandate of Heaven.[10] The deposed Song Emperor Gongzong disappeared into a Buddhist monastery and eventually became a monk. The elderly empress entered a nunnery and died there, peacefully, in 1283.

To Qubilai and to Bayan it must have seemed that the Song Dynasty had been placed quietly into the sarcophagus of history. They had miscalculated. The war against the Mongols, and against northern barbarians before them, had gone on for so long that it had become almost the natural state of things for the *nanren* or southern Chinese. The wanton death and destruction that the Mongols had wreaked upon China perhaps also made submission to them an unattractive option, as it appeared unlikely to secure peace for ordinary Chinese and safety for members of the aristocracy. These powerful notions, harnessed to the deep reverence that many *nanren* felt for the Song Dynasty, and the fact that two Song princes still remained beyond the Mongols' grasp, meant that the war would continue and would cost the lives of many, many more.

~ 8 ~

Child Emperors and Suicides

The End of the Song Dynasty

Stake Everything on a Single Throw

A warning made to minister Kou Zhun of the Song Dynasty by minister Wang Qinruo[1]

Miao Zaicheng, a Song commander who was still quixotically defending Zhenzhou despite the fall of Hangzhou, welcomed Wen Tianxiang and his fellow escapees and enrolled them in assisting him in his self-appointed task of defending the Huai River east and west of Zhenzhou. Then, however, Miao Zaicheng received orders from General Li Tingzhi, the ex-military commissioner for the Xiangyang region, to arrest and execute Wen Tianxiang. Li Tingzhi was at Yangzhou, but was preparing to move to meet up with the fugitive party that was escorting the two young princes after their flight from Hangzhou. Li Tingzhi wrote to Miao Zaicheng, saying that Wen Tianxiang had surrendered to the Yuan and must therefore be considered a spy. Miao Zaicheng did not arrest Wen Tianxiang and his followers, but he did trick them into leaving the city and then refused to let them return. Wen Tianxiang and his twelve men then headed towards Hangzhou, but upon hearing that they had been indicted by the new Yuan-controlled Hangzhou government they fled east. They disguised themselves but were still nearly caught by a Yuan cavalry patrol and at some point Wen Tianxiang also avoided being killed by assassins sent after him by Li Tingzhi. He was, surprisingly, able to convince them that he was not among the men who had weakly surrendered Hangzhou to Bayan whilst Li Tingzhi had been fighting furiously to keep the Song cause alive in Yangzhou. Eventually the little group of men made it by boat to Wenzhou and from there they travelled on to Fuzhou after Wen Tianxiang heard that the prince Zhao Xia was being set up there with the throne name of Emperor Duanzong.

The sheriff of Hangzhou, Yang Zhen, had led the princes' escape party and had needed to work hard to avoid its capture by the Yuan. As discussed above, the northern fleet now controlled the sea east of Hangzhou and the river delta around it, but Yang Zhen took the princes west on the Qiantang River to Wuzhou. Mongol patrols chased the little party through the mountains and came close to capturing it beyond Wuzhou, but one week later the princes reached the safety of Wenzhou. From there the party took ship for Fuzhou. By June 1276 a court was crystallising around the two princes. The man who had finally secured the peaceful capitulation of Hangzhou with Bayan, Lu Xiufu, was perhaps the first to join the new government. He had obviously dissembled his antipathy towards the Mongols during his negotiations with them, whereas the second man to join the court, Zhang Shijie, had never shown any such inclination.

Word of the new Song court spread rapidly through southern China and inspired resistance even in areas such as Fujian that were under tight Yuan control. Li Tingzhi even attempted, at the head of some forty thousand irregulars, militia and regular Song army troops, to free Emperor Gongzong from his Mongol guards as he was being taken to Beijing on the Grand Canal. The attempt failed chiefly because the emperor's mother had no particular interest in being rescued, or in allowing her son to be taken from her.

Bayan, for once, was caught by surprise and was unprepared for this new upsurge in resistance. He also appears to have prepared no contingency plan for the unlikely event that Song resistance should continue beyond the fall of Hangzhou. The Mongol general must, however, have been pleased to hear of the capture and execution of Li

Tingzhi, who had been made a counsellor of the new court in absentia but had continued to fight the Yuan in the field and far beyond the safety of the new Song court's walls. Li Tingzhi had tried to commit suicide to avoid capture after a defeat to the north of Hangzhou in August 1276. With his death the year-long resistance to the Yuan in the area collapsed. The citizens of Yangzhou may actually have been glad of the heroic general's death. Li Tingzhi's long opposition and refusal to hand the city over to the Yuan had caused an appalling level of suffering for its people, and the city's strategic value had essentially been lost once Hangzhou had fallen. Li Tingzhi's second-in-command manufactured a surrender to the Yuan commanders, and doubtless saved the population from a very severe reprisal. Mongol sacks of rebelling cities were commonly deliberate affairs involving a systematic annihilation of the population.[2]

What Li Tingzhi would have made of Chen Yizhong's reappearance in the Song government after his desertion of Hangzhou we will never know, but Chen Yizhong was appointed as counsellor of the left almost as soon as he arrived at the court. His appointment also caused probably one of the quickest resignations from senior office in Chinese history. Wen Tianxiang had not been particularly welcome at the new court because it was, in the main, the creation of men who had fled Hangzhou before it fell. They made excuses for their cold-shouldering of Wen Tianxiang, suggesting that he may have been 'turned' by his Yuan captors, but in truth they were more likely to have been fearful of the way that his name had become a byword for defiance at the old capital when they had so rapidly deserted the Song cause, and because his reputation had been further enhanced among the people by his subsequent escape from the Yuan. Despite this mutual antipathy, Wen Tianxiang had been offered, and had accepted, the role of military affairs commissioner in the summer of 1276. He resigned the post upon Chen Yizhong's appointment, after he had hunted down and executed a false emperor. A certain Huang Cong of Tingzhou had caused an uprising against the new court and claimed to be a true descendant of the Song line. After seeing Huang Cong done to death, Wen Tianxiang left Fuzhou to gather forces to defend his home province of Jiangxi. He also proposed an expedition aimed at the liberation of Jiangsu and Zhejiang from the sea, but these plans were rejected by Chen Yizhong as too risky. Wen Tianxiang set up his first command in Nanping, Fujian, and began recruiting an army.

Zhang Shijie took a government appointment – after all, he had been the catalyst for its creation – but he spent more time away from the court on the battlefield than attending court. With Wen Tianxiang and Zhang Shijie away from Fuzhou the bungling of Chen Yizhong went largely unchallenged. Furthermore, the contentious appointment of Chen Wenlong, another man who had fled Hangzhou before its capitulation, damaged the legitimacy of the court in many men's eyes, so whilst the Song name was still revered and men were prepared to battle the Yuan on the dynasty's behalf, the court itself was often looked upon with disdain.

In the early part of the Song military resurgence Wen Tianxiang and Zhang Shijie won striking if costly victories in Fujian and around Guangzhou and pushed into central Jiangxi province. Late summer, however, saw a series of reverses, starting with the death of Li Tingzhi and the loss of Yangzhou. Having stabilised the Yangzi front, the Yuan then went onto the offensive. General Aju and General Dong Wenping swept south from Zhenjiang, and their march south was accompanied by the Yuan navy off the coast. This was matched by a further assault through Jiangxi, headed by Generals Lu Shikui and Li Heng. A huge pincer attack was therefore applied to the Song forces and when the Yuan armies met at Jianning in north Fujian at the end of 1276 the court was forced to retreat from Fuzhou.

Fuzhou fell early in 1277, but by then the court had relocated further down the coast of Fujian, via ships, to Juanzhou. The government's stay in Fujian was over by the spring of 1277 and the court fled to Guangzhou. Chen Wenlong had not sailed with the court and had remained in Fuzhou. He was captured there and sent to Bayan at Hangzhou. However, he committed suicide by starvation before he reached the former capital. The year 1277 went from bad to worse for the Song government, and from the middle of the year there was essentially no safe refuge where the court could establish itself for any length of time. It relocated eight times in the course of one year and the emperor may have spent more time at sea than he did on dry land. The Song armies were still fighting but could not hold any territory, and even their hold on the southern coastal strip was tenuous. Heroic efforts by both sides at Guangzhou meant that it was retaken from the Yuan some five times by the Song, but each time it was lost again, once in late 1277 as the result of a lethal pandemic infection among its Song defenders. Again and again it was recovered by the Song and then finally taken by the Yuan forces at the end of 1278. The loss of Guangzhou, a major revenue-yielding port with access to southern China via the Pearl River, essentially extinguished any hope of the Song ever re-establishing themselves. And yet resistance continued and the Yuan resorted to atrocities in an attempt to burn the loyalty of the *nanren* to the Song out of existence. Massacres replaced moderation as *zhongtong* was abandoned. Yuan General Li Heng captured practically all of Wen Tianxiang's family as he pushed the Song out of Jiangxi and he decimated the populations of any Song city that refused to heed calls to surrender as he moved south.

Li Heng's appalling tactics seem to have borne fruit in the responses they engendered at the Song court. Amid acrimonious arguments Chen Yizhong deserted once more and sailed to Vietnam, from where he travelled to Laos to seek sanctuary. The court also relocated once more at this juncture, to an island off modern Aomen (Macau). One month later it became ever more obvious that the end of the dynasty was at hand. Lu Xiufu tried hard to hold the court together despite his own fractious condition but the near-death of the child emperor Duanzong after his ship was hit by a cyclone and sank and the realisation that even Aomen was not a safe refuge must have made this an almost impossible task. The nine-year-old Son of Heaven died soon after the cyclone on 9 May 1278, and the court finally sailed, or perhaps rather limped, to Yashan Island south of modern-day Xinhui in Guangdong province, where the little emperor's body was laid to rest.

The third little prince, Zhao Bing, was not yet six years old, and had never been designated heir, as it was unpropitious for a brother to succeed a dead emperor, and the court nearly dissolved itself rather than place him on the throne. It was only the powerful intercession of Lu Xiufu and Zhang Shijie that persuaded the prince's step-mother, Dowager Consort Yang, to allow him to be recognised as Emperor Dibing under her regency, two days after his brother's death.

Meanwhile, Wen Tianxiang had made a fighting retreat following the disasters of 1277 when he had been pushed from Jiangxi by

General Li Heng, a Tangut serving under the banners of the Yuan. Wen Tianxiang had retired with his army to the coast of Guangnan and, still loyal to the Song cause, was trying to raise new forces for its defence and to hold on to southern Jiangxi. He rarely visited the new court on Yashan Island and spent most of his energy attempting to defend or retake territory. His defence of the south was vital as Yashan Island lies only about 90 kilometres south of Guangzhou and the Song court had evidently decided that it was to be their last stopping point. An extensive programme of building was undertaken on the island and the population grew, with craftsmen building barracks for the soldiers who had come with the court and who had spent an uncomfortably long period aboard the dynasty's last ships. 'Several tens of thousands' of militia[3] may also have billeted on the island, though whether they had attended the court all the way from Fuzhou or were local levies from Guangnan is hard to determine.

Yashan Island was, in many ways, a natural fortress. It was ringed by small islands which could be occupied by defending troops and was surrounded by waters that were shallow on its northern side, and so precluded an army landing on that part of the coast. It was perhaps apt that the Song court should have one place of relative security, because in every other part of southern China their empire was being rapidly dismembered.

In Sichuan major Yuan assaults against Chongqing and Hezhou had begun in 1277. Resistance had been fierce, possibly because the Song defenders did not know of the fall of Hangzhou and thought they were still fighting as part of an undefeated Song empire. In 1278, however, as more and more Yuan forces were released from the eastern campaigns, the cities began to fall one after the other. Chongqing and Luzhou fell early in the year, and this essentially gave Qubilai's commanders unimpeded control of all of the Yangzi River. Hezhou, the city that had seen the death of Mongke Khan in 1259, was, perhaps fittingly given its long history of resistance to the Mongols, the last major city in Sichuan to fall to the Yuan. It did not fall until early 1279, and only then because famine and disease had made any further opposition untenable for its citizens and soldiers.

The year 1278 saw Wen Tianxiang's forces effectively knocked out of the war by a series of superbly coordinated Yuan campaigns that saw their fleet and ground forces working with one accord. Guangxi was attacked from the north, from the Yuan's Sichuan bases and through Yunnan to its west. Then in the summer of 1278 a massive assault was made in the southeast. General Li Heng was supported by the Yuan fleet commanded by Zhang Hongfang, the uncle of the Song commander Zhang Shijie. The Yuan forces swept down through Fujian and Guangdong, and all the coastal cities were lost by the end of 1278. Then the Yuan armies closed on Wen Tianxiang's last remaining army at Caozhou. Wen Tianxiang retreated into the mountains near Huizhou but was now trapped inland and could not call on the Song fleet for support, though it is doubtful whether it could have offered any help given the size of the Yuan land and sea forces now committed to the final eradication of the Song. Zhang Hongfang captured Wen Tianxiang during a surprise attack on 2 February 1279. Zhang Hongfang then took his prisoner to a rendezvous with Li Heng at Guangzhou, which had once more fallen to the Yuan. Wen Tianxiang would therefore have witnessed the Yuan commanders' preparations for their final assault on Yashan Island, and was treated with great respect by Zhang Hongfang.

Zhang Hongfang then sent word to his nephew that he should surrender. Zhang Shijie replied, 'I know that by surrendering to the Yuan army, I can not only be spared my life but will be richly rewarded. But I would rather die than betray my country.' Zhang Hongfang knew that Zhang Shijie, like so many other military men, held a profound admiration for Wen Tianxiang. He therefore attempted to get Wen Tianxiang to write to Zhang Shijie to encourage him to capitulate on honourable terms. Wen Tianxiang did indeed then write to Zhang Shijie: 'Man is mortal to be sure; a pure heart would longer endure.' Both Zhang Shijie and Zhang Hongfang would have realised exactly what this short note meant. No surrender.

Qubilai, now recorded as the Great Yuan Emperor Shizu, gave very specific orders to his generals, Li Heng and Zhang Hongfang, that there was to be no bombardment of the Song navy before any assault for fear that it would break up and flee. The Yuan emperor wanted Song to be finally extinguished in this one engagement, and for that to occur the Song navy would have to be totally destroyed. He evidently feared that the Song line could still attract loyalists to its standard if the Song emperor continued his fugitive existence.

The Yuan fleet sailed for Yashan at the end of February 1279. Zhang Hongfang took Wen Tianxiang with him on his flagship in order to allow the former minister a fine view of the end of the Song Dynasty. Zhang Shijie had prepared for the coming assault by assembling his fleet in Yashan's harbour mouth. The one thousand ships of the Song fleet outnumbered the Yuan fleet by some three hundred ships but were at a disadvantage in terms of weaponry and supplies from the outset of the contest. The Song ships were anchored together, and matting and caked-on mud was applied to the sides of every vessel as protection for the expected *huihuipao* and fire-bomb assault by the Yuan navy. Zhang Shijie had also constructed forts in the shallow waters of the bay and Song ships anchored to these as well as to each other. The child emperor, Dibing, was guarded by Lu Xiufu and kept aboard a large war junk in the centre of the line. It might be suggested that the little emperor was taken into the fleet to facilitate his escape should defeat loom, but Zhang Shijie's decision to shackle his ships together and to stay within the harbour and not on the open sea rather negates this theory, and it seems more likely that Dibing was present to help rally the flagging morale of the troops.

Zhang Hongfang pressed Wen Tianxiang once more to compel Zhang Shijie to surrender, and, when he refused, Zhang Hongfang launched dozens of fireships loaded with dry straw and kerosene towards the Song fleet. These were repelled by the wet mud covering the Song ships and by troops armed with long poles. With the option of a bombardment – the staple of medieval Chinese ship warfare – denied them, the Yuan generals chose instead to try to starve and thirst-out the Song fleet. They first sealed off any option of escape to the north and west, and then began harassing the Song flotilla from the south. Zhang Hongfang used the tide to support his attacks. At low tide his ships attacked from the north, and at high tide the attacks came with the incoming force of the sea from the south.

The blockade and harassing attacks were continued for half a month, and it is to be wondered why the Song navy did not cut and run with the tide. It may have been that the Yuan had done an excellent job of closing all options, or perhaps that even if the emperor, his court and his navy could escape battle at Yashan there was simply nowhere else left to go. Furthermore, whilst the outcome of this one battle was uncertain, the fate of the court and the dynasty was surely sealed. Why Zhang Shijie, Lu Xiufu and the other Song loyalists fought to the death at Yashan can never be fully ascertained, but given that the tactics they deployed denied them almost any hope of escape, or even of attack, the Battle of Yashan Island has all the distinct characteristics of a ritual sacrifice.

The Song troops were soon reduced to dry rations and were extremely short of fresh water. The Yuan assaults continued without making much headway but they did keep the Song from being able to leave the line or to attempt re-victualling, and undoubtedly further eroded the morale of Song's already exhausted and homesick troops. On 12 March some Song ships defected, and an attempt by a Song squadron to get past the Yuan patrol boats and to break out was quickly beaten back. On 17 March Li Heng and Zhang Hongfang called in their commanders and told them to ready themselves for an attack within the next few days. The Yuan fleet was then divided into four. Li Heng was to command the north and northwest flotillas, Zhang Hongfang took personal control of the southwest flotilla, and the west and south were assigned to junior commanders.

On 19 March 1279 the attacks came and they were perfectly timed to exploit the incoming tide for the southern attack, and the ebbing tide for the attack from the north. Heavy rain and winds lashed at both fleets but this did not deter Li Heng, and his attack began at daybreak. The powerful southern current and tide made his descent on the Song fleet incredibly fast, and he then turned every one of his vessels around in order to approach the Song stern-first. This gave his men the advantage of being able to fire down onto the Song ships from the high stern castles of the Yuan junks. Seven or eight expert archers were assigned to the rear of each ship. The Song sailors fought back hard with a missile barrage but Li Heng's marines managed to cut the ropes securing Song vessels to each other and to board several of them. Casualties in this violent engagement and in the hand-to-hand fighting that ensued were high on both sides. Song lost three ships and by noon Li Heng's flotilla had broken through the outer line of the Song fleet with two of its squadrons and had shattered the northwest corner of the Song formation. As the tide then began to shift, Li Heng's fleet broke away from the engagement.

Then music was heard from Zhang Hongfang's flagship. The Song sailors thought this was a signal for the Yuan fleet to leave the battle and to return to the mainland for re-victualling and rearming, but it was actually the general calling his ships to an all-out assault. Zhang Hongfang's force arrived on the swift north-flowing current and smashed into a cluster of Song ships. Zhang Hongfang himself headed for the Song admiral Zuo Tai's ship. From morning until evening the fight continued with showers of Yuan arrows and Song missiles filling the sky. Zhang Hongfang's ship was said to have been like a porcupine at the end of the day, but his bravery paid off and he captured Admiral Zuo Tai's flagship. Li Heng then re-entered the fray, and Song ships began to surrender en masse. Zhang Shijie watched Song flags being lowered one after another as his ships and men ceased fighting. Zhang Shijie was saved from defeat only by the coming of night, but the next morning, despite a heavy fog, there was no hiding the fact that the navy had been destroyed and only about ten ships remained either able or willing to fight. Zhang Shijie put his best troops into the centre of what remained of his formation and then tried to organise a breakout. He sent a light skiff to the emperor's junk, intending to pick up Dibing and spirit him away from the battle. A traditional tale has it that Lu Xiufu saw the small boat coming towards the emperor's ship and feared that it was a Yuan trick designed to secure the emperor. What is more likely is that Lu Xiufu realised, with absolute clarity, that the Song Dynasty was lost. He is said, again traditionally, to have shouted these words: 'There's no hope now for our country. His majesty has no alternative but to die for the country!' Holding the little emperor, who was dressed in his imperial robes and carrying the imperial seals, Lu Xiufu plunged into the sea.

On Yashan Island and on the remaining vessels of the Song navy, tens of thousands of Song officials and their women reportedly followed their emperor into the sea to drown themselves. Only a hundred or so military and civilian officers chose to surrender. According to both the *Songshi* and *Yuanshi*, one hundred thousand soldiers killed themselves in the same fashion. Zhang Shijie sailed what remained of his fleet to bring the news of the emperor's death to his stepmother, Dowager Consort Yang. Distraught, she, too, took her own life and was interred on one of the beaches of Yashan by Zhang Shijie. He then also committed suicide by drowning.

Wen Tianxiang outlived the dynasty he had served so passionately and loyally, and he was the only witness of the final battle to commit it to written record. He was invited by the cordial Zhang Hongfang to a banquet of all the Yuan generals to be held by Qubilai in Beijing. At the dinner Wen Tianxiang was offered service under the Yuan as chief minister. His answer is traditionally recorded as being both simple and unambiguous: 'My country is no more, I could not prevent its destruction, and even my death will not begin to redeem my guilt. How could I prolong my existence in ignominy?'

Qubilai managed to get Wen Bi, Wen Tianxiang's brother, to work in the Yuan government but the former Song minister refused all offers. Qubilai was, however, afraid to execute Wen Tianxiang for fear of rebellion in southern China, and instead he kept Wen Tianxiang captive for three years. Initially, Wen Tianxiang was treated well but when he refused to kneel before the judge at his trial and had to be forced to kowtow, and it became obvious that he would continue to resist, he was transferred to the warden's direct care. He was kept chained at all times and his cell flooded in winter and was baking in summer. Wen Tianxiang slowly deteriorated under these conditions, but still penned one of China's most famous poems, 'Zhengqige', 'Ode to Virtue's Force', from his cell. Then in January 1283 a peasant uprising in Zhongshan, Hebei province erupted. Its leaders claimed descent from the Song royal line and called for a march on Beijing to free Wen Tianxiang. Qubilai became fearful once more of Wen Tianxiang's potential as a rallying point for all of China's disaffection for its new rulers. He arranged a personal audience for Wen Tianxiang and had the prisoner brought to his palace. Wen Tianxiang refused to kneel before the Yuan emperor but he did bow. Qubilai then offered Wen Tianxiang the post of chief minister again. The response was terse: 'I am the chief minister of the Song government. There is no way I am going to serve two governments. Only by dying now would I feel comfortable in the company of the patriots and heroes who died before me.' Qubilai made one more attempt to convert Wen

Tianxiang. He offered him the post of military affairs commissioner, but Wen Tianxiang's reply left Qubilai in no doubt that he would never submit: 'All I want now is to die. I have no more to say.' He was executed the next day. A howling north wind was blowing and the day was grim and overcast. The Yuan had not given any indication that Wen Tianxiang was to be executed, but a crowd of ten thousand people gathered at Chaishi execution ground to see the patriot die. Wen Tianxiang asked the crowd which way was south. He made several bows in that direction, and then calmly offered himself to the executioner's blade.

~ 9 ~

The Phoenix and the Dragon

The Ghosts of the Song and the Fall of the Yuan

Heaven be my Witness.

Yue Fei

The Yuan Dynasty collapsed in 1368 after ruling China, uncontested, for less than a century. In many ways its demise after only a brief life was made inevitable by the long war it had undertaken against the Song for China and for the Mandate of Heaven. The contest with Song, as we have seen, involved every evil of war, the extensive militarisation of Chinese society and the near-destruction and stagnation of the economy of all of China as both sides diverted funds from almost all other activities to pay for the long war.

In the short term the southern Chinese reaction to the Yuan victory was dramatic and overwhelmingly nihilistic. Many minor and middle-ranking *nanren* Song officials retired from public life and many among the Confucian literati who had not even served the Song adamantly refused to serve the new rulers. It was also not uncommon for such men to set up their schools of learning away from the imperial universities, now under the control of the Yuan. This meant that men of talent commonly did not enter the imperial exams system. The scholars' non-violent protests therefore deprived the Yuan civil service of both fresh talent and experience – two attributes that would be sorely needed as the Yuan government began, later, to unravel.

These responses were, however, mild compared to the many, many suicides that also occurred in this early period among southern Chinese. Desperation certainly paid a part in individuals' decisions to take their own lives, but equally important was the 'example' of the ruling court and leaders of the Song state. The voluntary death of Wen Tianxiang, and the suicide of Liu Xiufu and Zhang Shijie, and of many others at Yashan, may have excited a 'Werther Effect' among those with even the slightest connection to the dynasty.[1] One historian's suggestion that the loyalism that drove many of these individuals to take their own lives was 'a product of the Song dynasty's unique cultural traditions, and a testimony to the government's effectiveness in using education to mould culture'[2] seems entirely justified. This, allied to a general feeling of resignation about Mongol brutality and that atrocities and horrors such as those committed at Changsha and Changzhou were all that could be expected from the new dynasty, were perhaps enough to make many more wish to depart this cruel world by their own hand.

A Yuan assault on the legacy of Song, instigated at a level of government well below that of Emperor Qubilai and perhaps designed partly to eradicate sites that might act as foci of remembrance, reverence and thereby revolution in the name of the old dynasty began in January 1279. The royal tombs of Baoshan, 'Mountain of Treasures', just to the east of Hangzhou, were ransacked under the leadership of a Tangut Buddhist monk. Simple greed and Buddhist revenge for the Song's destruction of temples in order to build their tombs have also been cited as possible reasons for the desecration, but the fact that the half-decomposed body of Emperor Lizong was left exposed and his head was kicked about the place like a football indicate that a powerful political statement on the complete extinction of the Song Dynasty was also intended. Any hopes that the sacrilegious act would cause the population of south China to discard their devotion to the Song were soon dashed, however, by the reaction of local people. Many of the emperors' and empresses' remains were rescued before the Yuan grave-robbers could get to them and moved to secret locations. The royal tombs themselves were barbarously looted and wrecked, as were the palaces of Hangzhou that Bayan had tried so hard to preserve upon his entry to the city in 1276. It is reported that Qubilai tried to prevent the wholesale looting that was now occurring all over southern China, but the Mongols had opened a Pandora's box with their seventy-year war on Chinese civilisation and even the great khagan could not now stop his own men from wanting to continue in the old, well-known and comfortable way of life they had long enjoyed – that of looting, destruction and malice.[3]

As noted above, the immediate reaction among the *nanren*, especially those in positions of authority prior to the Yuan conquest, was to refuse to engage with the new rulers in any way. Desecration of the royal Song tombs and other Yuan outrages of this ilk, however, stirred up an active resistance at grassroots level in the old lands of Song. In 1281, Yuan troops beheaded twenty thousand demobilised Song troops who had taken up arms once more in rebellion, and one hundred thousand Yuan troops were mobilised in order to bring order back to Fujian province, which had also revolted.

Continued troubles throughout the restive south required large-scale garrisoning by the Yuan of the whole region, an expense they could barely afford after the decades of war that they had funded and the abject failure of an expensive expedition against Japan in 1281. Qubilai should perhaps have known better than to entrust a large part of this expedition to the care of Fan Wenhu. Jia Sidao's brother-in-law, who had failed the Song at Xiangyang and at Anqing, now failed the Yuan whilst leading a southern army to Japan's shores. Like a cat with nine lives Fan Wenhu managed to survive the debacle and went on to be an active and brutal suppressor of domestic rebellions for his new employers. Needless to say, the failure of the Japanese expedition also made it very plain in China that the Mongols were not invincible. It is notable that the rebellion of soldiers from the disbanded Song army began in this same year.

The garrisons required in the south were just another expenditure that added to a precipitating financial crisis that began to overwhelm the state towards the end of Qubilai's reign. The industrious and rapacious tax-collector Ahmad, whom Qubilai had appointed in 1262, was already infamous throughout China for increasing the number of taxed households by half a million, and now he turned to raising taxes on merchants; arguably one of the groups most responsible for the Yuan's victory over the Song. The merchants had supplied much of the navy that defeated the Song on the Yangzi and which also effectively closed the campaign through its support of the southeastern campaign of General Li Heng. Now these men found themselves facing ruinous duty rates and, through another of Ahmad's initiatives, competing against state monopolies controlling salt, alcohol and tea prices. Ahmad's assassination in April 1282 must have pleased almost every taxpayer in China, and Qubiliai's later decision to have his body exhumed and hung in the market and eaten by dogs indicates the emperor's realisation that his giving licence to a foreign and corrupt minister to extort funds from a fiscally exhausted country was, in fact, counterproductive, as it simply made for more rebellion in the south and banditry in every region.

Yet, Qubilai continued to spend on military expeditions that had little hope of success and would gain the Mongol empire little in return even if they were successful. The failure of the expeditions to Indonesia and Vietnam are cases of this, and it seems evident that such endeavours were related more to the problem that an outlet was desperately required for Mongol aggression and expansion, and that expansion and aggression were essentially core policy in all Mongol governments. Continual territorial gain was the *sine qua non* of the Mongol state, as Mongol tribesmen wanted and needed plunder in the form of ready gold, slaves and new lands. There was no profit in peace and no honour either. One of the chief charges made against Qubilai by Ariq Boke and by Qaidu was that Qubilai had abandoned the way of the steppes for a sedentary Chinese existence. Even as late as 1287 Qubilai faced rebellion from within his own lands and from his own people when Nayan, the Mongolian military commissioner of Manchuria, joined Qaidu's anti-Qubilai confederacy. Controlling the dogs of war and subduing them to the service of the state and financially feeding an almost unending war against northern invaders whilst still maintaining the domestic economy had been the Song state's greatest achievements. The Mongols proved themselves unable to do any of the above; they had wrecked the economy of northern China, were now killing the golden goose of mercantile trade in the south, and could only look to new conquests to feed their financial needs as they could not successfully manage what they had conquered.

Voracious tax collection methods did not cease with the death of the foreigner Ahmad. Chinese ministers such as Lu Shirong further increased foreign trade levies and gained a reputation for hounding men to their deaths in the pursuit of payment and for devaluing the paper currency at every juncture and solely to the government's advantage. The emperor's direct intervention mitigated some of the harm of these policies, and in truth Qubilai did waive taxes during extreme times and attempted to revive trade in the south. The emperor, of course, only extended such 'kindnesses' out of concern not only that the south should begin to pay for its own occupation but also that it should begin to pay for the north too. From the reign of Qubilai onwards the south began to support the north in rice, the region having been famine struck ever since the first Mongol pony's hoof landed on it in the early thirteenth century. The Grand Canal was extended in 1289 to serve this end and to deliver grain to the new Yuan capital in the north. This experiment in feeding the north from the south's fields was successful but the monopoly on transport that it handed over to ex-pirates caused almost unlimited corruption at every level of Yuan government and in every department involved in the process. Arguably, the 'trial of the century' occurred in 1303 when two pirates were arraigned on corruption charges. They were executed and their families perished with them, but they also named and doomed a string of high officials within the Yuan government.

The year 1285 saw the execution of Lu Shirong and the appointment of a new minister whose reputation, if such a thing was possible, was perhaps even more odious to the Chinese than that of Ahmad. Minister Sanga added a reputation for the kind of carnality that the Song minister Han Tuozhou had been famous for to the avarice and corruption that his Yuan predecessors had been renowned for. His sponsorship of the attacks on the Song royal tombs was well known throughout China, and whilst his favouring of foreigners over Chinese was perhaps not surprising as he was of Tibetan origin, it was still politically naive. The opening-up of government to foreigners who had not passed through the Chinese exam system began in this period, and later Yuan legislation that allowed foreigners to graduate with lower marks than Chinese students was certainly not viewed as a particularly positive form of discrimination by the Chinese population of the empire.[4]

The Yuan government's reduction in the number of capital offences and generally increased leniency towards offenders might have been welcomed by the Chinese population, but the positive effects of these changes were completely neutralised by the concurrent implementation of the Mongol system of blood money payment for murder or other grievous crimes. This essentially made such crimes, when committed by non-Chinese, unpunishable and completely eroded the rule of law. Jurisprudence was replaced by a crude system that might conveniently be labelled with the Latin idiom *quod principi placuit legis habet vigorem* or 'what pleases the prince has life in law'. Achieving justice when a Mongol or *semuren* was involved in a criminal case was therefore extremely unlikely, and by all accounts the use by petty officials of forged documents and lawsuits to extort bribes from citizens was also widespread. The justice system, such as it was, also seems to have been so clogged with such cases that those awaiting justice whilst imprisoned, often following false accusations, either faded away waiting or were executed without trial.

Sanga's sponsoring of a college for the study of Muslim script was also unpopular but not as damaging to both the country and Yuan rule as his manipulation of the currency and the forced exchange of old Yuan tender for new currency notes at rates that were highly unfavourable to those forced to trade in their now worthless 'old' paper money.

Qubilai Khan died in February 1294 and was, without doubt, one of history's most remarkable men. The problem was that he was just that: a man. As discussed earlier, the difficulty for all the steppe confederations, right from the Xiongnu of the fourth century through to the Mongols, was that they could not effectively move from the rule of man to the rule of government and law. Tribal customs, including the patrimonial share-out and equality of inheritance between sons, meant that the transference of power from a deceased monarch was always a risky manoeuvre. 'The king is dead, long live the king!' was an unlikely shout at any tribal meeting upon the death of the monarch.[5] This was manageable in an uncomplicated polity such as Mongolia – although arguably it nearly destroyed all the Mongol states at one time or another, and certainly ended the Mongol world empire in 1260. However, if the same confused accessional politics were applied to a complex state such as post-Song China, which was used to a strong, autocratic, body politic and an extensive bureaucracy, it was a recipe for chaos.[6] The road to the Yuan collapse was paved by the political turmoil that this system engendered after the death of Qubilai and throughout the reigns of some nine khagans before the last Yuan emperor ascended the throne in 1333. The seizure of the throne in 1308 by Qayshan Guluk with the backing of an army that marched on Beijing from Mongolia is just one example of business as usual in terms of Yuan successions.

Experienced men of government who might have been able to assist the Mongol royalty to govern their Chinese state did exist, but, as we have seen, in the early years of the Yuan state they refused to serve. Later, as the Yuan colonisation of China became an obvious, if unpalatable, fact, these men might have served but Yuan policy now practically precluded such a thing from occurring. As the *nanren* had been the last people to submit to Mongol rule, they were effectively placed at the bottom of the Mongol political hierarchy, beneath Mongols, *semuren*, northern *hanren*, Kitan and Jurchen. The Yuan set a quota for all government posts, with only a fraction of the most junior local administration positions open to *nanren*. Government ballooned in size as ineffective civil servants were supplemented by the addition of assistants and overseers. The curious logic of this seemed to be that three unskilled men could be sent to fix a problem that one talented man could have rectified with ease. For example, the Yuan Beijing court's official quota was for two thousand six hundred personnel, but a census of 1294 reported that the numbers had swollen to over ten thousand, presumably fairly idle, men and that this was replicated throughout the country, with even more duplication occurring in the provinces. Moving the vast personnel of the Yuan court every year between the winter and summer imperial capitals, Beijing and Shangdu, must have been incalculably expensive and just one more drain on the treasury.

An attempt was made in 1303 to cut the payroll of administrators but to little effect. Many Mongol officers doubtless looked upon the civil service as a way to milk the system rather than a route to civic duty. 'Employment' was, however, only one source of income for Mongol aristocrats who felt they were owed something from the Yuan state. In fact, the best way to become wealthy without working for it was to apply directly to the khagan-emperor for a grant. This entailed large payments from the government purse, and was another hangover from primitive steppe government. Again, this was not a problematic process for a war leader of a steppe confederation who might distribute gifts for loyalty and service to a select group of followers, but in Yuan China this effectively meant that many entitled individuals drew comfortable pensions for long periods of time from a state that could barely support itself. That the Yuan emperors continued with these divestments of favour right until the end of their line tells us of the fear they had of rebellion from within their own military. Appeasement of the horde was, however, expensive and tended to inflame rather than diminish its cupidity.[7]

A convenient characterisation of the series of succession crises that the Yuan fell into in the years after Qubilai's death is to view them as the result of a Janus-faced administration that sometimes looked to the steppe and sometimes to the governmental culture of China for its policy and philosophy. That several Yuan emperors also showed a strong inclination for the kind of heavy drinking that their steppe ancestors had been famous for also tended to slow down any process of reform or productive government. The policies of the Yuan emperors swung wildly between engaging more fully with their Chinese state and blindly exploiting it as one would a colonial possession. Neither of these directions was ever fully embraced and this confusion over the state's purpose meant that both the native Chinese and the Mongolian 'aristocracy' were eventually alienated from the central government. Bloody purges of a predecessors' ministers, whether they were *semuren* or Confucian scholars, were practically the norm and added to the ad hoc nature of government.

The long war with Song exerted a further malign influence on Yuan politics, as 'heroes' of the great conflict such as General Bayan became veritable kingmakers. Their extensive fame throughout the

Mongol Empire, a result of their deeds in the Mongols' greatest theatre of war, carried enormous weight, and their backing of a candidate almost guaranteed him the throne. The early Song emperors had worked hard to defang the army that had brought them to mastery of China. The Yuan never showed either the inclination or the political ability to do the same. The growth of this alternative power within the state and its later disassociation from it was another cause of the collapse of the Yuan Dynasty before it could complete even a century of rule.

Yuan rule became increasingly ramshackle over the first half of the fourteenth century with hyperinflation taking the currency to a level of worthlessness that made the 1280s crisis look tame. Actors and butchers served in the highest offices of state, and massive disbursements were made to the Mongol aristocracy from a state treasury that had to issue IOUs to the recipients for half the amounts promised. Attempts at reform in both legal codes and financial management were made but essentially failed against the vested interests of the Mongol military class. The princely Mongol class and its senior military officers were essentially autonomous in their appanages and resisted all changes to this status quo; they still, however, happily indulged in the securing of ever larger grants from the state whilst refusing to involve their possessions directly in it. They also retained direct and total control over their local military forces. No Yuan emperor was ever likely to challenge this group, and a grim display of the danger they held for the leadership of the country was made in September 1323, when the Emperor Suddhipala and his entourage were murdered by the imperial censor's personal guard at the instigation of a host of Mongol princes whose personal annual grants had been cancelled by the unfortunate emperor.

A desperate casting about for new ways to raise funds caused a large-scale revolt in Jiangxi province, in the old Song lands, in 1315. Land duties based on a new survey of Jiangxi and Hunan were challenged by former Song aristocrats, and the leader of the revolt declared himself the king of the newly independent state of Cai. It took two months to crush the revolt and further attempts at land tax reform were abolished. The problem was that landowners in the south could not see a great deal of value for their tax money as the dynasty could not even guarantee law and order. From the first decades of the dynasty there had been problems maintaining security in the northern plain from Beijing down to the Huai River line. Beyond this point the situation deteriorated further, with merchants in Jiangxi and Fujian province having to dodge gangs both in the city and in the countryside. By 1315 the Yangzi was difficult to navigate because of the sheer volume of pirates that plied its length looking for merchantmen to rob, and by the 1320s and 1330s commercial traffic along the great river was virtually stalled by the brigands' vessels.

The tipping point for the Yuan Dynasty was 1328. By this juncture the ascendancy of steppe politics and *semuren* ministers was complete, and the death of Emperor Yesun Temur on 15 August brought about a civil war that had all the hallmarks of the bloody internecine conflicts of the Mongolian steppe and the thirteenth-century wars that led to the near extermination of the Ogedei and Chagatai clans by the Toluids, and of Ariq Boke and Qubilai's long war. Fratricide and the further exhaustion of the state's finances in putting down Mongol princes' rebellions in Sichuan and Yunnan in flare-ups of dissent that lasted until 1332 were the sequelae to this eruption of Mongol blood feud and steppe politics inside the borders of China. The direct result of the 1328 war was that Yuan emperors were also made into the puppets of powerful non-Chinese military men. A Turk, al-Temur, and a Merkit, Bayan, effectively ran the state until 1340. The selling of political office to the highest bidder also became the standard government method of raising funds in this period, and of course these offices were then used as vehicles for extortion of funds from the populace. In fact this had begun as early as 1291, when the scholar Hu Zhiyu had observed that eight out of every ten local posts in Jiangnan were sold for bribes to butchers, wine peddlers, brokers and other 'riff-raff'. These men then used their office to rape and seize men's wives, to commandeer property and to bend the law to their own ends.

Discounting the wave of suicides and revolts that had occurred in the early years of the Yuan Dynasty and the brief life of the kingdom of Cai, the populace of the old Song lands had been somewhat quiescent during the first decades of the fourteenth century. This state of affairs also changed after 1328, and a wave of natural disasters that struck China in this period became the catalyst for popular revolts across southern China. Droughts and floods across the country led to famine and the loss of arable land and homes. Funds to support affected areas were virtually impossible to find as the exchequer had been drained by the Mongol civil war, and the costs of suppressing multiple rebellions among the non-Han peoples of the south who, if truth be told, had been even more badly treated by the Yuan than even the *nanren* had. National relief efforts were sponsored by the central government but any goodwill these may have garnered from the peasantry was soon dispersed by Yuan landlords who actually managed to benefit from these same natural disasters. Landlords used usury as a weapon to both appropriate their tenants' land and also force them to sell the members of their family into slavery. Regional government reports of the period recognise the problem, but it seems that their authors were essentially either unwilling or unable to change this situation.

Revolution now also stood a chance against the once mighty Yuan military machine. Corruption at all levels of the military commissions and officer corps had weakened the army's leadership, and garrison duty and living had softened the once adamantine men that made up its rank and file. Furthermore, the military system that the Yuan had established after the conquest of China was not strongly centralised. The Bureau of Military Affairs, in fact, only directly controlled the imperial guard and a few other contingents in north China. Even the guard was not dissimilar to a mercenary force made up of regiments that recruited men from areas as distant as the Caucasus Mountains. Large feudal armies attached by loyalty and by interest to Mongol princelings were in reality the 'army' of the Yuan and were as likely as not to refuse the call to arms of the central government. The Mongols had also failed to make up for the new failings of their troops in other ways. Fortification had been neglected throughout China. The Mongols commonly did not repair a city's walls once it had fallen to them. This was not a problem as long as a Mongol field army was at hand and the 'terror of their arms' – to borrow a phrase from Gibbon – was evident to all likely enemies. But, as with the Roman legions of the late empire, once the Mongols' military fragility was exposed they should have looked to mortar and stone to make up for this loss in martial capacity. They did not, and the often rapid loss of cities to rag-tag rebel armies was a direct result of this.

The last Yuan emperor, Toghan Temur, ascended to the throne of the Son of Heaven in July 1333 at the age of 13 and inherited a wealth of problems, most self-inflicted by the dynasty, others perhaps external to its direct governance but often worsened by the rulers' handling of crises. Chancellor Bayan ran the early part of the new emperor's reign and it was business as usual for the Yuan elite as Bayan carried out a bloody extermination of his erstwhile rival al-Temur's family on charges of treason. The chancellor, now unopposed, then attempted to take the dynasty back by some fifty years to the immediate post-conquest days. Admittedly, Bayan also tried to reduce waste in government, to relieve famine-struck areas and to reinvigorate the economy, but all of this was aimed at re-establishing a strong government that rejected any Chinese influence and was, to all intents and purposes, de-Sinicised. This was clearly impossible for, as we have seen, the Yuan victory over Song had relied more on Chinese infantry and engineers than on Mongol cavalry, and on Chinese merchants, sailors and admirals and their ships. Furthermore, fairly extensive intermarriage had occurred between Mongols and Chinese and, despite their egregious attempts, it had soon become obvious that the Mongols could not govern China at either national or regional level without Chinese know-how.

Bayan attempted to disarm all Chinese, and to ban them from riding horses and hunting. The order on weaponry confiscation was perhaps deliberately misinterpreted by many local officials, who also took away dangerous-looking hoes and shovels from bemused Han farmers. Provincial Yuan governors also used Bayan's edict as an excuse to ban Chinese opera. This is not surprising. One of the most popular entertainments in Yuan cities was *zaju* theatre, poetic drama set to music. Chinese intellectuals used this particular art form extensively as a very subtle method of mocking their Mongol overlords. Attacks on the Yuan government and exposure of the venal nature of many of its public servants were, in fact, perpetuated across the arts. Guan Hanqin's 'Dou E's Grievance' is a classic example, showing a young girl's collision with corruption at every level as she seeks justice. The piece ends with only nature responding to the young girl, Dou E's, misfortunes as it covers her executed body with a light coating of snow. The punishing three-year drought that the gods then send against the heartless governors who have destroyed Dou E was, in fact, already striking Yuan China, as real events made a curious imitation of Guan Hanqin's art.

The Mongols appear to have been much more tolerant of literature, although, as one eminent scholar has argued, this was very possibly because they could not read Chinese, and would therefore have been ignorant of the sedition that was being propagated by Han writers of the time.[8] Furthermore, much of the subversive literature of the time transposed the corruption of the Yuan onto older times. Memories of a particularly harsh period of government during the old Song Dynasty, after the fall of Wang Anshi (1085) and before the first of the Jin attacks on Song, were used as an artistic vehicle for criticism of the current dynasty. One minister, Cai Jing, who ruled Song through puppet emperors, just as Bayan ruled the Yuan state through Toghan Temur, was the villain of several literary pieces devoted to telling the story of the rebellion of the peasants of the lower Yangzi under their leader Fang La. Similarly, and more memorably, the bandits of Liangshan, though easily suppressed by a Song army in 1119, were immortalised in the violent, bloody and heroic tale 'Shuihuzhuan', or 'Outlaws of the Marsh' of the late Yuan period.[9] That these tales were circulating around Yuan China long before they were written down seems implicit given their popularity once they were placed in print. The extreme violence of many later Yuan *zaju* operas and literature in the form of popular 'penny dreadfuls' also captures absolutely the nihilism, horror and bathos of the last years of Mongol rule in China.

Bayan's 'reforms' caused a mass panic across China as there were rumours that he would solve the problem of excessive Sinicisation of the state through the execution of all unmarried Chinese children and of all individuals carrying the family names of Zhang, Wang, Liu, Li and Zhao. This would have amounted to about nine-tenths of the population. Chinese town dwellers commonly revenged themselves for Bayan's policies on Muslim neighbours; in Hangzhou an entire Muslim wedding party was beaten to death by a mob. In fact, Bayan probably never had any intention of carrying out a holocaust of the scale described above, but his cancellation of the examination system, presumably on the basis that it was too expensive to maintain, was viewed as a very major step towards cultural genocide by the Yuan's Chinese subjects and also brought a great deal of violent opposition to the chancellor's rule from Mongols with a vested interest in the system.

Hunan, Guandong and Jiangxi began to quiver with peasant uprisings as resentment against Bayan grew, and in 1339 a Chinese clerk named Fan Meng killed a large number of the bureaucrats of the provincial capital of Hunan. Bayan responded to all these events by quickening the pace of his purges of Chinese from positions of any kind of influence in the local government system, but it was a coup from within the Mongolian elite that finally finished the minister, in March 1340. Bayan died in April that year before reaching his place of banishment and was succeeded by his nephew, Toghto, who had in fact been the instigator of his downfall.

Minister Toghto 'ruled' with the slightly less invisible Emperor Toghan Temur making public appearances, if little else, for four years before handing over power to minister Berke Bukha, and then reclaiming his first man at court status in 1349. The Yuan government, in this period at least, attempted to remedy the ills of the country, and all of Bayan's policies were reversed. In truth, it was too little too late. The structural flaws in the state were too great, and although it may be argued that the plagues and famines, with attendant depopulation, that struck China in the Yuan period were enough to overwhelm any polity, the fact remains that the men who formed the rebellions that finished the Yuan Dynasty achieved their coalition building and maintenance of armies in the field under the same conditions in which the Yuan government failed to hold the state together.

Certainly this period was exceptionally cruel to China, with brutal winters being almost the norm. Yellow River floods alternating with droughts were common, and both of these caused recurrent famines in the north. The Black Death epidemics that racked China in the 1340s may have been the unwitting gift of the Mongol invaders. Certainly the marmot, the small rodent that Mongols today still hunt to eat as a steppe delicacy, carries an abundance of fleas, which in turn carry bubonic plague. The *Pax Mongolica* was arguably the great conduit through which the Black Death entered the cities of China and spread through the Middle East and into Europe via Venetian trade with the Levant. Without the Mongol empire linking East to West and China to Mongolia it is to be wondered if the deadly contagion would have remained isolated and able to bring harm to only very few humans in the thinly populated steppe.[10] As it was, the disease killed millions. The censuses of the year 1200 give us an approximate population for China of about one hundred and twenty million people; in 1393 this number had been almost halved to sixty-five million. Needless to say, the drop may reflect mass death due to the miseries of famine and other assorted pestilences caused by the conquest and civil wars of the Mongols, but the numbers killed by the plague were still immense. In the midst of this maelstrom of misery, in 1344 the plague erupted in Anhui province in the old Song territories, and visited the home of a certain young man named Zhu Yuanzhang. He was sixteen and the Black Death killed his immediate family, leaving him destitute and without even the funds to bury his mother, father and brother with an appropriate level of filial piety. He entered a Buddhist monastery as a novice, and was put to work cleaning and cooking.

The census would have recorded many, many people who had lost families just as Zhu Yuanzhang did, but countless others within the Yuan state simply did not want to be found by census takers, as head counts meant taxation, and for families who had lost everything such payments were untenable. The simple volume of natural disasters that struck China during the Yuan period is almost unbelievable but they have been carefully catalogued and include ninety-two floods, eighty-six droughts, sixty-one locust epidemics, fifty-six earthquakes, forty-two typhoons and twenty extensive epidemics including, of course, the Black Death that decimated the population of the old world. During the last decades of the Yuan huge numbers of itinerant people roamed over China and frequently either joined revolts that were inspired by a diverse range of religious outlooks or simply turned to banditry.[11]

In June 1344 the Yellow River breached its banks once more. It shifted its course and from this point it on it no longer joined with the Huai River. Droughts struck hard at Hunan, Anhui and Jiangxi, whilst further north the Grand Canal became impossible to navigate due to flooding. The north's lifeline to the south's harvests was cut. Thousands of families were made homeless and many more starved. Men in these communities were literally forced into banditry. This was the point of no return and the Yuan state went from endemic disorder into outright civil war. A series of local rebellions broke out all over China and, whilst the Yuan government struggled mightily to bring these to an end and applied strategies first of centralisation and then dissemination of power to the affected provinces, nothing worked. The second half of the fourteenth century in China has been characterised as 'a half-century of intensifying chaos, an age of breakdown in which throughout most of the country the conduct of daily life increasingly depended on direct recourse to violence'.[12] The beginning of this period of anarchy and its brutality is recorded by the writer Kong Qi. He wrote of the widespread famine in the north in 1345 and how boys and girls fleeing south across the Yangzi River were sold as slaves. The condition of these young people was evidently not good as the writer goes on to tell us that the best of the bunch were taken off to become prostitutes or actors by the very rich, but the rest looked lucky to have even made it to the south without dying en route.

The Mongol military was ill prepared and poorly positioned to meet this upsurge in violence throughout the country, especially as the majority of these new eruptions began in the former territories of the southern Song empire. The Yuan's Mongol troop contingents were garrisoned in the Yellow River region and, whilst they might make forced marches to troublesome regions, they were not deployed for long-term suppression of the rumbling banditry and low-level acts of sedition that were now occurring constantly all over Hubei, Anhui, Jiangxi and Guangdong. They were only deployed to undertake action in the southern provinces when there were spikes in the 'normal' level of chaos and disorder.

The Yuan's policing of the south was also, logically, arranged around the protection of the major cities of the rich Yangzi delta area. Yangzhou, Nanjing and Hangzhou all maintained large garrisons of former Song battalions under the stewardship of Mongol officers. Other areas were much more thinly manned or effectively abandoned to the brigands. As discussed above, the

Yuan military establishment was, by this point, debilitated by its corrupted and ineffective command structure and rotten from within by the character of its troops. The provincial armies, even when bolstered by previously elite forces such as the Yuan Asu army, proved themselves again and again to be something of a paper tiger in their attempts to suppress banditry and local rebellion in the former Song lands. Given this fact it is therefore not surprising that, despite Yuan attempts to disarm every Han Chinese within the confines of their empire, self-defence leagues formed all over the south. The sixty years of brutal war that the Mongols had forced upon the Middle Kingdom had militarised Chinese society.[13] We have already looked at the Clausewitzean impossibility of closing this process down inside the Mongol military society, but 'total war' had also ingrained violence into every area of Chinese life. The *baojia* system of Wang Anshi that had helped maintain Song's long fight against the northern army even after the fall of Hangzhou and the disintegration of the dynasty's armies would have been the ideal model for the orderly recruitment and organisation of a local militia. With the disintegration of central control such a system could never evolve in the Yuan state. Therefore, towns and villages set up their own militias without reference to even a regional level of command and control. Needless to say, such self-reliance soon felt in need of reward, and this was often found in casting away all attachment to the central Yuan government, and in the non-remission of taxes and duties to the apparently redundant government of Beijing.[14]

The evolution of the bandit bands that were erupting all over southern China was not dissimilar to that seen in the Song period with individuals such as Li Quan. However, the simple lack of reverence for the Yuan Dynasty, which was distinctly the opposite of the devotion that so many *nanren* had felt for the Song even during their most repressive and dysfunctional phases, meant that these petty bandit kingdoms enjoyed a far greater popularity among the people. Furthermore, the leaders of these little 'statelets' had no desire to rejoin the failing Yuan state even when amnesties were offered. The best the Yuan government could hope for was to buy off the bandit chieftains with titles and autonomy, and the same practice was applied to the Mongol princelings with their independent armies and appanages. The conversion of the Mongol princelings into warlords was a rapid process, but Mongols were not the only men in China who made this conversion. Powerful regional Chinese warlords also emerged south of the Yangzi River among *nanren*. In the 1350s, a ship-owner and trader, Fang Guozhen, wrested control of the rich prefectures and shipping lanes of Zhejiang and Hangzhou and took all of the trade revenue of the region into his coffers. In the same period a salt smuggler, Zhang Shicheng, had virtually unchallenged control over the cities and canal routes of the Yangzi delta.

The self-defence leagues, warlords and bandits organised or abrogated authority out of self-interest. One other very different sector also existed and began to grow at a rapid pace in this period. This was made up of the sectarian movements which emerged from mainstream Buddhism and movements which claimed direct lineage from the Song royal family. These were the groups that were in fact the greatest danger to the Yuan state. The bandits, warlords and self-defence leagues aimed at the preservation of their territory. Movements such as the *bailianjiao* or White Lotus Society and the *hongjinjun* or Red Turban Army aimed at nothing less than the total remaking of China.

The White Lotus Society was forced, due to Yuan persecutions, to become a secret society in the late thirteenth century, but by the late 1330s its metamorphosis into the Red Turban Army had occurred in the Huai River valley region, and it had spread over half of China. It was a dispersed movement, and entirely heterogeneous in some places, with doctrines that fell well outside those of the original White Lotus Society. The Red Turbans were therefore, even at their outset, a diverse confederation and the lack of direction and leadership within the 'group' was always a major stumbling block to its military endeavours. The induction of peasants and lower-class workers into creeds such as the White Lotus Society that took place in many provinces was undoubtedly assisted by the passage of famine and epidemics through those areas, and the ensuing misery that they brought into being. As starvation and pestilence affected all parts of China it was perhaps natural that the movement would spread right across the central and western reaches of the Yangzi and the eastern provinces of Anhui, Hubei, Shandong and Jiangsu. Identifying the

Red Turbans as 'eastern' and 'western' is useful at this juncture as we try to make sense of this chaotic period and the large geographical spread of the movement. These labels do also, in fact, describe with some degree of accuracy how the movement was split into two bodies that would eventually come into direct conflict with each other. The prize for the victor of this contest was the right to rule China.

The year 1338 saw probably the first peasant rising in the Red Turbans' name, in Yangzhou. This uprising was short-lived and suppressed by the local authorities, but more than three hundred other peasant uprisings occurred in 1341. It would be reasonable, given the prevalence of the Red Turban movement in this period, to associate the continuance of many of these revolts directly with its doctrines and leadership even when, as in Hebei, the actual catalysts were simple economic ills such as hyperinflation. Part of the movement's appeal was its 'neo-Buddhist' doctrine and its proclamation of the expected return of a Bodhisattva named Maitreya, who would bring wealth to the suffering multitudes who followed the creed. At first glance the battle cry used by the society in Hebei in this early period seems strange as it was made in the name of the old Song Dynasty, and Hebei had not been under the control of the Song since 1125. The organisation in the east had first, however, become a militant force in Yingshang and Fuyang. These were cities in Anhui province and very much within the old boundaries of Song. The society also, of course, used red turbans and banners to mark out its followers; red had been the traditional fire colour of the Song court.

The Yuan government's decision to use corvée labour to attempt to 'straighten' the Yellow River in 1351 gave the Red Turbans their chance. The work lasted eight months and was undoubtedly technically successful. The Yellow River was contained and the Grand Canal became functional again. The problem was that compelling unwaged men to work on the project handed the Red Turbans a gift-wrapped propaganda vehicle. Peasant revolts erupted in all the areas of Hebei that were close enough to the river to be affected by the Yuan's policy. Yingzhou was chosen to be the headquarters of the revolution and was immediately inundated by swarms of Yellow River workers. The Red Turban Army was now a very major force and within months its ranks had swollen to some one hundred thousand men. The alarmed Yuan Beijing government deployed the Asu army, hoping that the elite force would crush the large rebellion swiftly, but the troopers of the Asu were by now corrupted by drink and more interested in loot than in doing their government's bidding against peasants who had nothing worth plundering. Six thousand Asu troopers were sent but were defeated and scattered by the sheer number of Red Turbans sent against them and by the religious fervour of their opponents.

Other societies were now also springing up all over the Huai River region and in north Jiangsu province. Further west, in 1351 the Tianwan or 'heaven perfected' Red Turbans formed in the central Yangzi region under Xu Shouhui, a former street peddler, and in Sichuan the Xia kingdom, which certainly followed different doctrines to the 'true' Red Turbans, came into being under a peasant leader, Ming Yuzhen, in 1362.

The society's huge success in Hubei was the creation of a man who was in fact named Han Shantong, but who claimed to be of the Zhao lineage and an eighth-generation descendant of Emperor Huizong of Song. On 16 March 1355 he took the throne name of Longfeng, or 'dragon-phoenix'. His associate Liu Futong also claimed to be a descendant of Liu Guangshi, a Song general and a contemporary of Yue Fei. On 11 June 1358 Liu Futong took Kaifeng. The significance of 'reclaiming' the original Song capital that had been lost to the Jurchen northern invaders in 1126 was undoubtedly large, given that the dynasty was now being reincarnated. Buoyed by this success, Liu Futong attempted to take Beijing and in an unrelated event the Mongol summer capital of Shangdu in modern-day Inner Mongolia was attacked by Chinese rebels. However, by September 1359 even Kaifeng was under immediate threat of being lost as a counterattack by the Yuan-sponsored warlord Chagan Temur drove into Hunan.

Han Shantong was captured and killed by the Yuan at some point, but his wife and son, Han Lin'er, avoided capture and fled through Hebei. Little of the ritual of the society has come down to us, but the sacrifice of a white horse and a black ox to the gods of sky and underworld was certainly undertaken before Han Lin'er was then identified as the prospective Song Emperor Mingwang, literally 'bright-shining king', under Liu Futong's close guardianship.

The Huai River White Lotus society quickly joined with Han Lin'er's Red Turbans but other groups, such as Zhang Shicheng's men of north Jiangsu, which sat somewhere between straightforward bandits and anti-Yuan revolutionaries, stayed outside the confederation that was growing around Han Lin'er. Perhaps because it was isolated in this way, the Yuan government next sent troops against Zhang Shicheng's men. This Yuan force failed, however, as its leader refused to take direction from Beijing and actually disbanded his own forces without Zhang Sicheng having to do anything to send it into disarray.

Then Liu Futong broke out of Kaifeng, where he had been besieged by Chagan Temur, and brought Han Lin'er back to Anhui. Han Lin'er was then formally proclaimed as a new Song emperor with the throne name of Xiao Mingwang. Now the armies of Han Lin'er and Liu Futong began a march north. The Yuan government scrambled around for troops to meet this threat and eventually managed to conscript sufficient forces from levies raised by landowners. The Yuan records describe how effective salt-field workers were against bandits in this period and, given the militarisation of all levels of Chinese society that we have discussed above, the fierceness they exhibited was almost certainly just as evident in other field workers. Needless to say, the landlords for whom these men worked had decidedly more interest in defeating the 'millenarian' troops of Han Lin'er than the 'nomads' of the Asu army ever would have. There was a distinctly proto-communist edge to at least some of the fringe societies that made up the Red Turbans; communal ownership of property was a central tenet of many of the societies' politics, and this was certainly the antithesis of the feudal society that made up the fragile Yuan body politic.[15]

The Red Turbans were defeated by this new Yuan land army, and Zhang Shicheng, the bandit 'king' of Suzhou and now a Yuan ally, then turned his forces on Liu Futong and defeated and killed him in 1363 near Anfeng. We will describe Zhang Shicheng's 'private' wars a little later, but it is enough to note at this juncture that the northern insurgency now began to falter seriously after twelve years of successes.

Even with this major setback it is unlikely that the Yuan government could have held back the Red Turbans and other insurgent groups from an immediate resurgence in the early 1360s without the 'assistance' of the quasi-independent warlords who were by now well established throughout much of China. One such warlord has been briefly introduced above as Chagan Temur. It seems likely that Chagan Temur first started to form a private army in the 1340s with the simple intention of defending his lands in northern China from the increasing threat of the insurgents of Anhui and Hunan. He first tackled the Red Turbans in 1352 and found success where regular Yuan forces had failed. He was, in fact, even able to extend his territory in Hunan and Shandong, and to take personal control of Kaifeng in 1358. At this point the Yuan government recognised his right to the lands he had conquered and conferred legitimacy on his army and on his newly won lands. However, despite its acknowledgement that Chagan Temur was effectively an independent ruler in his own right, the Yuan court, or rather the factions and self-seeking ministers that made up the remnants of its governing body, still remained jealous of the warlord's progress and of any expansion of his power.

Chagan Temur was of the Naiman tribe, and despite the fact that he was therefore a *semuren* and probably as close to being 'Mongol' as it was possible to be, it seems that it was the envy of a Mongol aristocrat, Bolod Temur, the father of the empress, that caused his downfall. Bolod Temur attempted first to choke off supplies to Chagan Temur's army, and to use what was left of the dynasty's imperial authority as an obstacle to Chagan Temur's operations against the Yuan's own insurgent enemies. Then, in 1361, the vicious politics of the time were shown in all their grim squalor. Two Yuan generals who had failed dismally against the Red Turbans were captured by them in Shandong. They then left a suspiciously comfortable captivity, following the securing of their release under an amnesty agreement made in the name of the Yuan government and brokered by Chagan Temur. The two generals fought alongside Chagan Temur as he expanded his own lands, and the influence of the Yuan court, further into Shandong. In the summer of 1362 the two generals assassinated Chagan Temur, claiming that they were acting under instructions from Beijing. However, when the deed was done, the pair fled to the Shandong Red Turbans rather than to

Bolod Temur in the Yuan capital, even though it seems likely that he was their paymaster. Honours were then piled, posthumously, and somewhat bathetically given the circumstances of his death, upon Chagan Temur by the emperor.

The Yuan government continued to seesaw between such extremes; it found itself kowtowing to warlords as they were the only effective force in the field who could hold back the insurgents, whilst secretly plotting their destruction for fear that they might become too powerful and aim to replace the Chinggisid line on the throne. This schizophrenic policy was applied to the succession to Chagan Temur in Hunan and Shandong. Chagan Temur's adopted son, Koko Temur, was confirmed in all the various government positions that his father had held. This rapid affirmation of Koko Temur as the 'court's man' may, of course, have been pure realpolitik, as he was also acclaimed in the field by his father's generals. Koko Temur then went on to do both his own bidding and that of the Beijing court's through a drive into eastern Shandong. He was also able during this successful campaign to capture the two assassins of his father. Koko Temur sent two hundred rebel leaders to Beijing for execution but retained the two ex-generals for his own personal revenge, and finally sacrificed their hearts to the memory of his father.

Bolod Temur's malign influence finally pulled Koko Temur more closely into the orbit of court politics than Chagan Temur would ever have wished either for himself or for his adopted son. Bolod Temur made a bold attempt to disinherit Emperor Toghan Temur's chosen successor, Ayushiridara, in 1364. Bolod Temur was driven to this audacious move by a number of defeats that he suffered in a war he had forced upon Koko Temur in 1363. In desperation, Bolod Temur fled from the battlefield and seized Beijing, hoping perhaps to use Toghan Temur and the imperial family, if not as hostages, then at least as bargaining chips in any negotiations with Koko Temur.

Ayushiridara fled Beijing upon Bolod Temur's arrival in the city and took refuge with Koko Temur. This desperate act of the heir-apparent seems to have at last stirred action from the emperor, and Bolod Temur was judicially murdered by axe men on Toghan Temur's orders as he was travelling to court in August 1365. The arrival of his head at Koko's camp was enough to convince Ayushiridara that it was now safe to return to Beijing. The gratitude of the Yuan court was shown to Koko Temur through the granting of further titles, but as he was now effectively master of northern China these were empty trophies and, given the poisonous atmosphere of the Yuan government, a counsellor's role was something to be shunned rather than embraced.

Even without taking a court position Koko Temur could not avoid entanglement in the disintegrating politics of the Yuan, which centred largely, as discussed above, on maintaining a balance between domination by, and reliance on, warlords. At one point four warlords of the northwest were engaged in full-scale assaults on Koko Temur with the tacit approval of at least a part of the Yuan court, even while he was under imperial commission to make war on the Red Turbans in the Yangzi delta in the late 1360s. Such obvious contradictions to what should have been the Yuan's most simple policy – to destroy the insurgency in the east – ensured the immediate survival of the disparate and at this time wavering eastern Red Turban movements, and ultimately the victory of these groups over the Yuan. Arguably, the defeats of the early 1360s by the Yuan 'land army' and Chagan Temur, and the defection of Zhang Shicheng, could have been enough to kill off the eastern Red Turbans had the Yuan been able to push into Anhui to destroy the movement in the place where it had begun. This did not occur, in simple terms, because men such as Koko Temur, who may have been capable of completing this arduous task, were distracted from it by the all-against-all swordfight that was dominating northern China.

With the Yuan infighting in the north, and the Beijing government concentrating on destroying the eastern Red Turbans, the western 'arm' of the Red Turban movement was able to grow with relatively little interference from outside forces. The Tianwan Red Turbans made Xu Shouhui into an emperor, and again the Song Dynasty was chosen as the royal line he had supposedly sprung from. By 1357 the Tianwan state had expanded into Anhui and Jiangsu, where it collided with the ambitions of eastern Red Turban leaders. The Tianwan movement's leading general at this point was Chen Youliang who, in 1360, had Xu Shouhui assassinated. Chen Youliang changed the title of the 'dynasty' to Great Han, and made a rapid advance on the eastern Red Turbans' new capital of Nanjing. He was defeated at the city's walls but remained strong in Jiangsu province. He then founded a capital for his Great Han dynasty in modern Wuhan, at the point on the central Yangzi where Qubilai had been forced to turn back from his invasion of Song in 1260.

Sichuan also slipped from Yuan control in 1357 as Ming Yuzhen's followers built a fleet and used it to conquer long reaches of the Yangzi River valley. They captured Chongqing and fought through the valleys of the province to clear it of Yuan resistance. The Xia state, as discussed earlier, seems to have been an offshoot of the western Red Turban society but, whilst Yuan resistance in Sichuan was paltry at best, Ming Yuzhen's men also had to dislodge elements of other independent Red Turban forces in order to gain total control of the province. Ming Yuzhen also refused to acknowledge Chen Youliang after the murder of Xu Shouhui, and the Xia kingdom of Sichuan, proclaimed in 1362, would follow an independent and somewhat detached path of history from the rest of China until 1371. Ming Yuzhen reigned until 1366 and was succeeded by his son in a fairly orderly and peaceful manner. The people of the Xia kingdom during this time were living in something of an oasis of pacific and good governance compared to the rest of China.

Peace and good government were things that were very much denied the people of northeastern China in this period, and this may be one reason why the eastern Red Turbans, despite their setbacks in the field in the early 1360s, were at least able to maintain their ideological base in the region. Certainly, having an incarnation of the Song emperor, Xiao Mingwang, would have helped too. The memory of Song's resistance to the by now thoroughly detested Mongols would have continued to be a powerful spur for recruitment. The child Han Lin'er survived until 1367, and he was identified not only with the Song line but also with the still awaited Bodhisattva Maitreya. This said, defeat in the field had fractured the eastern movement even to the extent of causing fratricidal warfare between the various branches of the Red Turbans. Independent leaders existed in Xuzhou in northern Jiangsu, in Hunan, Shandong and Manchuria. Every branch north of Anhui had also been shattered by the series of hammer blows they had received from Chagan Temur in the early 1360s.

Therefore, by 1363 the eastern Red Turban movement had faded as a real military and political force in the northeast. It remained strong in Anhui, however. In fact, the Anhui movement was in certain ways different by the 1360s from the heterogeneous organisation that had fought the Yuan in Hunan and beyond. Back in 1352 two men from the very bottom of Chinese society who were to be pivotal to its future had met in Anhui. Guo Zixing came from a low-class family and had joined the White Lotus society as a young man with few other options in life. He was obviously a natural, if somewhat irritable and impatient, leader, as by 1352 troops under his command took Haozhou from its Yuan garrison. A Yuan counterattack on the city made no headway and in order to please their masters in Beijing the Yuan troops took civilians as prisoners back to Beijing in an attempt to fool the court that they had been successful against the insurgents. In Haozhou Guo Zixing met the junior monk Zhu Yuanzhang, whose family had all been killed by the plague and whose new home, the temple, had now been burned down and plundered during Yuan attacks on the city. Zhu Yuanzhang was quickly taken under the older man's wing and almost as rapidly became his son-in-law through marriage to Guo Zixing's adopted daughter, and was made into a military man. He swiftly rose to the rank of corporal of a guard squad, and then became a member of Guo Zixing's personal bodyguard. Perhaps the fact that his grandfather had been a Song soldier who had fought the Yuan even after the fall of Hangzhou and had filled the young Zhu Yuanzhang with tales of military adventure and valour helped in this transformation.

Guo Zixing's famous temper soon caused fallouts between him and every one of the other five marshals of the Red Turbans in Haozhou. He was nearly killed after being kidnapped by two of the other leading Red Turban generals, but Zhu Yuanzhang was able to save his father-in-law in the nick of time. Zhu Yuanzhang also seems to have taken this sign of the growing chaos within the leadership of the Red Turbans as a poor omen for the future of the movement and returned to his hometown to recruit for his own army.

The epidemics that were once more raging all over eastern China at this point provided the apocalyptic conditions in which millenarian movements flourish and certainly helped in the re-emergence of the cults devoted to the 'coming' of the Bodhisattva that had assisted Han Shantong in first creating the White Lotus Society. Certainly, large numbers of men came to the standards of the Red Turbans at this time and this allowed the rebuilt army to take Xuzhou, the old Han Dynasty capital in northern Jiangsu province. Within this composite army, made up of loyalties to many different ideologies and religious ideals, Zhu Yuanzhang's force of seven hundred men, led by his most trusted lieutenant, Xu Da, and twenty-four of his closest friends from his youth, stood out through their loyalty to him as a 'hometown' leader and also because, unlike the undisciplined Yuan armies and the uncoordinated Red Turbans, this new model army had extensive organised training and iron discipline as its hallmarks. It became a nucleus around which defectors from the Yuan and from within the amorphous Red Turban confederation were soon recruited. In another way it was unusual for the period, in that Zhu Yuanzhang had to rely on 'friends' rather than relatives. Of course, he had practically no family to speak of, having lost virtually all of them to the plague, but generally armies and the rebel bands that came into being all over China in this period were based on kin. Perhaps one of the appeals of Zhu Yuanzhang's outfit for dispossessed men and unattached soldiers was that it would have been more egalitarian than other armies that were based on family ties.

Zhu Yuanzhang's army grew and by 1353 Guo Zixing had granted him a commission. He was then sent south by the political enemies of Guo Zixing. They obviously hoped that Zhu Yuanzhang would fail and be destroyed by the warlords of Jiangsu, but he pushed quickly through the province and in 1354 he entered the Yangzi River valley. By 1355 he had both an army of some thirty thousand men and a functioning local government in the region. He was joined by Guo Zixing in 1355. The older man was essentially fleeing the murderous atmosphere among the Red Turban marshals and did not live long after reaching Zhu Yuanzhang's army. The death of Guo Zixing in 1355 did not immediately bring Zhu Yuanzhang to the top of the heap. Guo Zixing's eldest son and one of his brothers-in-law were appointed as grand marshals by Han Lin'er, and they led the Red Turbans' assault on the city of Nanjing in 1356. However, it was now obvious that Zhu Yuanzhang, by virtue of the personal following that he had accrued and his innate military ability, was a major power broker within the movement. He was named as second-in-command of the army of the Red Turbans by Han Lin'er.

The Red Turban army crossed the Yangzi River on 10 July 1355 with the intention of making a base in the rich and fertile region of its valley. They made an immediate attempt on Nanjing that was beaten off, but Zhu Yuanzhang's men did not retire from the region as many of the other Red Turban contingents did. Zhu Yuanzhang had been successfully recruiting among the naval squadrons and merchantmen of the lower Yangzi River. He had also, with slightly less success, been negotiating for ships and men with the fishermen of Lake Chao. He obtained some support from these fiercely independent and suspicious-minded men, but many of the fishermen also joined Chen Youliang's forces. The addition of small ships and boats to Zhu Yuanzhang's army gave him the ability to stay on the river and strike at the Yuan's smaller towns and strongpoints on the Yangzi even when the main contingent of the Red Turbans had withdrawn. Through his refusal to retreat Zhu Yuanzhang obtained a greater degree of influence in the area and on the direction of the campaign, and in October, when both of Guo Zixing's sons were killed in another unsuccessful attack on Nanjing, full command of the eastern Red Turban army now fell to Zhu Yuanzhang. It is possible that Zhu Yuanzhang used a Mongol deserter to hoodwink Guo Zixing's sons into a position where they were then cut off and killed, but the evidence for this is tenuous at best. Guo Zixing's final surviving son became Zhu Yuanzhang's second-in-command, but was soon after executed for treason. A Yuan fleet was defeated by Zhu Yuanzhang's new navy on the Yangzi in March 1356 and Nanjing fell to Zhu Yuanzhang on 10 April 1356 after its Mongol garrison, some thirty-six thousand men, surrendered without offering a fight. Local Chinese Yuan forces put up some resistance but after a day of fighting the city was in Zhu Yuanzhang's hands. In the very same week Zhang Shicheng's independent army took Suzhou and the Tianwan Red Turbans conquered Hanyang.

Perhaps it was because of his experience of anarchy, chaos and death at an early age, or because he could clearly see that the struggle for supremacy among the Red Turbans would be the struggle for China, that Zhu Yuanzhang set out at this point to underpin his military achievement with a civil government that would bring order, law and a degree of prosperity to each of the regions that he conquered. Needless to say, the structure of Zhu Yuanzhang's government was military in character with generals also holding civilian office – he was, after all, now at the head of an army of some one hundred thousand men – but he recruited scholars into his fledgling administration from those who had served the Yuan as well as those who had refused to serve or had been barred from government by the Yuan's employment policies.

Zhu Yuanzhang's efforts to preserve and improve the economies of the areas he conquered have left him with the reputation, perhaps not totally deserved, of a leader who stressed the importance of disciplined soldiering that did no harm to peasants or to land, and of avoiding exploitation through heavy taxation. He also generously rewarded those who gave service to his army and to himself. Needless to say, this stood totally at odds with the experience of the peasantry with the Yuan Dynasty. His 'enlightened' governance also stood him in good stead to succeed in the power struggle that was about to take place within the wider Red Turban organisation and to allow the eastern provinces under his control to flourish as compared to the northeast, which, as we have seen, began to slip away from the movement in the early 1360s.[16]

The late 1350s saw Zhu Yuanzhang make extensive gains in south Anhui and Zhejiang, and the army doubled in size through defections from Yuan forces and local militias. Zhu Yuanzhang's original twenty-four companions were now all divisional generals in the army and many of the fishermen of Lake Chao had also risen to high rank. Zhang Shicheng and the pirate Fang Guozhen still controlled China's richest provinces and the coast, and further expansion by Zhu Yuanzhang to the west was blocked by Chen Youliang.

Chen Youliang, it will be remembered, had been extending the western Red Turban state into Anhui and Jiangsu, and made an attempt on Nanjing in 1360. This was entirely unsuccessful as Zhu Yuanzhang had done what the Yuan had neglected to do and invested in refortifying his capital, and Chen Youliang fell into a skilfully set trap. Zhu Yuanzhang had spies working for him among the fishermen of Lake Chao who had joined Chen Youliang in the 1350s, and they informed him of a planned surprise attack by Chen Youliang against

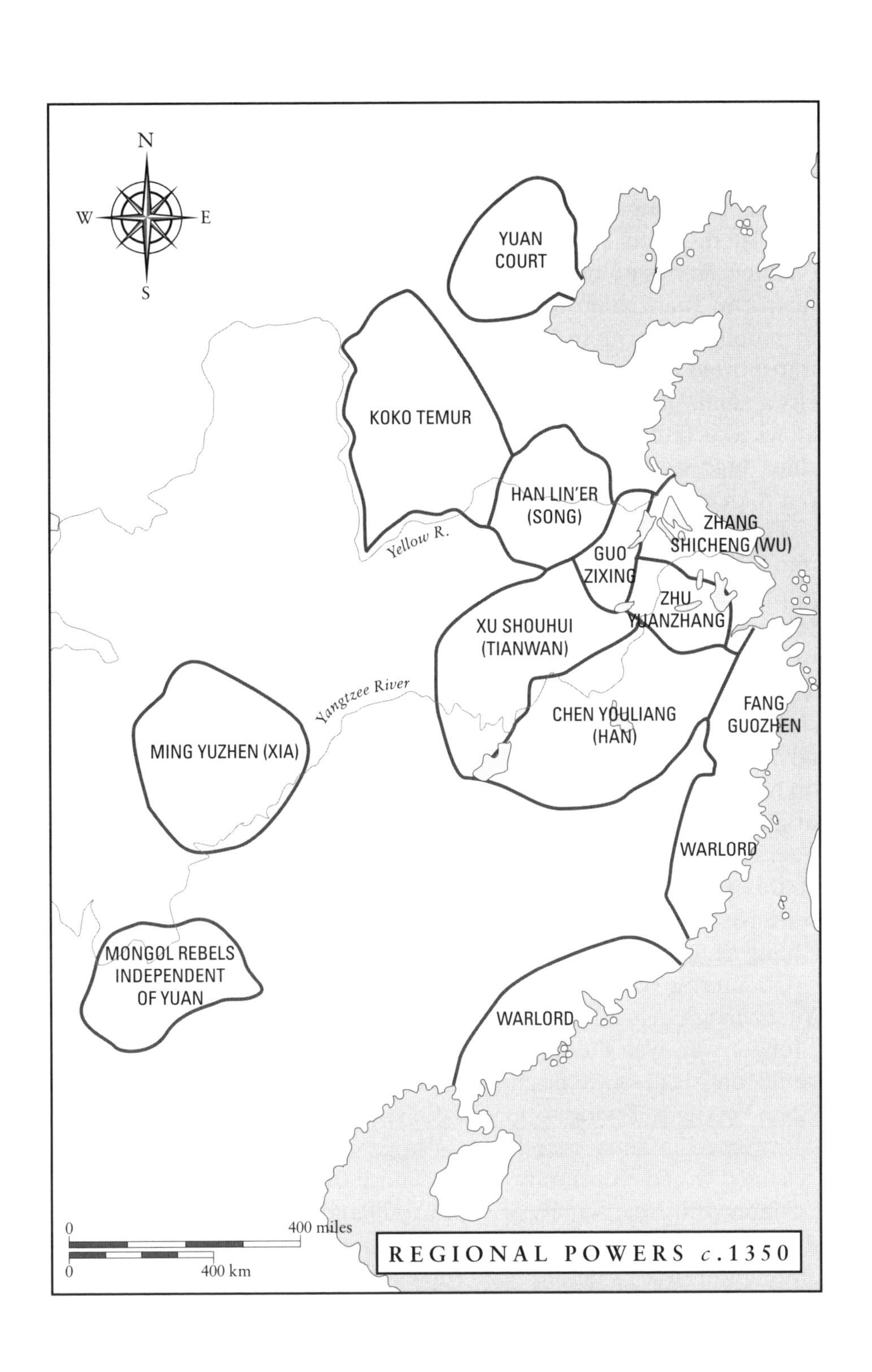

REGIONAL POWERS *c*.1350

general Xu Da at Chizhou. Xu Da was immediately reinforced, and when Chen Youliang's assault was launched it was heavily defeated in an ambush. Zhu Yuanzhang's generals then provoked Chen Youliang by killing almost all of the three thousand prisoners they had taken. Infuriated, Chen Youliang launched an immediate strike towards Nanjing. At this point, Chen Youliang was militarily far more powerful than Zhu Yuanzhang, but such was his haste to attack that he failed to mobilise any more than one hundred thousand men. His fleet transported this force down the river to Taiping on 11 June 1360. The city's small garrison refused to surrender, but after Chen Youliang attacked it both from the landward side and from the river using his ships' high sterns as siege towers it was taken and its commander was put to death.

This easy victory obviously imbued a great deal of confidence into Chen Youliang, for it was at this point that he disposed of the puppet emperor, Xu Shouhui, and crowned himself as the Great Han emperor. Envoys were then sent in the new emperor's name to Zhang Shicheng, seeking a short-term alliance against Zhu Yuanzhang and with a suggestion that Zhang Shicheng should simultaneously attack Nanjing from the rear as Chen Youliang's fleet advanced towards it along the Yangzi. Zhang Shicheng, however, sat on his hands at this time. His fear may have been that the destruction of Zhu Yuanzhang would simply tip the balance of power against his own state and make Chen Youliang impossible to restrain. Certainly, at this point, Chen Youliang was the most powerful of the three warlords in southern China and therefore the greatest danger to Zhang Shicheng's territories.

Countering Chen Youliang was not going to be easy for Zhu Yuanzhang's generals. The river, as it had been back in the long Song–Mongol war, was the key to victory or defeat, and Zhu Yuanzhang could only call on a fraction of the number of ships available to Chen Youliang. Trying to match the speed of any river-borne attack with forced infantry marches was impossible and Zhu Yuanzhang's generals would constantly have found themselves drawn out of position whilst the targets of Chen Youliang's campaign, the cities of the delta such as Yangzhou and Jiangyin, would fall to his ships and amphibious troops before relief forces could arrive.

Zhu Yuanzhang and his generals, Li Shanchang and Kang Maocai, overcame this problem by ensuring that Chen Youliang landed his troops at a specific spot and by gathering forces nearby to ambush the Han army. This was achieved through double-bluff and devious intrigue. One of Kang Maocai's servants was ostensibly spying for Chen Youliang, but was in fact passing far more valuable information than he ever gave him back to Kang Maocai. Kang Maocai had also fought alongside Chen Youliang in the past and his loyalties would have been easily presented as being conflicted, to say the least. He sent to Chen Youliang, through his servant, a letter offering to defect to his former employer and also to destroy a wooden bridge on the Sancha River, which would then allow Chen Youliang's fleet to moor directly up against Nanjing's walls, and for his troops to storm the city from this position. Chen Youliang agreed immediately to the scheme but then Zhu Yuanzhang added another level of complexity to what had been, so far, a simple double-cross. He ordered the bridge destroyed, as agreed between Kang Maocai and Chen Youliang, but for it also to be immediately restored as a stone structure. It seems that Zhu Yuanzhang was aiming for a more extensive destruction of Chen Youliang's forces than could be achieved at the city's walls. Certainly, it would have taken Chen Youliang's men several hours to disembark fully from their ships on the River Sancha and onto the city's walls. Any ambush would therefore only be able to assault the leading troops before all surprise was lost. Open space was needed if a true killing ground was to be created by Zhu Yuanzhang's men.

Zhu Yuanzhang evidently felt that he could outguess Chen Youliang and decided to arrange his main forces near a point called Dragon Bay. He evidently hoped that Chen Youliang could be directed to a large-scale landing there through the denial of any other favourable options following his disappointment when Kang Maocai did not defect. Three divisions were placed at points that could give Chen Youliang direct access to Nanjing's walls and 'lotus flowers' – sharpened stakes driven into the riverbanks – were placed at every point where an army might try to disembark. Chen Youliang's brother, Chen Yuren, reached Dragon Bay and put ashore with a large force that captured a small contingent of Zhu

Yuanzhang's men. Chen Yuren's ten thousand men then fortified their position and awaited reinforcements.

Meanwhile, Zhu Yuanzhang had divisions hidden in hills to the north of the bay, and on hearing of Chen Yuren's disembarkation he strengthened them further to prepare for a large-scale ambush if Chen Youliang should bring the rest of his forces to the bay. Thirty thousand men were hidden in the hills and Xu Da's corps was deployed to the south wall of Nanjing, from where he could aid in cutting the Han army off from the river. Zhu Yuanzhang took a further reserve division and went northwest of the city's walls; from the hills there he could view the entire plain and direct the coming battle. His signallers used red flags to indicate to his generals the full disembarkation of Chen Youliang's army, and yellow to order them to the attack.

Zhu Yuanzhang had ordered his small navy to avoid contact with Chen Youliang's large fleet, and on 23 June 1360 the Han army did exactly what Zhu Yuanzhang had predicted it would. Chen Youliang attacked several other points but was repelled either by the narrowness of the rivers that denied access to his large troop transports, or by stout resistance and the lotus flowers. When he saw the new stone bridge he realised that Kang Maocai was not coming over to him and decided against a direct attack on the walls, fearing that his men would be trapped on two sides, and instead sailed for Dragon Bay, where his men disembarked.

Zhu Yuanzhang waited until the afternoon and then sent his own force to march across the plain to provoke Chen Youliang. Despite a heavy rainstorm and the summer heat, Chen Youliang's army set off in pursuit of this little contingent. Then the rain stopped, Zhu Yuanzhang ordered all his drums to be beaten and for the yellow flags to be raised. It was all over very quickly. The Han forces broke under the assault of Zhu Yuanzhang's generals and fled for their boats and ships. Around one hundred of the larger ships and many of the smaller craft stuck in the mud and passed over to Zhu Yuanzhang's ownership. The majority of Chen Youliang's men got away, crowded uncomfortably onto the remaining vessels, but twenty thousand lay dead on the field, and over seven thousand of the Lake Chao men defected from the Han to Zhu Yuanzhang.

The victory was followed up by a rapid invasion of Jiangxi and the capture of Guangxin. Zhu Yuanzhang now threatened Chen Youliang's lands and had gained the initiative, but held back from an immediate full-scale invasion of Jiangxi for fear of denuding his defences against Zhang Shicheng. He was able to press Chen Youliang back to his capital through a limited river campaign based around his newly enlarged fleet but a series of serious rebellions in the recently conquered areas around Nanchang and in Zhejiang and the discovery of a conspiracy among his generals compelled Zhu Yuanzhang to withdraw from nearly all of Chen Youliang's lands and to concentrate on preventing what he already had from slipping away.

Zhu Yuanzhang was therefore unable to prevent Chen Youliang from reasserting himself, and Anjing was lost to the Han after a surprise attack in August 1361. The loss of this major city seems to have brought Zhu Yuanzhang to the conclusion that a major attack on Han was required if he was to have any hope of coming out on top in the three-sided war that he, Chen Youliang and Zhang Shicheng were engaged in. On 11 September Zhu Yuanzhang sailed with his fleet to Anjing. He failed to take the city but burned the Han fleet anchored there before moving on and entering Lake Poyang. Zhu Yuanzhang's campaign seems to have unsettled the Han leadership, and two Han commanders immediately defected to him along with their men and ships. Despite this, and the fact that his fleet was now numerically inferior to that of Zhu Yuanzhang, Chen Youliang offered battle but was rapidly outflanked and lost over one hundred ships. He fled to the smaller lakes connected to Poyang and during the night slipped away with the remainder of his men and ships. Zhu Yuanzhang sent vessels to pursue Chen Youliang but failed to prevent him from reaching his capital. Xu Da blockaded Chen Youliang there until April 1362.

Zhu Yuanzhang then attempted to reconstitute the authority he had lost in Jiangxi during the recent rebellions, endeavoured to bring Chen Youliang's Anhui cities over to him and also had to respond to reports of movement on the northern Jiangsu front as Zhang Shicheng mobilised around Lake Tai. Both the army and the authority of Zhu Yuanzhang's state were certainly overstretched and at this point he perhaps came the closest he ever would to losing everything.

In February 1362 Zhu Yuanzhang entered Nanchang after negotiating its surrender, and the chances of pacifying Anhui quickly seemed good. The threat of Zhang Shicheng in Jiangsu also seems to have been rapidly neutralised after the dispatch of an army to the region, but by March 1362 Zhejiang was aflame with rebellion. Miao troops transplanted by the Yuan from their homelands in Guizhou, Yunnan, Hunan and Sichuan to Zhejiang province rose in a well-coordinated insurrection possibly instigated by agents of Zhang Shicheng. They killed their general, Hu Dahai, and fortresses protecting the border with Zhang Shicheng were also taken by the rebels.

Zhu Yuanzhang appointed his nephew Li Wenzhong to supreme command in Zhejiang and he recaptured the key centres of the province, but many of the rebel Miao troops eluded capture and went over to join Zhang Shixin, the brother of Zhang Shicheng, who was now invading Zhu Yuanzhang's lands from the north. Li Wenzhong showed as much artifice as his uncle in dealing with this new threat. He contrived to have Zhang Shixin believe that general Shao Rong was in two places at once with a vast army and this was enough to force Zhang Shixin to retreat to the border.

Zhu Yuanzhang had expanded his lands quickly and had had little time to consolidate them or to disarm the various petty warlords whom he had left in semi-autonomous control of many of his newly acquired cities, but it is still hard to decide exactly what the root causes were of the fleeting but violent rebellions that erupted all over his territories in this period. Just as he put down one revolt, another head of the beast, like a hydra, would rise up. Next Jiangxi revolted against his rule and, having denuded its cities of garrisons to reinforce the blockading of Chen Youliang by Xu Da, Zhu Yuanzhang struggled to contain the rebellion. Two former enemy generals who had reluctantly joined Zhu Yuanzhang after his capture of Nanchang in February 1362 were the locus of the rebellion this time and they turned back from joining Xu Da with their fleets and made a successful attempt on Nanchang in April as Zhu Yuanzhang's army had already left the city and the garrison was undermanned. Xu Da had to retire from his siege of Chen Youliang but was able to retake Nanchang by May 1362.

Zhu Yuanzhang allowed Chen Youliang some peace whilst he concentrated on refortifying Nanchang and Anjing. Then Zhu Yuanzhang had one more conspiracy to quash, but this time it came from within the ranks of his own army and from among his original twenty-four companions. In the summer of 1362 General Shao Jung, with the support of General Zhao Jizi, planned the murder of Zhu Yuanzhang. The generals' ire may have been fired by envy at the accelerating career of Zhu Yuanzhang's two nephews. Zhu Wencheng had been given command of Nanchang upon its recovery and Li Wenzhong had gained much credit for suppressing the rebellion in Zhejiang.

The two generals plotted to kill Zhu Yuanzhang in Nanjing as he returned from a review of the army in August 1362. Zhu Yuanzhang was obviously a superstitious man, and when a review flag, caught by the wind, flew about his body as he entered the main gate of the city he changed his plans and entered the city at another point and far away from the waiting assassins. The plot then collapsed amid mutual denunciations and confessions and the generals were arrested. Its 'harmless' outcome would suggest that the conspiracy of Shao Jung and Zhao Jizi lacked any real degree of support from within Zhu Yuanzhang's army and state, but it still shook him and restrained him from further action against his external enemies for the rest of 1362.

Therefore a standoff between the three main players in southern China took hold for the rest of the year. We need, however, to concentrate on this region a little longer, as the future of China and who would rule the Middle Kingdom was to be decided in 1363. The north of China, as we have seen, had become increasingly irrelevant to the decision on who would succeed to the Yuan's wrecked state after the murder of Chagan Temur and the coup of Bolod Temur in 1364.

In February 1363 Zhu Yuanzhang met the challenge of Zhang Shicheng, who had attacked Anfeng in Anhui after accepting the bribe of a Yuan government post. As discussed earlier, Han Lin'er's 'Song' court had settled in Anfeng after the failure of the northern insurrections. Zhu Yuanzhang, despite the threat of Chen Youliang's army and navy, of which he may in fact have been ignorant due to a failure of his normally efficient intelligence network, was able to send enough men under Xu Da's command to Anfeng to attempt a rescue of the court. Though he was unable to save Liu Futong from Zhang Shicheng, Xu Da did return with the emperor. Anfeng was then 'abandoned' by both sides and was subsequently garrisoned by

Yuan loyalists; its strategic significance was lost once Han Lin'er had been removed from it.

Zhu Yuanzhang's 'possession' of the emperor was of immense value in his new moves to consolidate his powerbase and to begin to mould the Red Turban revolution to his own vision of China's future. That he had now reached the decision that he had already or would very soon receive the Mandate of Heaven is clear from his actions over the next few years. First he founded an office of Confucian academies in Nanjing; not only was this a break with the neo-Buddhist millenarian theology of the Red Turbans but it also meant that the traditional 'breeding ground' for government ministers to serve a dynasty had been established within his lands. Zhu Yuanzhang then began to appoint counsellors and administrators using titles derived from Yuan bureaucracy. He was already evidently aiming at creating legitimacy for a future reign in the mid-1360s, and his statement on religious rites and standing laws, made in this period of construction of the apparatus that would bring the Ming Dynasty into existence, is indicative of his thinking at this point: '[They are] the network [*jigang*] sustaining the state . . . When a state is being newly established, they constitute the first order of priority.'[17]

Chen Youliang returned to the fray in 1363 with a vast fleet and a large army. The sources are not particularly helpful in deciding quite how Chen Youliang achieved this military renaissance, but do tell us a great deal about the impressive vessels that made up his fleet. It consisted of many tower-ships of three decks with iron-plated turrets manned by contingents of archers. The sterns of the vessels were also impressively high, and we have seen earlier how the Han used these to deploy troops onto the walls of enemy cities. Chen Youliang took personal command of the enterprise and probably had about three hundred thousand men with him and numerous craft in addition to the tower-ships. He had regained naval superiority over Zhu Yuanzhang once more and aimed to use this armada to take Nanchang and then to move on through the Yangzi delta to topple more cities. The Han fleet arrived off Nanchang on 5 June 1363.

The first obstacle to this grand strategy was that Nanchang's walls had been rebuilt in 1362 and had actually been moved back and away from the river's edge. This stymied Chen Youliang's 'high sterns' tactic and forced him into a blockade of the city, and the attendant loss of momentum to his campaign that this entailed. An attack on the city's walls on 9 June 1363 brought down a section of wall but the garrison repelled the Han troops with a gunpowder fusillade and built a makeshift palisade behind the fallen section. A further attack on the city's main gate was repelled later in the month and desperate Han attacks on the few water gates that the city retained in July also failed and resulted in heavy losses.

Chen Youliang was now bogged down at Nanchang and the river level was dropping, reducing the manoeuvrability of his larger vessels. When he was offered a truce and the vague possibility of surrender by the starving city he agreed with alacrity. The Nanchang garrison used this breathing space to get a message through to Nanjing which arrived there on 4 August.

Zhu Yuanzhang was at this point still entangled in the aftermath of the Anfeng conflict with Zhang Shicheng and putting down yet another rebellion in Zhejiang. Despite protests from his senior generals, who retained a romantic attachment to the Anfeng Song Dynasty and wished to continue the war on that front to seek revenge for the killing of Liu Futong, Zhu Yuanzhang stopped all offensive action against Zhang Shicheng and ordered General Hu Deji to march to the relief of Nanchang.

Zhu Yuanzhang's fleet of about one thousand mostly small ships and perhaps as many as two hundred thousand men sailed for Nanchang. It arrived at the mouth of Lake Poyang on 24 August and the troops dug in. The Han fleet was at anchor in the lake and the only route out was past Zhu Yuanzhang's ships, which sat in a narrow stretch of water linking the Yangzi to the lake. Having now secured a base, Zhu Yuanzhang's fleet moved into the lake to relieve Nanchang. On 30 August the two fleets closed to begin a series of battles that would decide the future of China.

Zhu Yuanzhang put his heaviest ships in the centre of his line under his direct control and those of Xu Da and Chang Yuchun and his lighter vessels on the wings of the fleet. Some immediate successes were scored with catapults and fire, and Han ships were set aflame, but once the line reached close to the Han tower-ships Zhu Yuanzhang's fleet was immediately pushed onto the defensive and started to take heavy losses. Both Zhu Yuanzhang and Xu Da's ships were lucky escapees from several attacks and the attack was broken off. Zhu Yuanzhang took his fleet into shallow water to avoid further battle with the large Han ships. He had lost the first engagement.

Xu Da sailed overnight to Nanjing with the unbattleworthy ships, and Zhu Yuanzhang had to resort to summary executions of several officers before he could force the remainder of his fleet into battle the next morning. He incurred more losses in the ensuing fight, but as the Han ships pulled closer together to bear down upon Zhu Yuanzhang's diminished line they became vulnerable to fireships. Fishing boats were packed with reeds and gunpowder, crewed by 'dare to die' sailors and dispatched with a strong following wind towards Chen Youliang's ships. Hundreds of Han ships went up in flames, and the battle reports speak of sixty thousand Han troops lost, along with two of Chen Youliang's brothers. The battered and burned fleets separated and there was no engagement the next day as each side licked its wounds.

The morning of 2 September saw the Han fleet advancing in an open formation and, although Zhu Yuanzhang's smaller ships could now penetrate the Han line and take advantage of their greater manoeuvrability, no decisive action could be achieved by either side. Word must also have come at some point that Hu Deji's army had relieved Nanchang as Zhu Yuanzhang's fleet began to sail out from the lake in the late evening, with the intention of preventing the Han fleet from entering the Yangzi.

Chen Youliang was now trapped in the lake. His still superior numbers of ships would count for nothing in the narrow channel where Zhu Yuanzhang was waiting for him. Plans were made and then rejected for abandoning all the ships and marching overland to escape the blockade, and then two of the Han's senior generals went over to Zhu Yuanzhang as morale deteriorated in the beleaguered fleet. Over the next month Zhu Yuanzhang sent a series of letters to his temperamental opponent, seeking to irritate him and force him to a rash attack.

Chen Youliang was eventually forced into an attack and it is clear that even at this juncture Zhu Yuanzhang was not assured of victory as his generals, with the exception of Chang Yuchun, had to be coerced into engaging the Han fleet on 30 October. Chen Youliang attempted to make for Wuchang but Zhu Yuanzhang was upstream of his fleet and soon numerous fireships were being carried by the current into the Han fleet, which then broke apart and fled down the river. Individual Han ships were pursued by packs of smaller enemy vessels, and troops garrisoned on the riverfront also added their catapult fire to that of Zhu Yuanzhang's ships as the Han fleet was decimated. The final blow to the Han's hopes in the battle came with the death of Chen Youliang, who was killed by arrows whilst crossing from one crippled vessel to another ship. Han morale collapsed and some fifty thousand men surrendered with their ships to Zhu Yuanzhang.

An infant son of Chen Youliang was rescued from the carnage and spirited away to be crowned in his father's place, but the Great Han would never again be a force in southern China. For Zhu Yuanzhang, empire now beckoned and his generals did not dare to defy him again.

Nanjing underwent a large-scale building programme to ready it for the role of imperial capital, including the construction of altars to earth and heaven, and in 1367 civil service examinations were begun there. Zhu Yuanzhang took a new title for himself in 1364. He had been acclaimed as the duke of Wu by his generals back in 1356, and naming himself as *wuwang*, the prince of Wu, may have been a simple response to the taking of the same title by Zhu Yuanzhang's only remaining rival within the rebels, Zhang Shicheng. However, the title also had ancient connotations dating from the Spring and Autumn Period (771 to 403 BC), and would have identified Zhu Yuanzhang as the main pillar of the state simply because the region at that time controlled by the Dragon-Phoenix Song court of Emperor Mingwang was Wu – the area today covered mostly by Jiangsu and Anhui province. The Wu princedom of Zhu Yuanzhang grew quickly and by May 1366 Jiangxi and Hunan were incorporated, as were Chen Youliang's old lands in the central Yangzi region and the newly reconquered Anfeng. The population under Zhu Yuanzhang's care had now tripled and his state was the strongest regional power in China, with armies twice the size of Zhang Shicheng's.

Zhu Yuanzhang's coldly political dealings with, and disposal of, his nephew Zhu Wencheng and very possibly Emperor Han Lin'er during this period indicate something of the character of the man making the transition from a successful warlord to a political leader vying for the great prize of 'all under heaven'. In February 1365 in Jiangxi province Zhu Yuanzhang appeared at the head of an army with his general Tang He and summarily dismissed Zhu Wencheng from his command of Nanchang and every other position that he had been granted by his uncle. Zhu Yuanzhang then accused his nephew of kidnap, rape, plotting to surrender to Zhang Shicheng and of an act of *lèse-majesté* as he had ornamented his home with dragons and phoenixes. Zhu Yuanzhang sought the death penalty for his nephew's supposed crimes but finally settled for exile after appeals from men from all ranks of the army. We can only conjecture about Zhu Yuanzhang's motivation for the attack on his nephew but it seems likely that it was fear of the younger man's popularity among the troops.

In early January 1367 Zhu Yuanzhang sent an escort to bring Han Lin'er across the Yangzi to meet with him in Nanjing. The boat carrying the party overturned and the emperor drowned. The accident may very well have been arranged by Zhu Yuanzhang, but even if it was not it came at a serendipitous moment. The new lunar year was due to begin on 31 January, and with the death of the Emperor Mingwang the prince of Wu was able to proclaim his own calendar for the year without reference to the rites of the now twice-demised Song Dynasty. Proclaiming the new calendar was a significant step towards announcing heaven's favouring of Zhu Yuanzhang with its mandate. Only Zhang Shicheng now stood in the way of Zhu Yuanzhang's imperial destiny.

Zhang Shicheng had formerly been a potential alternative to Zhu Yuanzhang as the man who would wrest China back from alien hands, even though, with the hindsight that six hundred years gives us, his failings are startlingly obvious. His 'resistance' to the Mongols dated from the 1350s, when he was active around Yangzhou in Jiangsu province. Ambushes of Yuan patrols and the murder of envoys sent to try to coax him into joining the Yuan body politic seem to have been the hallmarks of his warfare at this point. His control over the lucrative salt production industry in the Yangzi delta was enough to bring the Yuan chancellor, Toghto, into the field at the head of the last great army of the Yuan Dynasty. He besieged Zhang Shicheng at Kaoyu city, west of Nanchang in Jiangxi province in late 1354. Zhang

Shicheng was repeatedly defeated by Toghto as he tried to break the siege, and his lands were slipping away from him by January 1355. The poisoned chalice that was high office in the Yuan Dynasty then saved Zhang Shicheng. Toghto received an imperial order to turn over command of the army, to surrender all insignia of office and to submit to arrest and exile. Toghto's enemies in Beijing had engineered his fall by complaining to the emperor that he had held back from storming a city, and had instead chosen to starve it out. The emperor swallowed this nonsense and his courtiers' explanation that such sluggishness indicated that devious plans were being played by Toghto. Toghto's political enemies also saw to it that he was murdered during his exile in Yunnan. Zhang Shicheng was offered amnesty by the same men. Then, when further envoys were sent to confirm him in a government position, he returned to his old habit of murdering such emissaries, and went to war to regain everything he had lost to Toghto in the summer of 1355.

Zhang Shicheng then sent his brother, Zhang Shide, across the Yangzi, where he would be in almost direct competition with Zhu Yuanzhang for new territories to conquer. By March 1356 Zhang Shide had taken Suzhou. It would be Zhang Shicheng's capital for the next eleven years. Expansion of Zhang Shicheng's newly inaugurated kingdom of Great Zhou continued despite facing opposition from both Zhu Yuanzhang in Nanjing and local Yuan forces in Hangzhou. Zhang Shide even managed to capture Hangzhou for a brief period.

Zhang Shide was then captured by Zhu Yuanzhang during a battle north of Suzhou. A letter from the captured brother told Zhang Shicheng never to surrender to Zhu Yuanzhang and Zhang Shide then starved himself to death in prison. Zhang Shicheng then offered to enter service under the Yuan once more, presumably to improve his chances in a contest with Zhu Yuanzhang. The local Yuan governor almost refused his offer, as previous behaviour stood against placing any trust in Zhang Shicheng, but by 1357 he was named as a grand marshal, and made responsible for the shipment of rice from his prefectures north to Beijing. His power in the region remained undiminished. As we have seen, he was responsible for the killing of Liu Futong, the eastern Red Turban leader, in 1363, but then slipped away from his Yuan masters again in the autumn of the same year, and it was at this point that he declared himself prince of Wu and ceased all grain shipments from his lands to Beijing. He was now at the height of his power, with Hangzhou and much of Zhejiang under his control. He then began to take advantage of the conflict between Zhu Yuanzhang and Chen Youliang by undertaking a series of attacks against Zhu Yuanzhang's flank in Anhui. Zhang Shicheng's greatest error was that he failed to exploit Zhu Yuanzhang's difficulties fully in 1363, and when Zhu Yuanzhang had dispensed with Chen Youliang once and for all at the end of 1363 Zhang Shicheng was in terrible peril, for Zhu Yuanzhang had created a level of discipline and purpose among his men and commanders that the bandit king Zhang Shicheng had never achieved, and Zhu Yuanzhang's military reforms of 1364 bound his armies and generals even more tightly to his will.

Zhu Yuanzhang's oldest troops, the men he had personally led, were divided into seventeen guard regiments with barracks and lands near Nanjing. They were maintained as military muscle should anyone dare to contest Zhu Yuanzhang's rule from within the state. Soldiers with a shorter history of loyalty to the regime were deliberately relocated to reduce the risk of local rebellions forming as they had in the early 1360s in Zhejiang and Jiangxi. Men from Anhui and Zhejiang were sent to Hunan and Jiangxi, or were mixed in among older veteran regiments to serve in the coming invasion of Zhang Shicheng's lands. Field units were regulated as to their size, with each being made up of five battalions of one thousand men divided into ten companies of one hundred. New officer ranks were also created, and based not on historical or hereditary rank but entirely on the number of men commanded.

The two self-declared princes of Wu went to war in the autumn of 1364 and it was an entirely unequal fight. Zhu Yuanzhang had numbers on his side but also had personal discipline and intelligence far outweighing that of Zhang Shicheng. After the death of his brother, Zhang Shide, who was undoubtedly the brains of the family, Zhang Shicheng allowed indiscipline to spread through his army. Even his generals, three of whom were his brothers, regularly had to be coaxed into battle through bribes and gifts. These three brothers were nicknamed the 'claws and teeth of Wu' but often the positions they defended were abandoned without a fight during the war with Zhu Yuanzhang, and the home front was little better given that avarice and licentiousness were the hallmark of the late administration of Zhang Shicheng and his household. Oddly enough, during his early bandit years Zhang Shicheng had attracted a number of sober and responsible Confucian scholars to his court, but perhaps it was his contact with the Yuan that fatally corrupted him, and by 1363 his court was filled with artists and musicians rather than with counsellors and clerks.

Serious men of business and politics had been attracted instead to Zhu Yuanzhang's government in Nanjing. The Confucian fundamentals required for true imperial ambition were therefore in place at Zhu Yuanzhang's court long before he began his contest with Zhang Shicheng. His deft political touch and military success, in fact, also assured him of an almost unanimous following from former Red Turbans and he retained just enough religious revelation in his political philosophy to keep the more radical elements within the movement on board.

Zhang Shicheng initiated the inevitable war in November 1364. In March 1365 an attempt was made by his general, Li Bosheng, to advance in Zhejiang. Zhu Yuanzhang's nephew, Li Wenzhong, defeated this army when he led a single cavalry charge against it. Zhang Shicheng's spring offensive was a debacle, and later in 1365 Zhu Yuanzhang's generals went on the offensive. Zhu Yuanzhang's strategy seems to have been to take progressive rings of territory away from around Zhang Shicheng's capital of Suzhou, somewhat like slowly peeling an onion. The lands north of the Yangzi were first to submit, followed by those in central Zhejiang. With the reduction of the prefecture around Yangzhou in December 1365 Zhu Yuanzhang's army and fleet obtained access to the Grand Canal. An amphibious operation up the canal captured Kaoyu on 24 April 1366 and destroyed a major part of Zhang Shicheng's fleet. Many cities in north Jiangsu submitted to Xu Da, and the general then captured Anfeng from the Yuan in May of the same year. There was no response from the Yuan as Koko Temur, the quasi-independent warlord of eastern China, could not convince the petty Yuan lords of the region to follow him in attempting to repulse Xu Da's armies from the region. Zhu Yuanzhang was now able to make a journey of filial piety back to his home village near Anfeng. He dined with his distant family and honoured the graves of his parents.

Only the summer heat stopped the advance of Zhu Yuanzhang's armies and he returned to his cautious strategy of stripping Zhang Shicheng of his possessions layer by layer. Perhaps, after enduring the constant risk of a joint attack by Chen Youliang, Zhang Shicheng and the Yuan warlords for so many years, Zhu Yuanzhang worked hard now not to shake the princelings and loyalists of the Yuan into action by too rapid an advance on Zhang Shicheng's heartland.

Northern Jiangsu was attacked towards the end of 1366. Xu Da and Chang Yuchun besieged Huzhou, and Li Wenzhong brought his army to the gates of Hangzhou. Both cities surrendered peacefully before the end of December. Fang Guozhen, the 'pirate king', had offered tribute to Zhu Yuanzhang back when Chen Youliang had been defeated and killed, and had also agreed to surrender if Hangzhou was taken by Zhu Yuanzhang's armies. He now reneged on his promise, however, and refused to submit.

Suzhou was invested by Xu Da on 27 December. This finally stirred Zhang Shicheng into action and the city resisted under his animated and passionate leadership for some ten months. He personally led sorties against the besieging army despite the fact that it was well dug-in and battered at his capital's walls with an impressive array of artillery on a daily basis.

On 1 October 1367 Suzhou fell and Zhu Yuanzhang proclaimed a war of liberation against the Mongols. Zhang Shicheng's wives and concubines were voluntarily immolated in a tower, and Zhang Shicheng attempted to hang himself, but was cut down and sent to Nanjing. He successfully hanged himself there a few days later. With his death, the field of battle was cleared of domestic danger and Zhu Yuanzhang prepared to bring all of his forces to the battle against the foreign invaders. Another two hundred and fifty thousand men now joined his army from Zhang Shicheng's disbanded battalions and he had also acquired the revenues of China's richest prefecture to add to his war chest. Policies of 'divine clemency' instigated by Zhu Yuanzhang, but put into practice through the iron discipline of Xu Da, brought the twin rewards of rapid realignment of loyalty among military men and minimal disturbance in the agrarian economy.

Back in 1356, when Zhu Yuanzhang had conquered Nanjing, he had issued a proclamation declaring that his sole object was to expel the foreigners and to restore a national form of government:

> It is the birthright of the Chinese to govern foreign peoples and not of these latter to rule in China. It used to be said that the Yuan or Mongols, who came from the regions of the north, conquered our empire not so much by their courage and skill as by the aid of Heaven. And now it is sufficiently plain that Heaven itself wishes to deprive them of that empire, as some punishment for their crimes, and for not having acted according to the teaching of their forefathers. The time has now come to drive these foreigners out of China.

The Great Ming dynasty was officially inaugurated with the announcement of the new year calendar on 20 January 1368. Caesar-like, and as traditional imperial custom required, Zhu Yuanzhang had thrice rejected the pleading of his court officials to take the throne. Eventually, however, he accepted the fact that the Mandate of Heaven was shifting to a former peasant and homeless monk.

Following the Yuan emperor's killing of Bolod Temur, the Yuan court gave command of all military units in north China armies to Koko Temur, but, impressive as this sounds, it was an empty gesture. Koko Temur, despite his successes in the northeast, could not hope to control the warlords in the central north of the country. He certainly tried and, as we have seen, the distracting civil war that ensued allowed the issue of who was to control southern China to be played out with relatively little interference from what remained of the Yuan body politic.

Imperial orders to Koko Temur that he should desist from war with Chagan Temur and Bolod Temur's surviving lieutenants and attend to the 'southern question' were blithely ignored and, finally exasperated by Koko Temur's stubbornness, Toghan Temur deprived him of all his official titles and possessions in February 1368. The Yuan emperor then switched his support from his erstwhile ally to the northern warlords, but Koko Temur still remained the most powerful lord in northern China.

That Toghan Temur should act in such a dramatic fashion was not surprising. In November 1367 an army had begun a march from Nanjing to conquer north China. By January 1368, of course, this army was fighting under the banners of the newly established Ming Dynasty, and word of Zhu Yuanzhang's claiming of the Mandate of Heaven would have made for unpleasant and fearful reading at the Beijing court.

Zhu Yuanzhang's plans for the reduction of the north were similar to those that he had employed in dismembering Zhang Shicheng's Wu state. Shandong was slated for conquest first, then Hunan and Beijing. Securing the Tong pass during these phases would then allow for the army's entry into Shanxi and Shaanxi. Xu Da and Chang Yuchun were given two hundred and fifty thousand men for the campaign.

Resistance from the northern warlords was fierce, but their armies could be fought piecemeal as they refused to unite. By March 1368 Shandong was conquered. Hunan was next, and Kaifeng endured a short siege before submitting on 16 April. Koko Temur took the field but was heavily defeated near Luoyang. Luoyang was the second of the old northern Song capitals to be reclaimed by a Chinese dynasty.

The Tong pass was captured in mid-May, and Zhu Yuanzhang consulted with his generals at Kaifeng over the capture of Beijing. The Ming army then halted their war and sowed and gathered a harvest. They were not like the Mongols who had entered China at the beginning of the thirteenth century and who fought all year, but then neither were the Mongols of the fourteenth century, and no counterattack came from the Yuan.

In August the Ming crossed the Yellow River. Xu Da led his army through Beijing's gates on 20 September, and again an approach of clemency was taken, with a complete absence of looting, rape or murder. The peaceful conquest stood completely at odds with the city's plight during the Mongol sack of 1215. Zhu Yuanzhang changed the city's name to Beiping or 'northern peace' in reference to the fact that the city had been conquered by an army from the south.[18] Many of the buildings of the city of Qubilai were deliberately demolished. The Yuan emperor fled, along with his heir, Ayushiridara, to Mongolia but China would not be free of the remains of the Mongol dynasty or of the threat of a counterstrike from the steppes for a number of years yet. Other dangers in the south and east had by this time been eliminated, however.

Just as the northern expedition had set out, another army had marched into Fujian, and the fleet had also been dispatched to assist in the province's reduction. Guangdong was also assaulted by the Ming armada. Fuzhou fell on 18 January 1368 and the petty warlords of Fujian, leftovers of the 1350s, surrendered one by one. Canton, a Yuan outpost in Guangdong, submitted on 18 April. Mopping up continued in Guangxi province until July.

Fang Guozhen was also brought to heel. He was pincered between an advancing army and Zhu Yuanzhang's fleet. He sailed from Ningbo upon the city's fall but had surrendered by December. Loose ends were being tied up all over, but even though the Ming emperor was undisputedly the ruler of China, much of the country was still to be mastered.

The conquest of Sichuan, and the reduction of the Xia kingdom – the breakaway Red Turban state established there by Ming Yuzhen – took place between 1370 and 1371. Ming Yuzhen had written to Zhu Yuanzhang after the defeat of Chen Youliang in 1363, offering an alliance, but no reply had been received. Zhu Yuanzhang probably felt that the little state was far enough away and isolated enough to be ignored, and in many ways the kingdom of Xia simply atrophied in the 1360s. As discussed earlier, the area was relatively peaceful and Ming Yuzhen ruled quietly until his death, probably by poisoning, in 1366. His young son succeeded to the throne under the tutelage of the dowager empress, but the warlordism that had torn the Yuan state apart then infected the Xia kingdom. By the end of the 1360s it was a collection of petty feudal estates under only nominal control from the Xia court.

The Ming saw their opportunity to conquer the now fractured Xia kingdom in 1370. A series of victories against the Mongols in Shanxi and Shaanxi had opened up a northern approach into the hard to conquer province. Generous terms for surrender were sent to the Xia court but now it was Zhu Yuanzhang's turn to be kept waiting for a reply. He did not wait long. Xiangyang was the main staging post for supplying the Ming army that invaded Sichuan from the north and for the fleet, which followed the same route that Ming Yuzhen's ships had taken in 1357 when they had wrested control of the province from the Mongols.

Rapid progress was made in the north, but the bulk of the forces available to the Xia court had been placed in the Yangzi gorges. Strength in numbers, added to the natural defences of the region and the artifice of Xia engineers, who placed catapults on suspension bridges above the river from where they could fire down upon the advancing ships, was enough to halt the Ming fleet's progress. It was only when accurate cannon fire had cleared the gorges of the Xia's catapults in the sky that progress could be made. The Xia then attempted to redeploy forces to the north but the war was already lost. Hanzhou fell in the north, leaving the major city of Chengdu open to assault, and the Ming Yangzi fleet reached Chongqing on 3 August. The Xia emperor was treated with respect and confined in Nanjing, and Sichuan was incorporated into the Ming empire.

Going back a little in time, we need now to look at how the Mongols were expelled from Shanxi and Shaanxi and how the Ming, like so many dynasties before it, took armies into the Mongolian steppe in an attempt to take China's timeless war with the barbarian away from its own fields and cities.

The invasion of Shanxi and Shaanxi was the first military action undertaken by the Ming after the fall of Beijing. The reduction of these two provinces was important in its own right for the ridding of the last vestiges of Mongol rule from 'China proper', but it would also give access to a northern invasion route into Sichuan, as noted above, and to the Hexi Zoulang, literally the 'west river corridor', commonly denoted as the 'Gansu corridor'. The Hexi Zoulang was a double-ended spear that pointed into the heart of China and also into Central Asia and held a series of oases on which any invading army coming from Mongolia would be dependent. Possession of it meant that the Ming could stab into their enemy's lands, but if the Mongols kept control of it the risk of invasion, or at least large-scale raids into the Wei River valley and Yellow River plains, would be ever present.

Chang Yuchun advanced through Hubei whilst generals Feng Sheng and Tang He pushed into Shanxi from the south. Then in January 1369 Xu Da became the central prong of the campaign and invaded Shanxi from the east. Taiyuan fell to the Ming armies in March and now they were fighting in the cradle of Chinese civilisation, where the first dynasty of China, the Xia, had been formed. By April Mongol resistance was crumbling and the Ming armies entered the Wei valley. Once more Mongol petty lords had refused to combine forces and to submit to being led by Koko Temur, who still retained a large army. Koko Temur retreated to northern Gansu, and the warlords of Shaanxi were, one by one, eliminated by Xu Da.

The Ming conquests of 1369 brought the lands beyond the line of fortifications that would later become the Great Wall within striking distance, and the war was taken to Toghan Temur's refugee court by Li Wenzhong and Feng Sheng in the spring of 1370. Xu Da and Tang He took on the arguably greater challenge of dislodging Koko Temur from Gansu, from where he had been raiding the new Ming frontier over the winter.

Li Wenzhong routed a large Mongol force and pushed on for Yingchang, where on 23 May 1370 the last Yuan emperor, Toghan Temur, died. Li Wenzhong moved with incredible speed and stormed into Yingchang on 10 June. Ayushiridara escaped, but some fifty thousand Mongol troopers were captured. With this one victory Li Wenzhong secured Ming dominance in Neimenguo or Inner Mongolia for the next thirty years and secured China's borders more firmly than the Great Wall ever could.

Xu Da matched Li Wenzhong's lightning speed by his diligence in pursuing the elusive Koko Temur. His army was engaged by Koko Temur on 3 May in eastern Gansu. The Mongol army was so large that Xu Da was forced to take up a defensive position and his men dug in. Koko Temur attacked and was able to turn the southwest end of the Ming line. Outraged by this and by the ineffectual response of General Hu Deji to the panic among his men, Xu Da put the general in chains and took personal command of the southwest. The day was saved, and the next day Xu Da led an attack that took the lives of some eighty-six thousand Mongols and saw Koko Temur fleeing the field in disarray.

The Hexi Zoulang was secured by Xu Da's great victory. The spear, at least for now, pointed not into China's heart but into the steppes of the barbarians. Zhu Yuanzhang had taken a throne name, as was customary, and now as Emperor Hongwu of the 'Brilliant' Ming Dynasty he ennobled and granted hereditary titles to thirty-four of the generals who, with him, had defeated the Mongols. At times it had looked to be an impossible task. Just as the Song had fought with tenacity and with every weapon that their state had in their desperate war to defend China and its civilisation, Zhu Yuanzhang and his companions had shown bravery and perseverance beyond limit during their contest. They were now finally rewarded with the guardianship of, and mandate to rule over, all that lay under heaven.

Epilogue

A Poisoned Wound?

China after the Expulsion of the Mongols

Anyone advocating running away should be decapitated. The capital is a central symbol of the state. If the central government pulls out from the capital, it will spell the end of the state. Have we forgotten the fate of the Song Dynasty?

Traditionally attributed to Yu Qian, Ming vice-minister for war, defending Beijing after the capture of the Ming emperor by Oirat Mongols in 1449

A story is commonly recounted from the Spring and Autumn Period of Chinese history. The son of a duke, whilst riding into the opposing army's line aboard his war chariot, found himself face to face with an enemy charioteer, who shot his crossbow at the noble duke's son. The crossbow bolt missed but the enemy charioteer reloaded with skill and alacrity and was ready to shoot again almost immediately. The duke's son calmly said, 'If you do not give me my turn, you are a base fellow.' His enemy consequently waited for the duke's son to raise his bow and take his shot and was killed. The truth of such a tale is hard to countenance but it is the product of a culture in which, even if such things did not really occur, it was felt that they *should*. Contrasting such ideals with those of Chinggis Khan is revealing. Hackneyed though it is, the quote traditionally attributed to Chinggis, 'the greatest happiness is to scatter your enemy, to drive him before you, to see his cities reduced to ashes, to see those who love him shrouded in tears, and to gather into your bosom his wives and daughters,' indicates a nihilism beyond the comprehension of the men who made China what it was before the Mongol invasion. China was, and is, not simply a country: it is a complex set of ideas, ideals and principles, as is any other cultured and sophisticated civilisation. The borders of China may change, modes of living may change, but the code of *wenming*, which is commonly and incorrectly translated simply as 'civilisation' is the very essence of China. A far more accurate definition of *wenming* is that it is the presence of a high level of ethics and the gentleness of a people. It is expressed in its most easy to understand form in Confucianism.

Though men might go to war for decades to obtain possession of the territory of China, each conquering dynasty, however driven by personal ambition or egotistical it might be, generally came to power with the desire to maintain such ideals and to become part of the pattern of *zhongguo wenming* or 'Chinese civilisation'. The Mongols were perhaps no different in the end, even though they initially came – as they came into another great world culture of the time, Islam – antagonistic to the religion and values of China, and looked only to plunder and destroy. The fact that they were held in check by the Song for so long on the Yangzi, allowing time for their fragile and immature polity to break apart, meant that they were forced to become Sinicised in order to be able to complete the conquest of China and for the Yuan emperor to use the resources of China in his battles for the Mongol homeland. Their rule was moderated a little at least by this fact, but the psychological scars left by them on the Middle Kingdom lasted far longer than their dynasty managed to endure.

The new Ming emperor, Hongwu, was certainly a product of the violent landscape of Yuan China but was fortunately also informed by the resistant undercurrent of *wenming* that had been nurtured by Song and had survived in southern China through the fond memory that the *nanren* held for that dynasty. That these two conflicting influences lay within Hongwu seems evident, as the emperor wrote a commentary on Laozi's *Dao De Jing* in 1375, and yet in the same year he executed hundreds of officials for slovenly clerical methods and had one of his ministers imprisoned and starved to death for questioning his judgement.

Under Hongwu China did emerge from the militarised society it had become under the Yuan, despite the continuing threat of a further irruption of barbarians and a crushing defeat inflicted by Koko Temur on General Xu Da's army in 1372 in the deserts beyond Ming China's northern border. Emperor Hongwu was therefore forced to maintain a permanent garrison on the Mongolian frontier, but still managed to bring his armies into a peacetime mode, and his officers began to give up their civil offices to the growing bureaucracy.

The Ming's requirement for a large military to meet the continuing threat of the Mongols that had to be maintained by the state was essentially the same problem that the Song had experienced. The Song 'solved' it by simply maintaining a large standing army with the attendant economic difficulties this entailed, but the Yuan had feudalised the army into a hereditary class with attached lands that would support the aristocrats of the army in peace and in wartime. The Song approach was a complex and modern one; the Yuan approach was primitive and medieval. The damage done to China's infrastructure and economy by the long Mongol war and the way that Zhu Yuanzhang's army was built step by step made the feudal approach the only possible option for the Ming. China was therefore effectively placed very firmly back in the Middle Ages from the demise of the Song until the end of the Qing Dynasty in 1911. I have written elsewhere of how the Mongol invasions and the assaults of the Crusaders on the Middle East caused a psychological inversion in that entire region and its society, and how that region's decline and the rise of the West can be marked from the end of the thirteenth century.[1] The same sad trend can also be seen in China from the beginning of the Mongol period. The Ming's necessary embracing of the feudal system, the economic miasma created by the Mongols, and the turning in upon itself that China's painful experience with the foreign invaders caused, effectively demodernised China. It is no coincidence that the Ming worked hard to seal off the world beyond their Great Wall and to build it ever stronger in the post-Mongol period,[2] just as the Mamluks of Egypt and Syria desolated Syria's coast in an attempt to prevent any invader from the West from ever again entering their lands from the Mediterranean.

Both the Ming and the Mamluks incurred self-inflicted wounds by their efforts to seclude their states from the rest of the world, and both effectively missed out on modernity. That, perhaps, was the Mongols' greatest and most poisonous legacy to China. China could very likely have produced an industrial revolution centuries before Great Britain did,[3] but any hope of that was effectively destroyed by the Mongol invasion and by the regressive Yuan Dynasty. As noted above, the Yuan state itself showed none of the modernist tendencies of the Song and furthermore destroyed the fiscal basis of the state. Emperor Hongwu's reputation for prudence, economy and frugality was a direct reaction to this and the insurrections that it had brought about. He could not, however, risk large-scale demobilisation of the huge and expensive Ming army, even if his northern enemies had faded away, for fear of the social chaos such a move would cause, and was therefore forced to embrace a feudal system. He also shunned the modernising trend of trade, possibly because of his own peasant background, but also because such a move would have required extensive contact for the Chinese with foreigners, and foreigners, under the Yuan, had caused enormous damage to China.

Emperor Hongwu had begun civil service examinations again by 1370, and had even modernised the system, with political analysis being required as an academic discipline along with archery, horsemanship, calligraphy, arithmetic and examinations on jurisprudence and the law. This was short-lived, though, and in 1373 the system was abolished in favour of personal appointments. This seems characteristic of the Ming Dynasty's ongoing suspicion of change, progress and also science. The wish for China to return to an idealised bucolic and certainly illusory state that the Ming believed had existed before the long Mongol war even drove the dynasty to discard the one positive legacy of the Yuan, though it was in truth a gift of the Song. The Ming inherited a navy that could control the trade of the South China Sea and beyond. The opportunity to dominate Asian maritime trade was rejected, however, by China's new masters after the extensive journeys and then abrupt recall of Admiral Zheng He in the first third of the fifteenth century. This took place just as Europeans were beginning to master the compass and portolan charts, and the Ming's abandonment of active sea trade allowed the Portuguese, Dutch and English to create a new world trade and geopolitical system. The West's global hegemony of the last five hundred years is directly related to China turning in on itself in the early fifteenth century.

The physical damage incurred during China's long Mongol war is probably incalculable, and the sheer volume of death and destruction is almost too horrific even to contemplate. Moreover, the seemingly indelible stain it left upon Chinese society and Chinese consciousness blighted the country's growth for the next five hundred years and changed the course of Asian and world history.

Notes

Introduction

1 From a letter of Engels to Nikolai Danielson, 24 February 1893, in K. Marx and F. Engels, *Correspondence, 1846–1895*, edited by D. Torr, New York: International Publishers, 1935, p. 510.
2 In B. Croce, *La Storia Come Pensiero e Come Azione*, Naples: Bibliopolis, 1938/2002, p. 42.
3 T. Cleary, *Mastering the 'Art of War': Zhuge Liang's and Liu Ji's Commentaries on the Classic by Sun Tzu*, Boston, MA: Shambhala Dragon Editions, 1990.
4 See Boccaccio's *Decameron*, edited by V. Branca, 2 vols, Turin: Einaudi, 1992, 'Prima Giornata, Introduzione'.
5 'Florio's translation' can most easily be found at the Brown University Internet Decameron Project, www.brown.edu.
6 J. Saunders, 'The Nomad as Empire-Builder: A Comparison of the Arab and Mongol Conquests', in G. W. Rice (ed.), *Muslims and Mongols: Essays on Medieval Asia*, Christchurch, NZ: University of Canterbury Press, 1977, p. 48.
7 J. Fletcher, 'The Mongols: Ecological and Social Perspectives', *Harvard Journal of Asiatic Studies*, vol. 46, no. 1, 1986, pp. 11–50; reprinted in J. Fletcher, *Studies on Chinese and Islamic Inner Asia*, edited by Beatrice F. Manz, Aldershot, Ashgate, 1995.

Chapter One

1 I use the term 'barbarian' extremely cautiously here. Certainly there was a certain snobbery among Chinese court officials about the Turco-Mongolic tribes, and my use of the term reflects that, but what we know of these tribes also indicates a large degree of influence by Chinese civilisation on the structure of their government and culture, and this extended to the

official titles they adapted, such as the Kitan title for general, *xinkun*, from the Chinese *jiangjun*. The Mongols trumped this with their adaption of the Chinese for king, *wang*, as *ong*. Of course, to Chinese villagers of the eighth century whose livestock was being plundered and whose family members were taken as slaves, Turco-Mongolian warriors would certainly have appeared fairly barbarous.

See *Cambridge History of China, Volume 6: Alien Regimes and Border States, 907–1368*, edited by H. Franke and D. Twitchett, Cambridge: Cambridge University Press, 1994, pp. 12–16.

2 See S. Jagchid, 'The Kitans and their Cities', *Central Asiatic Journal*, no. 25, 1981, pp. 70–88. The relocation of artisans seems to have been a major preoccupation of Central Asian conquerors. The Mongols, even during campaigns that were highly destructive, shied away from the slaughter of artisans who could then be transplanted to centres where their expertise was required. The transmission of medical thinking, art, agronomy and astronomy from China to Iran that took place under the *Pax Mongolica* is described in fine detail in T. Allsen, *Culture and Conquest in Mongol Eurasia*, Cambridge: Cambridge University Press, 2001. The process as described by Allsen evolved and became formalised under the Mongols' transcontinental empire, with extensive sharing of cultural resources, personnel and literature between the Ilkhanate of Persia and Yuan China.

The plundering campaigns of Timur Leng and his descendants of the late fourteenth and early fifteenth century also included forced relocations of artisans that led to both the magnificent Timurid architecture of Samarqand and the miniature-painting schools of Herat and Bukhara. Given Saunders's verdict on Timur Leng that he was, 'till the advent of Hitler . . . the supreme example of soulless and unproductive militarism', it is perhaps as well to remember that 'the *Pax* and the Yoke were not mutually exclusive'. See Allsen, p. 5, and J. Saunders, *The History of the Mongol Conquests*, London: Routledge & Kegan Paul, 1971, p. 174.

3 Of course the khan could not possibly have known what he was getting into, but given that by his actions Chinggis's descendants were handed another half-century of war in China after his death, Central Asia would slip from the grasp of those who eventually conquered China and the Yuan Dynasty was gone from China by 1370, the return on investment in terms of men and materiel expended does not appear to be a good one. Perhaps Timothy May is close to the truth when he writes: 'I am not convinced that Chinggis Khan even wanted an empire, but would have been quite content ruling Mongolia.' See T. May, *The Mongol Conquests in World History*, London: Reaktion, 2012, p. 22.

4 P. Lorge, *War, Politics and Society in Early Modern China. 900–1795*, New York: Routledge, 2005, p. 13.

5 See C. Wang, 'Towards Defining a Chinese Heroism', *Journal of the American Oriental Society*, vol. 95, no. 1, 1975, pp. 25–35.
6 See a masterly account of the Song's attempt to 'isolate [the army's] function to that of a static, reliable instrument of dynastic stability', in Lorge, pp. 1–17.
7 See D. McMullen, 'The Cult of Ch'i T'ai-kung and T'ang Attitudes to the Military', *Tang Studies*, no. 7, 1989, p. 62.
8 See H. Williamson, *Wang An Shih: Chinese Statesman and Educationalist of the Sung Dynasty*, London: Arthur Probsthain, 1935, pp. 186–7.
9 See Y. Lien-sheng, 'Numbers and Units in Chinese Economic History', in Y. Lien-Sheng, *Studies in Chinese Institutional History*, Cambridge, MA: Harvard University Press, 1961, p. 80.
10 The situation faced by Gaozong seems entirely similar to that faced by the Dauphin following King John II of France's capture by the Black Prince at Poitiers. King John's long captivity and the Dauphin's subsequent conduct in the war are quite illuminating when we consider Gaozong's policy problems. See J. Sumption, *The Hundred Years War, Volume 2: Trial by Fire*, London: Faber and Faber, 1991, chapter 10.
11 See R. Hartwell, 'A Revolution in the Chinese Iron and Coal Industries during the Northern Sung, 960–1126 AD', *Journal of Asian Studies*, vol. 21, 1962, pp. 153–62.
12 Chengda Fan, *Stone Lake: The Poetry of Fan Chengda 1126–1193*, translated by J. Schmidt and P. Hannan, edited by D. Twitchett, Cambridge: Cambridge University Press, 1992. Qin Hui was the minister who brought about Yue Fei's fall, partly for fear of Yue Fei jeopardising the peace with Jin but also for fear of Yue Fei's increasing influence over the army and the number of officers and soldiers who were personally devoted to him. The poetic sources commonly say that Yue Fei was hanged but it is more likely that he was poisoned.
13 See J. Waterson, *The Knights of Islam: The Wars of the Mamluks*, London: Greenhill Books, 2007, pp. 242 and 259.
14 The minister of the right generally had precedence over the minister of the left.
15 See W. Gong, 'The Reign of Hsaio-tsung (1162–89)', in *Cambridge History of China, Volume 5, Part 1: The Sung Dynasty and its Precursors, 907–1279*, edited by D. Twitchett and P. Smith, Cambridge, Cambridge University Press, 2009, pp. 722–3.
16 Gong, p. 730.
17 See R. Davis, 'The Reigns of Kuang-sung (1189–94) and Ning-tsung (1194–1224)', in *Cambridge History of China, Volume 5, Part 1*, pp. 756–838.
18 See Davis, 'The Reigns of Kuang-sung (1189–94) and Ning-tsung (1194–1224)', p. 774.

19 Lorge, p. 58.
20 In S. Griffith, 'Introduction', in Sun Tzu, *The Art of War*, translated by S. Griffith, Oxford: Oxford University Press, 1963, pp. 1–56
21 See Davis, 'The Reigns of Kuang-sung (1189–94) and Ning-tsung (1194–1224)', p. 812.

Chapter Two

1 One li is roughly equivalent to half a kilometre
2 The similar attitude of the Song court when Jin was later being devoured by the Mongol crocodile and of the English and French courts when eastern Europe was being scourged by the Mongols are both noteworthy. See R. Dunnel, 'The Hsi Hsia', in *Cambridge History of China, Volume 6*, pp. 154–214; and J. Waterson, *The Ismaili Assassins: A History of Medieval Murder*, London: Frontline Books, 2008, p. 143.
3 There would doubtless have been numerous other tribal allegiances to be found within Chinggis's army. See D. Morgan, *The Mongols*, 2nd edn, London: Blackwell, 2007, pp. 76–9 for an erudite and entertaining deconstruction of the difficulties of identifying what exactly constituted a 'horde'.
4 John of Piano Carpini, in M. Komroff (ed.), *The Contemporaries of Marco Polo: Consisting of the Travel Records to the Eastern Parts of the World of William of Rubruck (1253–1255); The Journey of John of Piano de Carpini (1245–1247) and the Journey of Friar Odoric (1318–1350)*, New York: Boni and Liveright, 1928, p. 41.
5 The only warriors who consistently succeeded against the Mongols were the Mamluks, Turkish warriors and sultans of Egypt and Syria. They retained all that was impressive in steppe soldiery and outdid the Mongols through a disciplined approach to warfare learned in the hippodromes of Cairo and Damascus. For their remarkable achievements and the martial science and art that made these possible see Waterson, *The Knights of Islam*, chapters 5 to 7.
6 For more on Mongol rations see J. Smith, 'Mongol Campaign Rations: Milk, Marmots and Blood?', *Journal of Turkish Studies*, vol. 8, 1984, pp. 223–8.
7 For a discussion of the equipment of the average Mongol warrior and the advantage that Chinggis Khan's troopers had over their contemporaries see M. Rossabi, 'All the Khan's Horses', *Natural History*, October 1994, pp. 48–57.
8 See D. Nicolle, *Medieval Warfare Source Book: Warfare in Western Christendom*, Leicester: Brockhampton Press, 1995, p. 136.

9 The Jurchen, of course, 'returned' from Manchuria to conquer all of China and form the Qing Dynasty in 1644. The 'Forbidden City' – essentially forbidden to Han Chinese – and the forcing of the native male population of China to wear their hair as 'queues' by the Qing give some indication of what the Jin's attitude to the Han Chinese would have been.
10 See T. May, *The Mongol Art of War*, London: Frontline Books, 2007, p. 38.
11 D. Graff, *Medieval Chinese Warfare, 300–900*, New York: Routledge, 2002, p. 5.
12 See Waterson, *The Ismaili Assassins*, p. 94.
13 The war had begun after Turks of the shah's army had plundered Mongol merchants and then Chinggis's envoy had been murdered by the shah's governor at Utrar, a city on the border between the two states. For the khan's terrible revenge see Waterson, *The Ismaili Assassins*, pp. 133–9.
14 The degree of influence of Chinese institutions on the Mongols before Chinggis is controversial. Song sources name the Mongols as a *guo* or state as early as 1147, when the Jin bestowed an imperial title on a Mongol who may or may not have been the grandfather of Chinggis. Song writers also recorded that Chinggis, before he became universal khan, attended the Jin court as a vassal. Some historians have refuted this and follow the line laid down in the 'Secret History of the Mongols', the single significant native Mongolian account of Chinggis Khan that the khan was 'purely' a steppe warrior and uncontaminated by the effete courts of China, but it is hard to believe that the Song writers of the twelfth century had any interest other than that of recording facts and that the authors of the 'Secret History' had any interest other than producing an encomium for the greatest Mongol ever known.
15 The tube was reloadable and its propellant was willow wood charcoal, iron filings, powdered porcelain and sulphur, and it was ignited with glowing embers carried in a small tin. See *Cambridge History of China, Volume 6*, p. 264.
16 Traditionally the messages are said to have read, 'If the Jin is conquered now, the next target will be the Song. An alliance between us will be in the interest of our two countries.' Myopic politics and posturing seem to have been the consistent hallmark of all of the Mongols' enemies, with the possible exception of the Crusaders of Acre, who allowed the Mamluk army to pass unhindered through their lands prior to its victory over the army of Hulegu Khan at Ain Jalut in 1260. Ironically, the Crusaders' eventual nemesis turned out not to be the Mongols but the Mamluk sultans they had assisted by this deed. See Waterson, *The Knights of Islam*, pp. 217–20 and P. Jackson, 'The Crisis in the Holy Land in 1260', *English Historical Review*, vol. 45, no. 376, 1980, pp. 481–513.
17 May, *Mongol Art of War*, p. 135.

Chapter Three

1 Ho Yenxi was commenting on Sunzi's maxim: 'In war, then, let your great object be victory, not lengthy campaigns'. See L. Giles (trans.), *Sun Tzu on the Art of War: The Oldest Military Treatise in the World*, London: British Museum, 1910, book 2. The work of Sunzi is only one of a long list of the definitive versions of Chinese classics created during the Song Dynasty that we read today.
2 See Lorge, p. 73.
3 See Waterson, *The Knights of Islam*, pp. 67–85.
4 See C. Peterson, 'First Sung Reactions to the Mongol Invasion of the North, 1211–1217', in John W. Haeger (ed.), *Crisis and Prosperity in Sung China*, Tucson, AZ: University of Arizona Press, 1975, p. 248.
5 Mongol integrity was certainly not entirely trusted by contemporaries, including the popes who attempted to convert them to Catholicism and to negotiate with them for an alliance against Islam. William of Rubruck, who spent a great deal of time at Qaraqorum, said of them: 'When they make peace with any one, it is only to destroy them'. See Komroff, p. 170.
6 Every society has struggled with the concept of 'just war' and whether it is a necessity, and it seems evident that no society can survive a war, even if it is victorious, without seeking an ethical argument for undertaking it. I would suggest that in purely practical terms the recriminations that occur once a state engages voluntarily in a war of aggression that turns into a long one are danger enough that any such undertaking should be avoided. See C. Guthrie and M. Quinlan, *The Just War Tradition: Ethics in Modern Warfare*, London: Bloomsbury, 2007, pp. 1 and 42.
7 I am reluctant to apply the term 'revolution' to the changes that gunpowder brought to China because these changes were incremental and, more importantly, even as late as the Qing Dynasty (1644–1912) gunpowder technology did not change the military establishment in the way that it had in the West at least a century before. It reinforced inertia in the military society rather than revolutionising it. See Lorge, p. 6.
8 See D. McCurley, '"Juedixi": An Entertainment of War in Early China', *Asian Theatre Journal*, vol. 22, no. 1, 2005, pp. 87–106.
9 C. Peers, *Imperial Chinese Armies (2): 590–1260 AD*, London: Osprey, 1996, p. 35.
10 From Graff, p. 194.
11 Wu Qi in M. Lewis, *Sanctioned Violence in Early China*, New York: SUNY Press, 1990, p. 114.
12 The bureaucracy was deliberately over-recruited both to ensure that a large number of talented individuals were available for the complex processes of government and also to provide the largest possible variety

of opinion within the higher echelons of government. See W. Lo, *An Introduction to the Civil Service of Sung China, with Emphasis on its Personnel Administration*, Honolulu: University Of Hawaii Press, 1987, chapters 1 and 2.

13 Needless to say the Song Dynasty's pursuit of policies contrary to their self-interest does not stand as a sole instance of 'wooden-headedness'. Examples abound: see B. Tuchman, *The March of Folly: From Troy to Vietnam*, New York: Ballantine Books, 1985.

14 There is some uncertainty over the population of Yuan China and subsequently how large China's population drop was in this period, but it was certainly precipitous. The Yuan government tried very hard to register subjects in order to tax them but the administrative machinery responsible for the census was notably inefficient. The most 'accurate' censuses from the reign of Qubilai give a figure of about sixty million people and this does concur approximately with the much more exacting census undertaken by the Ming in 1393. The northern Song government census of 1109 gave the state's population as one hundred million and the combined registered populations of Jin and southern Song in 1215 has been calculated to have been between one hundred and ten and one hundred and twenty million. The Yuan census of 1290 shows that the greatest losses occurred in the north China plain. The numbers for Shandong and Hubei are particularly distressing: these two areas were the theatre for most of the Jin-Mongol confrontation and then suffered even after the Mongols had won the war, as both areas slipped into warlordism. Neither region recovered in terms of its population count until the late sixteenth century, and the population of the entire country seems to have been reduced by about half.

'One must assume that there was a catastrophic reduction in China's population between 1200 and 1400, the most extreme in the history of China . . . the net loss from warfare and calamity plus the forestalled replacement attributable to long decades of hardship presents itself as the inescapable conclusion. Although the quantitative data have so far failed to resolve the riddles of the Yuan period's population history, fortunately the qualitative information allows historians to come to more satisfying, though by no means undisputed, conclusions about the life of Chinese society under Mongolian rule.' See *Cambridge History of China, Volume 6*, pp. 619–22.

15 See Morgan, pp. 72 and 89.

16 We have no reliable record of the arguments that were made in Qaraqorum for genocide or rapine in northern China, but further west and later in the Iranian Ilkhanate the Mongol's Persian minister Rashid al-Din had to work very hard to advance the argument that 'the exchequer of income is the peasants themselves, since the treasury is filled by their good efforts.'

Even though Ilkhan Ghazan was swayed by this argument he still appealed very much to his followers' self-interest rather than their humanity when he argued, 'I am not protecting the Persian peasantry. If it is expedient, then let me pillage and rob them all. But you must consider, if you commit extortion against the peasants, take their oxen and seed, and cause their crops to be consumed – what will you do in the future?' See Morgan, pp. 167–71.

17 See H. Franke, 'Siege and Defense of Towns in Medieval China', in F. Kierman and J. Fairbank (eds), *Chinese Ways in Warfare*, Cambridge, MA: Harvard University Press, 1974, pp. 151–201.

18 See J. Needham and R. Yates, *Science and Civilization in China, Volume 5: Chemistry and Chemical Technology, Part 6: Military Technology: Missiles*, Cambridge: Cambridge University Press, 1994, p. 105.

19 The traction trebuchet was invented by the Chinese sometime before the fourth century BC. The most powerful of these, with a two-hundred-and-fifty-man pulling crew, was capable of throwing a projectile of about 60 kilograms more than 75 metres. Many historians have suggested that the revolutionary counterweight trebuchet came to China first with the Mongols from Iran, along with its attendant Persian engineers in 1272, but there is considerable evidence for a similar device being used by the Jin against the Mongols at Luoyang in 1232. See P. Chevedden, 'The Invention of the Counterweight Trebuchet: A Study in Cultural Diffusion', *Dumbarton Oaks Papers*, vol. 54, 2000, pp. 71–116.

20 See L. Carrington-Goodrich and F. Chia-sheng, 'The Early Development of Firearms in China', *Isis*, vol. 36, no. 2, 1946, pp. 114–23. The Chinese love affair with pyrotechnics is summed up in the 1403 poem of Chang Xian: 'The black dragon lays eggs big as a peck. Crack goes the egg, the dragon soars away, the spirit of thunder departs. First it leaps up; light follows; the lightning flash reddens; The thunderbolt makes a single burst, and the earth is cloven in twain.'

21 See May, *Mongol Art of War*, p. 79.

22 The Mongol population was indeed small, but much of the 'Mongol' forces were by this point Chinese and Central Asian conscripts. The Mongols forced military service upon all conquered peoples and every household had to give up at least one male to conscription.

23 The Mongols had just inflicted a crushing defeat on the cream of the Polish nobility's armies and the Teutonic Knights at the Battle of Liegnitz. The whole of central Europe lay open to them but the Mongols retired from their march on Vienna and all offensive operations ceased. Upon the death of every khan all roads were closed to trade and wars stopped. This undoubtedly saved Europe from further Mongol incursions as I am certain that the Rhine and the western Europeans would have offered a lot less resistance to the Mongols than the Yangzi and the Song did.

24 The patrimonial share-out or division of political power upon Chinggis Khan's death was perhaps to blame for the Toluids' coup. They were essentially forced to undertake the action because when the empire was still expanding no one royal line from within could take a hold of the whole. The large-scale war that the Mongols had taken on against Song China required the either voluntary or involuntary submission of all the family branches, and their military resources, to the great khan. In Ogedei's reign this took the form of encroachments into the lands of his siblings both to reduce their territory and powerbase and to impel their followers to change their allegiance. In the 1230s Ogedei's campaign was chiefly directed at the 'sisters' of the Chinggisid line and culminated in the autumn of 1237 with the mass rape of four thousand Oirat Mongol girls. The chronicles of Juvaini and Rashid al-Din both describe how the mass rape was a punishment placed upon the Oirat for refusing to send girls to the khan's harem. Weatherford views this as a far wider assault on the lineage and holdings of Chingghis Khan's daughters and an attempt to extinguish the line of his deceased sister Checheyigen and for Ogedei to impose 'his own authority over her lands, her people, and her family'. See J. Weatherford, *The Secret History of the Mongol Queens*, New York: Crown, 2010, chapter 5. The accounts are found in the Persian chronicles of Rashid al-Din's *Jami al-Tawarikh* or *Compendium of Chronicles*, and Juvaini's *Chinggis Khan: The History of the World-Conqueror*. The place of mass rape in the arsenal of the ethnic cleanser and those interested in not just conquest but in the extermination of a people in the modern age is described in N. Fergusson, *The War of the World: Twentieth-Century Conflict and the Descent of the West*, New York: Penguin, 2007, pp. xlix–li and 629–35.

Chapter Four

1 In Graff, p. 29.
2 Book nine in Giles, *Sun Tzu on the Art of War*.
3 A tael is about 40 grams (1.4 oz) in weight.
4 The respite given to Song by the Mongol civil war was matched by the fighting chance it also gave the Mamluk Dynasty of Egypt far to the west. The Mamluks took their chance decisively and courageously. They comprehensively defeated the Mongols at the Battle of Ain Jalut, arguably one of the most important battles in history. The Mamluks' victory in Palestine and their subsequent stolid defence of Syria and Egypt until the collapse of the Mongol empire almost certainly preserved Islamic civilisation and very possibly saved Europe from a Mongol advance through the Mediterranean. See Waterson, *The Knights of Islam*, chapter 4 and Foreword by John Man.

5 The Song government, as evidenced in the way it – like every other Chinese dynasty – recorded its history of dealings with foreign peoples, essentially failed to change its theories and methods of dealing with barbarians with the changes *actually* occurring in the outside world. The ancient ideal was of the 'five zones of submission' in which China's ruling dynasty, which held the Mandate of Heaven, controlled mankind and had absolute political, cultural and moral authority over the Middle Kingdom. The barbarians and their states were viewed as satellites to this system that should willingly submit to vassalage; they should accept the emperor's moral authority even though they lay beyond the range of any real control. This attitude undoubtedly and fatally clouded the Song court's judgement over any offers of peace from the Mongols and often made the government blind to its own self-interest and that of the country. Even if the Mongol conquests marked 'the beginning of the modern world and the age of globalisation', as Timothy May contends, and ensured that 'unprecedented numbers of travellers, merchants, missionaries, and others criss-crossed the Eurasian land mass and even beyond', it would seem that the 'five zones' model persisted in the minds of the Chinese elite. I am confident that Dr May's globalisation hypothesis is absolutely correct for the rest of Eurasia but equally sure that China's relations with other peoples right down to the twentieth century continued to be coloured by attitudes forged in the time of the ancients. On the relative virtues or vices of globalisation, and whether the Mongols did mankind a kindness by either accidentally or purposely creating it, I will leave the reader to decide. See May, *The Mongol Conquests in World History*, pp. 1 and 8.

6 See J. Man, *Kublai Khan: The Mongol King who Remade China*, London: Bantam, 2006, pp. 187–8.

7 See Y. Lien-sheng, 'Hostages in Chinese History', *Harvard Journal of Asiatic Studies*, vol. 15, nos 3/4, 1952, pp. 507–21.

8 For example, the last Abbasid caliph of Baghdad was rolled in a carpet and kicked to death in 1258 by the Mongols because he was of a royal line.

9 The system seems to have evolved under the Qin Dynasty (221–207 BC). For the Mongol adaption of the system see D. Ostrowski, 'The *Tamma* and the Dual-Administrative Structure of the Mongol Empire', *Bulletin of the School of Oriental and African Studies*, vol. 61, no. 2, 1998, pp. 262–77.

10 The era in which a warship was constructed is practically academic when applied to naval warfare in Chinese history. A 'plateau' of technical excellence was reached very early and little changed after this. Even as late as the early twentieth century medium-sized traders of northern China were still prime examples of the ancient and quite peculiar Chinese shipbuilding tradition. See P. Manguin, 'Trading Ships of the South China Sea: Shipbuilding Techniques and their Role in the History of the

Development of Asian Trade Networks', *Journal of the Economic and Social History of the Orient*, vol. 36, no. 3, 1993, pp. 253–80.

11 J. Delgado, *Kublai Khan's Lost Fleet: History's Greatest Naval Disaster*, London: Bodley Head, 2009, p. 66.

12 Marines and sailors engaged in night actions in these small craft would bite on sticks to maintain silence as they approached enemy vessels.

13 Delgado, p. 32.

14 At times, in the late twentieth century, the Yellow River has failed to reach the sea by as much as 6 kilometres, such has been the degree of silting at its mouth. Its meanderings and shallow depth make it a very different proposition in sailing terms to the Yangzi.

15 J. Lo, 'Maritime Commerce and its Relation to the Sung Navy', *Journal of the Economic and Social History of the Orient*, vol. 12, no. 1, 1969, pp. 57–101.

CHAPTER FIVE

1 The Tai Kong is one of the seven military classics of China. See R. Sawyer, *The Seven Military Classics of Ancient China*, Boulder, CO: Westview Press, 1993.

2 See Cleary, *Mastering the 'Art of War'*.

3 Book nine in Giles, *Sun Tzu on the Art of War.*

CHAPTER SIX

1 From the opening lines of book one in Giles, *Sun Tzu on the Art of War.*

2 For the Mamluks' destruction of Acre and their application of counterweight trebuchets to the Crusader castles and cities of Crak de Chevalier and Tripoli see J. Waterson, *Sacred Swords: Jihad in the Holy Land 1097–1295*, London: Frontline Books, 2010, chapter 8 and Waterson, *The Knights of Islam*, chapters 6 and 7.

3 The difficulties of deciding who invented what and where, and who took the idea on to a higher level are well described in Chevedden.

4 By the time of the Mongol empire, 'China and Iran had been in political, cultural and commercial contact for more than a millennium', but it was the 'military challenge of rival cousins in Central Asia' that created the large and diverse exchange of materiel, men and resources between Qubilai's state and the Persian Ilkhanate of his brother Hulegu and his successors that began the extensive transmission of Chinese culture to Iran and from there further west that occurred during the Yuan Dynasty. That the West and Middle East benefited enormously from Chinese knowledge and techniques in 'art, medicine, agronomy and astronomy' seems beyond

doubt. I am also grateful to the Mongols for bringing the Chinese 'lotus motif' into Islamic art as its presence or absence made dating Iranian miniature pictures far easier during my time as a highly ungifted art history undergraduate. Whether or not the *huihuipao* was a positive contribution to China from the *Pax Mongolica* perhaps depended on which side of the Yangzi line one was standing in 1273. The best analysis of the enormous changes to the cultural history of Eurasia that the Mongol empire brought about is arguably Allsen; the above quotations come from the introduction.

5 L. Jieming, *Chinese Siege Warfare: Mechanical Artillery and Siege Weapons of Antiquity, an Illustrated History*, Singapore: Da Pao Publishing, 2006, p. 30.

6 Morgan, pp. 150–1.

7 Morgan, p. 74.

8 One argument for the 'rise' of the West and the hegemony that western nations have exerted on the world in the modern period is that the devastating impact of the Black Death in China and the reorientation of the Ming Dynasty to China's north rather than to the traditionally seagoing south meant that the South China Sea was essentially abandoned by the Ming, along with active sea trade, and that this allowed the Portuguese, Dutch and English to create a new world trade and geopolitical system. See J. L. Abu-Lughod, *Before European Hegemony: The World System, A.D. 1250–1350*, Oxford: Oxford University Press, 1989. For the journeys of Zheng He and the Ming Dynasty's isolationist policies see E. Dreyer, *Zheng He: China and the Oceans in the Early Ming Dynasty, 1405–1433*, London: Longman, 2006.

Chapter Seven

1 The *Yuanshi* or dynastic history of the Yuan Dynasty also records how land-based *huihuipao* destroyed elements of the Song fleet through exploding missile barrage. See Carrington-Goodrich and Chia-sheng.

2 From Zhao Hong's work, *Meng Da Bei Lu*. See May, *Mongol Art of War*, p. 76.

3 A. Chin-Wai Chung, 'Aspects of the Systems of Military Logistics during the Song Dynasty (960–1278): The Procurement of Horses, Military Agricultural Colonies, and the Imperial Ordnance Industry', unpublished MA thesis, Montreal, McGill University, 1999.

4 The life of a steppe pony both in the past and nowadays was and is not an easy one. The Song general Zhao Hong wrote that Mongol horses were never fed fodder, beans or grain and that when they were only one or two years old they would be ridden harshly in the steppe before being freed from service for two years and then trained again. He said that they 'do not kick or bite. Thousands and hundreds form herds but they

are silent and are without neighing or calling. When they dismount [the Mongols] do not rein them in and tether them, but they do not stray. Their temperament is very good.' See May, *Mongol Art of War*, pp. 55–6. Even today, although revered, their life is hard. See J. Man, *Genghis Khan: Life, Death and Resurrection*, London: Bantam, 2004, pp. 60–2 for a vivid description of their trials and triumphs during the Mongolian racing season and a tale of ultimately unsuccessful 'cardiac massage' performed on an apparently dying racing steed through a process of kicking him repeatedly in the chest.

5 P. Smith, *Taxing Heaven's Store House: Horses, Bureaucrats and the Destruction of the Sichuan Tea Industry*, Cambridge, MA: Harvard University Press, 1991.

6 See May, *Mongol Art of War*, p. 57.

7 The Jiangnan, literally 'south of the Yangzi', cities of Wuhan, Nanjing and Chongqing are known in China as 'the three furnaces'. The author has personally suffered several summers on the Yangzi; they are not to be recommended. Making war in such conditions must have been hellish.

8 One problem was that the racial make-up of the Golden Horde had changed dramatically during its conquest of southern Russia and its tribesmen were mostly Turkish rather than Mongolian. The Mamluks of Egypt and Syria were also Turks of Caucasian origin. Furthermore, many of the Golden Horde's tribesmen were Sunni Muslims, as were the Mamluks. Hulegu's Mongols had killed the caliph of Islam, burned the Great Mosque of Damascus and disestablished Islam as the state religion in every area of the Middle East that they conquered. The emergence of a mutual understanding between the rulers of the Golden Horde and the Mamluks, given the above and their mutual antipathy to the House of Tolui, was perhaps inevitable. See R. Amitai Preiss, *Mongols and Mamluks: The Mamluk–Ilkhanid War, 1260–1281*, Cambridge, Cambridge University Press, 1995 and D. Ayalon, 'The Mamluk Novice: On his Youthfulness and on his Original Religion', *Revue des Etudes Islamiques*, vol. 54, 1986, pp. 1–8.

9 From a palace notice posted at the empress' command. For the wrangling between ministers and desertions of petty officials that had driven the empress to these words see R. Davis, 'The Reign of Tu-tsung (1264–1274) and his Successors to 1279', in *Cambridge History of China, Volume 5, Part 1: The Sung Dynasty and its Precursors, 907–1279*, edited by D. Twitchett and P. Smith Cambridge, Cambridge University Press, 2009, pp. 920–40.

10 Confucian-trained historians always recorded reasons for a dynasty's fall and the 'bad' individuals within it that caused its loss of heaven's favour. The Ming undertook to record the history of the Yuan, the *Yuanshi*, and also altered the *Songshi* in order to make their own dynasty's ascendance

to the Mandate of Heaven appear as a logical and legitimate part of the imperial history of China. That this makes for a false system of history goes without saying. See A. Wright, *The Confucian Persuasion*, Stanford, CA: Stanford University Press, 1960.

Chapter Eight

1 Emperor Zhenzong was advised by Kou Zhun to meet a massive Kitan invasion in the field as commander-in-chief and not to seek safety by fleeing his capital. Almost every other counsellor disagreed with Kou Zhun and minister Wang Qinruo went as far as to warn the emperor that Kou Zhun was using the emperor as a stake as one might in a game of dice. Zhenzong took Kou Zhun's advice and won a great victory over the invaders. The saying has become a standard expression for admiration of dash and daring in China.

2 Weatherford has argued that the Mongols should be credited for killing their victims even during reprisals without inflicting torture on them. He suggests that the fear they inspired was not due to the 'cruelty of their acts so much as by the speed and efficiency with which they conquered and their seemingly total disdain for the lives of the rich and powerful'. The merit of this is of course dubious at best and the author's suggestion that the volume of killing undertaken by the Mongols given by the primary sources is untenable since the idea that 'the people could have merely run away' whilst awaiting murder at the hands of Mongol troopers is faintly ridiculous. The obvious question in an agrarian society tied for its survival to its crop production is – run where? The numbers given in the sources undoubtedly relate not just to those killed by Mongol sword or arrow but those who died as a result of the obliteration of cities and the agrarian infrastructure around them during such reprisals. See Weatherford's own recounting of the massacre of Nishapur following Juvaini's original account, in J. Weatherford, *Genghis Khan and the Making of the Modern World*, New York: Three Rivers Press, 2004, pp. 116–20.

3 Lu Xiufu, in Davis, 'The Reign of Tu-tsung', p. 958.

Chapter Nine

1 'Giving publicity to suicides may lead to an epidemic of suicides'. This claim was made in connection with the publication of Goethe's *The Sorrows of Young Werther*. The 'Werther Effect' is doubted by many modern psychologists, but one wonders about the powerful effect the mass suicide of the entire leadership of a country would have on its citizens, and whether

people of the past were affected more strongly with loss of 'nationality' than we might be today. I am certain that the 'Werther Effect' would have had more influence in the medieval than in the modern world. See J. Thorson and P. Öberg, 'Was there a Suicide Epidemic after Goethe's Werther?', *Archives of Suicide Research*, vol. 7, no. 1, 2003, pp. 69–72.

2 See Davis, 'The Reign of Tu-tsung', p. 953.

3 France experienced the same misery during the Hundred Years War as southern China did at the end of the Song Dynasty. Pillaging, kidnapping and extortion went on for some eight years after peace was signed simply because the war had become a way of life for twenty years. I would suggest that the average Mongol trooper was even more likely than any man of the Free Companies to ignore the benefits of a demobilised life. See Sumption, chapter 10.

4 Yuan rule saw the emigration to China of Italians as merchants and clerical staff, and of Arabs and Persians as 'leopard keepers' and artillerymen. It seems, however, that what really rankled with the Chinese and in particular with the Confucian scholars was the accelerated promotion of *semuren* gatekeepers and low-level clerks to top positions within the government. See Allsen, p. 6 for the movement east and west of people across the *Pax Mongolica*. It seems too that the Mongols preferred *huihuiyaofang* or Muslim medicinal recipes to Chinese medicine. See May, *Mongol Conquests in World History*, pp. 16–17 for some of the other products of the cultural synthesis of Chinese and Islamic scholarship that occurred during the Yuan period.

5 The lack of both longevity and fertility in Mongol rulers in both China and Persia also added to the problems of maintaining a stable polity. It has been argued that this was related to overeating and over-imbibing of alcohol by the members of the royal line. Short reigns were always likely to be destabilising in the medieval age, where so much depended on the skills and natures of individuals at the top. The Song bureaucratic system would have negated some of the effects of short-lived sovereigns but, as discussed, the Mongol polity was not developed enough to maintain smooth transitions or to absorb the workload of a debilitated monarch. See J. Smith, 'Dietary Decadence and Dynastic Decline in the Mongol Empire', *Journal of Asian History*, vol. 34, no. 1, 2000, pp. 35–52.

6 The problems of steppe polities being unable to manage what they had conquered and the tendency for Turco-Mongolic military men and minor nobles to hinder the practice of civil government persisted into the post-Mongol empire period. 'In [Timur Leng's] government, as in those of most nomad dynasties, it is impossible to find a clear distinction between civil and military affairs, or to identify the Persian bureaucracy as solely civil or the Turko-Mongolian solely with military government. Emirs were

often involved in civil and provincial administration and even in financial affairs, traditionally the province of Persian bureaucracy.' Timur Leng's empire was a fairly ramshackle affair within only a century of his death in 1405. See B. Manz, *The Rise and Rule of Tamerlane*, Cambridge: Cambridge University Press, 1999, p. 109.

7 Qubilai's successor, Temur, gave his 'relatives' four times as much gold and twice as much silver per year as Qubilai had paid them. He also gave additional vast one-off payments to these same individuals. See *Cambridge History of China Volume 6*, p. 501.

8 See Morgan, p. 113, and H. Franke, 'Could the Mongol Emperors Read and Write Chinese?', in H. Franke (ed.), *China under Mongol Rule*, Brookfield, VT: Variorum, 1994, chapter 5.

9 The tale remains popular in both China and in Japan even today and has been reproduced as a 1970s television show which western viewers might recognise as *The Water Margin*. The novel was probably first written down by the late Yuan writer Shi Naian, and, as if to make it clear that the tale had changed its original meaning beyond all measure to become a Chinese tale of resistance to foreign invaders, it was melded with legends of Yue Fei by the Ming Dynasty writer Qian Cai in his 1684 *Story of Yue Fei*.

10 The Black Death may alternatively have entered Europe via the Genoese slave port of Kaffa on the Black Sea coast in the 1340s. Genoese vessels possibly carried the infection from Kaffa to their mother port and into Europe.

11 It has been suggested that the earth suffered the beginning of a 'little Ice Age' in this period. See an ecological history of China in this period of climatic chaos in T. Brook, *The Troubled Empire: China in the Yuan and Ming Dynasties*, Cambridge, MA: Harvard University Press, 2010. A table of the sloughs of the Yuan and Ming Dynasties is given on p. 270. It is notable that there are nine periods during the period 1290 to 1643 of severe cold and wet leading to famines. Three of these periods of climate chaos occurred during the Yuan Dynasty whilst six occurred during the Ming Dynasty. It is interesting that the Ming Dynasty lasted over twice as long than the Yuan Dynasty despite suffering twice as many of these destructive periods.

12 See F. Mote's Introduction in *Cambridge History of China, Volume 7, Part 1: The Ming Dynasty, 1368–1644*, edited by D. Twitchett and J. Fairbank, Cambridge: Cambridge University Press, 1998.

13 'It is very noticeable, too, that the great majority of those personages of the Yuan empire whom Marco names in the book, other than Khans and other Mongol royalty, are soldiers, or at least are involved in some kind of military activity'. See S. Haw, *Marco Polo's China: a Venetian in the realm of Khubilai Khan*, London: Routledge, 2006, pp. 160–1.

14 It has been claimed that Mongol exactions in the form of taxes were no greater than those expected by the ruling dynasties that existed before their empire was formed. I would suggest the answer as to whether taxation is onerous relies as much on what the money is spent on as to how much is expected. As we have seen, the citizens of China received very little for their remittances in terms of security or mitigation of the consequences of natural disaster from the central government. See Haw, p. 213.

15 The Chinese Communist Party's view of Yuan society was neatly captured in 1967. A paper published on Chinese history in that year describes how a feudal nobility, the *noyan*, exploited the masses with the requirement for annual tribute. A further weakening of traditional clan life was created by the *nokor* or retainers in the service of the nobility. The Communist Party was also pretty confident that Song was conquered due to the 'rottenness and inability of the ruling class'. That the ruling Yuan were 'destroyed by peasant uprisings and large-scale feudal war among the Mongolian ruling class in the north', must having been a satisfying thought in China just as Mao's Cultural Revolution was gathering steam. See D. Farquhar, 'Chinese Communist Assessments of a Foreign Conquest Dynasty', *China Quarterly*, no. 30, 1967, pp. 79–92.

16 This portrait of Zhu Yuanzhang is certainly somewhat hagiographic. The similarity of his actions to those purported to be the progressive policy of the Communist forces of Mao Zedong in the 1940s are interesting. 'Wherever our comrades go, they must build good relations with the masses, be concerned for them and help them overcome their difficulties. We must unite with the masses, the more of the masses we unite with, the better'. See Mao Zedong, 'On the Chongqing Negotiations', in Mao Tse-tung, *Selected Works, Volume 4*, Beijing: Foreign Languages Press, 1961, pp. 53–64. The rather more grim reality of Mao's war is only beginning to be uncovered.

17 See F. Mote, 'The Rise of the Ming Dynasty, 1330–1397', in *Cambridge History of China, Volume 7*, pp. 55 and an extensive discussion of Zhu Yuanzhang's other concepts of statecraft in J. Dardess, *Confucianism and Autocracy*, Berkeley, CA: University of Berkeley, 1983, p. 196.

18 The city of Beijing has had many names throughout its history. It was Yanjing to the Song and Liao, although it was also designated as Nanjing by the Liao as it was their southern (*nan*) capital. It was Zhongdu (central city) to the Jin and Dadu (great city) to the Yuan, though technically Dadu was a new capital built alongside the old capital of Yanjing which retained its Song name. In 1403 the city was designated as Beijing, or northern capital.

Epilogue

1 See Waterson, *The Knights of Islam*, chapter 8 and *Sacred Swords*, chapter 8 and Epilogue.

2 The Great Wall as we know it today did not exist before the Ming. Evidence of fortifications of ramped earth and of fortresses and trading points along the border which the wall 'solidified', however, extends far further back in the country's history. See A. Waldron, *The Great Wall of China: From History to Myth*, Cambridge: Cambridge University Press, 1990.

3 See J. Yifu Lin, 'The Needham Puzzle: Why the Industrial Revolution Did Not Originate in China', *Economic Development and Cultural Change*, vol. 43, no. 2, 1995, pp. 269–92.

Bibliography

Abu-Lughod, J. L., *Before European Hegemony: The World System, A.D. 1250–1350*, Oxford: Oxford University Press, 1989.

Allsen. T., *Culture and Conquest in Mongol Eurasia*, Cambridge: Cambridge University Press, 2001.

Amitai Preiss, R., *Mongols and Mamluks: The Mamluk–Ilkhanid War, 1260–1281*, Cambridge: Cambridge University Press, 1995.

Ayalon, D., 'The Mamluk Novice: On his Youthfulness and on his Original Religion', *Revue des Etudes Islamiques*, vol 54, 1986, pp. 1–8.

Boccaccio, *Decameron*, edited by V. Branca, 2 vols, Turin: Einaudi, 1992.

Brook. T., *The Troubled Empire: China in the Yuan and Ming Dynasties*, Cambridge, MA: Harvard University Press, 2010.

Cambridge History of China, Volume 5, Part 1: The Sung Dynasty and its Precursors, 907–1279, edited by D. Twitchett and P. Smith, Cambridge: Cambridge University Press, 2009.

Cambridge History of China, Volume 6: Alien Regimes and Border States, 907–1368, edited by H. Franke and D. Twitchett, Cambridge: Cambridge University Press, 1994.

Cambridge History of China, Volume 7, Part 1: The Ming Dynasty, 1368–1644, edited by D. Twitchett and J. Fairbank, Cambridge: Cambridge University Press, 1998.

Carrington-Goodrich, L., and F. Chia-sheng, 'The Early Development of Firearms in China', *Isis*, vol. 36, no. 2, 1946, pp. 114–23.

Chevedden, P., 'The Invention of the Counterweight Trebuchet: A Study in Cultural Diffusion', *Dumbarton Oaks Papers*, vol. 54, 2000, pp. 71–116.

Chin-Wai Chung, A., 'Aspects of the Systems of Military Logistics during the Song Dynasty (960–1278): The Procurement of Horses, Military Agricultural Colonies, and the Imperial Ordnance Industry', unpublished MA thesis, Montreal, McGill University, 1999.

Cleary, T., *Mastering the 'Art of War': Zhuge Liang's and Liu Ji's Commentaries on the Classic by Sun Tzu*, Boston, MA: Shambhala Dragon Editions, 1990.

Croce, B., *La Storia Come Pensiero e Come Azione*, Naples: Bibliopolis, 1938/2002.

Dardess, J., *Confucianism and Autocracy*, Berkeley, CA: University of Berkeley Press, 1983.

Davis, R., 'The Reigns of Kuang-sung (1189–94) and Ning-tsung (1194–1224)', in *Cambridge History of China, Volume 5, Part 1: The Sung Dynasty and its Precursors, 907–1279*, edited by D. Twitchett and P. Smith, Cambridge: Cambridge University Press, 2009, chapter 10, pp. 756–838.

—— 'The Reign of Tu-tsung (1264–1274) and his Successors to 1279', in *Cambridge History of China, Volume 5, Part 1: The Sung Dynasty and its Precursors, 907–1279*, edited by D. Twitchett and P. Smith, Cambridge, Cambridge University Press, 2009, chapter 10, pp. 913–62.

Delgado. J., *Kublai Khan's Lost Fleet: History's Greatest Naval Disaster*, London: Bodley Head, 2009.

Dreyer, E., *Zheng He: China and the Oceans in the Early Ming Dynasty, 1405–1433*, London: Longman, 2006.

Dunnel, R., 'The Hsi Hsia', in *Cambridge History of China, Volume 6: Alien Regimes and Border States, 907–1368*, edited by H. Franke and D. Twitchett, Cambridge: Cambridge University Press, 1994, chapter 2, pp. 154–214.

Fan, Chengda, *Stone Lake: The Poetry of Fan Chengda 1126–1193*, translated by J. Schmidt and P. Hannan, edited by D. Twitchett, Cambridge: Cambridge University Press, 1992.

Farquhar, D., 'Chinese Communist Assessments of a Foreign Conquest Dynasty', *China Quarterly*, no. 30, 1967, pp. 79–92.

Fergusson. N., *The War of the World: Twentieth-Century Conflict and the Descent of the West*, New York: Penguin, 2007.

Fletcher, J., 'The Mongols: Ecological and Social Perspectives', *Harvard Journal of Asiatic Studies*, vol. 46, no. 1, 1986, pp. 11–50; ; reprinted in J. Fletcher, *Studies on Chinese and Islamic Inner Asia*, edited by Beatrice F. Manz, Aldershot, Ashgate, 1995.

Franke, H., 'Siege and Defense of Towns in Medieval China', in F. Kierman and J. Fairbank (eds), *Chinese Ways in Warfare*, Cambridge, MA: Harvard University Press, 1974, pp. 151–201.

—— 'Could the Mongol Emperors Read and Write Chinese?', in H. Franke (ed.), *China under Mongol Rule*, Brookfield, VT: Variorum, 1994, chapter 5.

Giles, L. (trans.), *Sun Tzu on the Art of War: The Oldest Military Treatise in the World*, London: British Museum, 1910.

Gong, W., 'The Reign of Hsaio-tsung (1162–89)', in *Cambridge History of China, Volume 5, Part 1: The Sung Dynasty and its Precursors, 907–1279*, edited by D. Twitchett and P. Smith, Cambridge: Cambridge University Press, 2009, chapter 9, pp. 710–55.

Graff. D., *Medieval Chinese Warfare, 300–900*, New York: Routledge, 2002.

Griffith, S., 'Introduction', in Sun Tzu, *The Art of War*, translated by S. Griffith, Oxford: Oxford University Press, 1963, pp. 1–56.

Guthrie, C., and M. Quinlan, *The Just War Tradition: Ethics in Modern Warfare*, London: Bloomsbury, 2007.

Hartwell, R., 'A Revolution in the Chinese Iron and Coal Industries during the Northern Sung, 960–1126 AD', *Journal of Asian Studies*, vol. 21, no. 2, 1962, pp. 153–62.

Haw, S., *Marco Polo's China: A Venetian in the Realm of Khubilai Khan*, London: Routledge, 2006.

Jackson, P., 'The Crisis in the Holy Land in 1260', *English Historical Review*, vol. 45, no. 376, 1980, pp. 481–513.

Jagchid, S., 'The Kitans and their Cities', *Central Asiatic Journal*, no. 25, 1981, pp. 70–88.

Jieming, L., *Chinese Siege Warfare: Mechanical Artillery and Siege Weapons of Antiquity, an Illustrated History*, Singapore: Da Pao Publishing, 2006.

Komroff, M. (ed.), *The Contemporaries of Marco Polo: Consisting of the Travel Records to the Eastern Parts of the World of William of Rubruck (1253–1255); The Journey of John of Piano de Carpini (1245–1247) and the Journey of Friar Odoric (1318–1350)*, New York: Boni and Liveright, 1928

Lewis, M., *Sanctioned Violence in Early China*, New York: SUNY Press, 1990.

Lien-sheng, Y., 'Hostages in Chinese History', *Harvard Journal of Asiatic Studies*, vol. 15, nos 3/4, 1952, pp. 507–21.

—— 'Numbers and Units in Chinese Economic History', in Y. Lien-sheng, *Studies in Chinese Institutional History*, Cambridge, MA: Harvard University Press, 1961.

Lo, J., 'Maritime Commerce and its Relation to the Sung Navy', *Journal of the Economic and Social History of the Orient*, vol. 12, no. 1, 1969, pp. 57–101.

Lo, W., *An Introduction to the Civil Service of Sung China, with Emphasis on its Personnel Administration*, Honolulu: University Of Hawaii Press, 1987.

Lorge, P., *War, Politics and Society in Early Modern China, 900–1795*, New York: Routledge, 2005.

McCurley, D., '"Juedixi": An Entertainment of War in Early China', *Asian Theatre Journal*, vol. 22, no. 1, 2005, pp. 87–106.

McMullen, D., 'The Cult of Ch'i T'ai-kung and T'ang Attitudes to the Military', *Tang Studies*, no. 7, 1989, pp. 59–103.

Man, J., *Genghis Khan: Life, Death and Resurrection*, London: Bantam, 2004.

—— *Kublai Khan: The Mongol King who Remade China*, London: Bantam, 2006.

Manguin, P., 'Trading Ships of the South China Sea: Shipbuilding Techniques and their Role in the History of the Development of Asian Trade Networks', *Journal of the Economic and Social History of the Orient*, vol. 36, no. 3, 1993, pp. 253–80.

Manz, B., *The Rise and Rule of Tamerlane*, Cambridge: Cambridge University Press, 1999.

Mao Zedong, 'On the Chungking Negotiations', in Mao Tse-tung, *Selected Works, Volume 4*, Beijing: Foreign Languages Press, 1961, pp. 53–64

Marx, K. and F. Engels, *Correspondence, 1846–1895*, edited by D. Torr, New York: International Publishers, 1935.

May, T., *The Mongol Art of War*, Barnsley: Pen and Sword Books Ltd, 2007.

—— *The Mongol Conquests in World History*, London: Reaktion, 2012.

Morgan, D., *The Mongols*, 2nd edn, London: Blackwell, 2007.

Mote, F., 'The Rise of the Ming Dynasty, 1330–1397', in *Cambridge History of China, Volume 7, Part 1: The Ming Dynasty, 1368–1644*, edited by D. Twitchett and J. Fairbank, Cambridge: Cambridge University Press, 1998, pp. 11–57.

Needham, J., and R. Yates, *Science and Civilization in China, Volume 5: Chemistry and Chemical Technology, Part 6: Military Technology: Missiles*, Cambridge: Cambridge University Press, 1994.

Nicolle, D., *Medieval Warfare Source Book: Warfare in Western Christendom*, Leicester: Brockhampton Press, 1995.

Ostrowski, D., 'The *Tamma* and the Dual-Administrative Structure of the Mongol Empire', *Bulletin of the School of Oriental and African Studies*, vol. 61, no. 2, 1998, pp. 262–77.

Peers, C., *Imperial Chinese Armies (2): 590–1260 AD*, London: Osprey, 1996.

Peterson, C., 'First Sung Reactions to the Mongol Invasion of the North, 1211–1217', in J. W. Haeger (ed.), *Crisis and Prosperity in Sung China*, Tucson, AZ: University of Arizona Press, 1975, pp. 215–52.

Rossabi, M., 'All the Khan's Horses', *Natural History*, October 1994, pp. 48–57.

Saunders, J., *The History of the Mongol Conquests*, London: Routledge & Kegan Paul, 1971.

—— 'The Nomad as Empire-Builder: A Comparison of the Arab and Mongol Conquests', in J. Saunders, *Muslims and Mongols: Essays on Medieval Asia*, edited by G. W. Rice, Christchurch, NZ: University of Canterbury Press, 1977, pp. 36–66.

Smith. J., 'Mongol Campaign Rations: Milk, Marmots and Blood?', *Journal of Turkish Studies*, vol. 8, 1984, pp. 223–8.

—— 'Dietary Decadence and Dynastic Decline in the Mongol Empire', *Journal of Asian History*, vol. 34, no. 1, 2000, pp. 35–52.

Smith, P., *Taxing Heaven's Store House: Horses, Bureaucrats and the Destruction of the Sichuan Tea Industry*, Cambridge, MA: Harvard University Press, 1991.

Sumption, J., *The Hundred Years War, Volume 2: Trial by Fire*, London: Faber and Faber, 1991.

Thorson, J. and P. Öberg, 'Was there a Suicide Epidemic after Goethe's Werther?', *Archives of Suicide Research*, vol. 7, no. 1, 2003, pp. 69–72.

Tuchman, B., *The March of Folly: From Troy to Vietnam*, New York: Ballantine Books, 1985.
Waldron, A., *The Great Wall of China: From History to Myth*, Cambridge: Cambridge University Press, 1990.
Wang, C., 'Towards Defining a Chinese Heroism', *Journal of the American Oriental Society*, vol. 95, no. 1, 1975, pp. 25–35.
Waterson, J., *The Knights of Islam: The Wars of the Mamluks*, London: Greenhill Books, 2007.
—— *The Ismaili Assassins: A History of Medieval Murder*, London: Frontline Books, 2008.
—— *Sacred Swords: Jihad in the Holy Land 1097–1295*, London: Frontline Books, 2010.
Weatherford, J., *Genghis Khan and the Making of the Modern World*, New York: Three Rivers Press, 2004.
—— *The Secret History of the Mongol Queens*, New York: Crown, 2010.
Williamson, H., *Wang An Shih: Chinese Statesman and Educationalist of the Sung Dynasty*, London: Arthur Probsthain, 1935.
Wright, A., *The Confucian Persuasion*, Stanford, CA: Stanford University Press, 1960.
Yifu Lin, J., 'The Needham Puzzle: Why the Industrial Revolution Did Not Originate in China', *Economic Development and Cultural Change*, vol. 43, no. 2, 1995, pp. 269–92.

Further Reading

The referenced books above are the obvious starting point for any reader wishing to pursue any of the themes covered in the text. For the slightly more adventurous reader the following books are suggested. I have made every effort to avoid including specialist and therefore difficult to obtain materials.

Barfield, T., *The Perilous Frontier: Nomadic Empires and China 221 BC to 1757 AD*, Oxford: Blackwell, 1992.
Breitman, R., 'Hitler and Genghis Khan', *Journal of Contemporary History*, vol. 25, no. 2/3, May–June, 1990, pp. 337–51.
Chang, S., 'Some Observations on the Morphology of Chinese Walled Cities', *Annals of the Association of American Geographers*, vol. 60, no. 1, 1970, pp. 63–91.
Cheng-Hua, F., 'Military Families and the Southern Song Court: The Lu Case', *Journal of Song-Yuan Studies*, vol. 33, 2003, pp. 49–70.
Creel, G., 'Soldier and Scholar in Ancient China', *Pacific Affairs*, vol. 8, no. 3, 1935, pp. 336–43.

Di Cosmo, N. (ed.), *Military Culture in Imperial China*, Cambridge, MA: Harvard University Press, 2009.

Dien, A., 'The Stirrup and its Effect on Chinese Military History', *Ars Orientalis*, vol. 16, 1986, pp. 33–56.

Elvin, M., *The Pattern of the Chinese Past*, Stanford, CA: Stanford University Press, 1973.

Fairbank, J., and F. Kierman, *Chinese Ways in Warfare*, Cambridge, MA: Harvard University Press, 1974.

Fried, M., 'Military Status in Chinese Society', *American Journal of Sociology*, vol. 57, 1951–2, pp. 347–57.

Gang, D., *Maritime Sector, Institutions, and Sea Power of Pre-modern China*, Westport, CT: Greenwood Press, 1999.

Gernet, J., *Daily Life in China on the Eve of the Mongol Invasion, 1250–1276*, Stanford, CA: Stanford University Press, 1962.

Golas, P. (ed.), *Change in Sung China: Innovation or Renovation?*, Lexington, KT: Heath & Co., 1969.

Graff, D., and R. Higham (eds), *A Military History of China*, Boulder, CO: Westview Press, 2001.

Holcombe, C., 'Theater of Combat: A Critical Look at the Chinese Martial Arts', *The Historian*, vol. 52, no. 3, 1990, pp. 411–32.

Hong, Y., *Weapons in Ancient China*, New York and Beijing: Science Press, 1992.

Jay, J., 'Memoirs and Official Accounts: The Historiography of the Song Loyalists', *Harvard Journal of Asiatic Studies*, vol. 50, no. 2, 1990, pp. 589–612.

Johnston, A., *Cultural Realism: Strategic Culture and Grand Strategy in Chinese History*, Princeton, NJ: Princeton University Press, 1995.

Lattimore, O., *Studies in Frontier History*, Oxford: Oxford University Press, London, 1962.

Levathes, L., *When China Ruled the Seas*, New York: Simon & Schuster, 1994.

Liu, J., 'Yueh Fei (1103–41) and China's Heritage of Loyalty', *Journal of Asian Studies*, vol. 31, no. 2, 1972, pp. 291–7.

Lo, J., 'The Emergence of China as a Sea Power during the Late Sung and Early Yuan Periods', *Far Eastern Quarterly*, vol. 14, no. 4, special issue on Chinese history and society, 1955, pp. 489–503.

Lorge, P., *Warfare in China to 1600*, Ashgate: London, 2005.

Lovell, J., *The Great Wall: China against the World, 1000 BC to 2000 AD*, New York: Atlantic Books, 2006.

Rossabi, M. (ed.), *China among Equals: The Middle Kingdom and its Neighbors, 10th–14th Centuries*, Berkeley, CA: University of California Press, 1983.

—— *Khubilai Khan: His Life and Times*, Berkeley, CA: University of California Press, 1988.

Sawyer, R., *The Seven Military Classics of Ancient China*, Boulder, CO: Westview Press, 1993.
Smith, J., 'The Mongols and World Conquest', *Mongolica*, vol. 5, no. 26, 1994, pp. 206–14.
Stroble, J., 'Justification of War in Ancient China', *Asian Philosophy*, vol. 8, no. 3, 1998, pp. 165–85.
Van der Ven, H., *Warfare in Chinese History*, Leiden: E. J. Brill, 2000.
Wallacker, B., 'Studies in Medieval Chinese Siegecraft: The Siege of Yu Pi AD 546', *Journal of Asian Studies*, vol. 28, no. 4, 1969, pp. 611–22.
Winthrop, J. (ed.), *Crisis and Prosperity in Sung China*, Tucson, AZ: University of Arizona Press, 1975.
Wright, D., 'The Sung-Khitan War of A.D. 1004–1005 and the Treaty of Shan Yuan', *Journal of Asian History*, vol. 32, no. 1, 1998, pp. 3–48.

Index